ADVANCE PRAISE

The Dravidian Model makes a compelling case for a development strategy powered by populist mobilization around regional cultural identity. Tamil Nadu, the authors argue, has created more effective institutions and delivered better outcomes on food, health, education and poverty reduction than other Indian states. This strategy has emphasised status inequalities of caste and gender rather than income inequalities with remarkable success. This book needs to be read and discussed.

Partha Chatterjee, *Columbia University*

Adopting a neo-Gramscian approach, Kalaiyarasan and Vijayabaskar have developed an original take on Tamil Nadu's economy, society and politics. With detailed attention to achievements in human development, structural economic change and accumulation, they reveal the ideas, politics and institutions distinguishing social populism from economic populism. Through both kinds of Dravidian left populism, countervailing power has been built and aspirations against entrenched inequalities have been simultaneously mobilised. The state is central to their co-ordination, continuities, relative success and limitations. This book is sure to generate the conversation the authors seek about the struggle for social justice that is now so urgently needed.

Barbara Harriss-White, *Oxford University*

The Dravidian Model breaks new ground, not only in making sense of Tamil Nadu's political economy but also in advancing our understanding of the possibilities for socially and economically inclusive development in the post-colonial world. The book exhaustively documents and explains the historical and cultural roots of Tamil Nadu's opportunity-equalizing politics and carves out new theoretical frontiers in the debate on left populism. This should be required reading for all those interested in the democratic possibilities of transforming deeply unequal societies.

Patrick Heller, *Brown University*

The Dravidian Model offers the most convincing explanation of the unmatchable level of development that south India has reached, compared to the rest of the sub-continent. It shows that political mobilization resulting in social change and less inequalities, makes redistribution more natural. And this process prepares the ground for real development—in terms of education and health, for instance—because of a certain democratization of growth. By contrast, Kalaiyarasan A. and M. Vijayabaskar expose those who claim that the economic trajectory of western Indian states are success stories–they are models of growth without development when the Dravidian model offers growth with development!

Christophe Jaffrelot, *CERI-Sciences Po*

The Dravidian movement has been studied extensively for its ideology and political mobilization. But its impact on social development and economic growth has rarely been subjected to such meticulous scrutiny. Of special importance here is the analysis of how the Dravidian movement brought lower castes into the entrepreneurial sphere, lifting Tamil Nadu not only socially but also economically. A compelling and much needed analysis.

Ashutosh Varshney, *Brown University*

THE DRAVIDIAN MODEL

The Dravidian Model adds to the growing literature on the dynamics of subnational development in the Global South by mapping the politics and processes contributing to the development trajectory of Tamil Nadu, south India. The book foregrounds the role of populist mobilisation against caste-based inequalities in shaping this development.

Subnational variations in economic and social outcomes across India, one of the fastest growing economies, continue to pose conceptual and policy challenges. States that do well on the growth front lag in human development, while human development in a few other states has not been accompanied by sustained growth in productive sectors. Tamil Nadu bucks this trend and has managed to combine relatively high levels of growth and sustained productive capacities with human development. Drawing upon fresh data, literature, policy documents and primary fieldwork, this book seeks to explain the social and economic development of Tamil Nadu in terms of populist mobilisation against caste-based inequalities. Dominant policy narratives on inclusive growth assume a sequential logic whereby returns to growth are used to invest in socially inclusive policies. By focusing more on redistribution of access to opportunities in the modern economy, the state has sustained a relatively more inclusive and dynamic growth process.

Democratisation of economic opportunities has made such broad-based growth possible even as interventions in social sectors reinforce the former. The book thus also speaks to the nascent literature on the relationship between the logic of modernisation and status-based inequalities in the Global South. Importantly, it contributes to the growing literature on how regional politics and political regimes shape global development trajectories.

Kalaiyarasan A. is Fulbright–Nehru post-doctoral fellow at the Watson Institute for International and Public Affairs in Brown University and Assistant Professor at the Madras Institute of Development Studies, Chennai. His academic interest lies in the intersection of caste and economic processes in India.

Vijayabaskar M. is Professor at the Madras Institute of Development Studies, Chennai. His research centres on the political economy of development with a focus on labour and land markets, industrial dynamics and rural–urban transformations.

THE DRAVIDIAN MODEL

Interpreting the Political Economy of Tamil Nadu

KALAIYARASAN A.

VIJAYABASKAR M.

CAMBRIDGE
UNIVERSITY PRESS

Shaftesbury Road, Cambridge CB2 8EA, United Kingdom

One Liberty Plaza, 20th Floor, New York, NY 10006, USA

477 Williamstown Road, Port Melbourne, VIC 3207, Australia

314–321, 3rd Floor, Plot 3, Splendor Forum, Jasola District Centre, New Delhi – 110025, India

103 Penang Road, #05–06/07, Visioncrest Commercial, Singapore 238467

Cambridge University Press is part of Cambridge University Press & Assessment, a department of the University of Cambridge.

We share the University's mission to contribute to society through the pursuit of education, learning and research at the highest international levels of excellence.

www.cambridge.org
Information on this title: www.cambridge.org/9781009413268

© Kalaiyarasan A. and Vijayabaskar M. 2021

First published 2021
First paperback edition 2023

A catalogue record for this publication is available from the British Library

ISBN   978-1-108-84413-0   Hardback
ISBN   978-1-009-41326-8   Paperback

To the 'Manure' of Anti-Caste Struggles

CONTENTS

1. THE DRAVIDIAN MODEL
An Introduction

1

2. CONCEPTUALISING POWER IN CASTE SOCIETY

26

3. DEMOCRATISING EDUCATION

52

4. DEMOCRATISING CARE

82

5. BROADENING GROWTH AND DEMOCRATISING CAPITAL

112

6. TRANSFORMING RURAL RELATIONS

144

CONTENTS

7. POPULAR INTERVENTIONS AND URBAN LABOUR
173

8. FISSURES, LIMITS AND POSSIBLE FUTURES
210

TABLES

FIGURES

ABBREVIATIONS

AIADMK	All India Anna Dravida Munnetra Kazhagam
AICTE	All India Council for Technical Education
AISHE	All India Survey on Higher Education
AITUC	All India Trade Union Congress
ANC	antenatal care
ANM	auxiliary nurse midwife
APL	above poverty line
ASER	*Annual Status of Education Report*
ASI	*Annual Survey of Industries*
BCs	Backward Classes
BEL	Bharat Electronics Limited
BHEL	Bharat Heavy Electricals Limited
BJP	Bharatiya Janata Party
BPL	below poverty line
BPSC	belated payment surcharge
CHC	Community Health Centre
CHN	Community Health Nurse
CITU	Centre of Indian Trade Unions
CODISSIA	Coimbatore District Small Scale Industries Association
CPI-M	Communist Party of India-Marxist
CSS	centrally sponsored scheme
CWSN	child with special needs
DICCI	Dalit Indian Chamber of Commerce and Industry
DK	Dravidar Kazhagam

DMCHO	District Maternal and Child Health Officer
DMK	Dravida Munnetra Kazhagam
DVTS	Dravidar Vivasaya Thozhilalar Sangam/Dravidian Agricultural Workers' Union
EU	European Union
EXIM POLICY	export–import policy
FCI	Food Corporation of India
FITE	Forum for IT Employees
FLFPR	female labour force participation rate
GER	gross enrolment ratio
GO	government order
GSDP	gross state domestic product
GST	goods and services tax
GVA	gross value added
HAL	Hindustan Aeronautics Limited
HCL	Hindustan Computers Limited
HHI	Herfindahl–Hirschman Index
HR	human resource
ICDS	Integrated Child Development Services
IDA	Industrial Disputes Act
IMR	infant mortality rate
INTUC	Indian National Trade Union Congress
IOT	Internet of Things
IT	information technology
ITES	information-technology enabled services
ITI	Indian Telephone Industries Limited
LFPR	labour force participation rate
LPF	Labour Progressive Front
MBCs	Most Backward Classes
MDGS	Millennium Development Goals
MHRD	Ministry of Human Resource Development
MLA	Member of the Legislative Assembly
MMR	maternal mortality ratio
MNC	multinational corporation

MNREGA	Mahatma Gandhi National Rural Employment Guarantee Act
MP	Member of Parliament
MRP	mixed reference period
MSME	Ministry of Micro, Small and Medium Enterprises
NABARD	National Bank for Agriculture and Rural Development
NAFIS	NABARD All-India Rural Financial Inclusion Survey
NCAER	National Council of Applied Economic Research
NCEUS	National Commission for Enterprises in the Unorganised Sector
NEET	National Eligibility Cum Entrance Test
NFHS	National Family Health Survey
NIES	newly industrialising economies
NITI AAYOG	National Institution for Transforming India
NMP	Noon Meal Programme
NRHM	National Rural Health Mission
NSDP	net state domestic product
NSS	National Sample Survey
NSSO	National Sample Survey Office
NUEPA	National University of Educational Planning and Administration
OBC	Other Backward Classes
PAC	Public Affairs Centre
PDS	Public Distribution System
PETA	People for the Ethical Treatment of Animals
PGI	Performance Grading Index
PHC	primary health centre
PPP	public–private partnership
PSE	public sector enterprise
SC	Scheduled Caste
SDP	state domestic product
SEQI	school education quality index
SEWA	Self Employed Women's Association
SEZ	special economic zone

SHN	sector health nurse
SIDCO	Tamil Nadu Small Industries Development Corporation
SIPCOT	State Industries Promotion Corporation of Tamil Nadu
SPIC	Southern Petrochemicals Industries Corporation Limited
SRM	Self-Respect Movement
TAMIN	Tamil Nadu Minerals Limited
TANSI	Tamil Nadu Small Industries Corporation Limited
TCMPF	Tamil Nadu Co-operative Milk Producers' Federation
TCS	Tata Consultancy Services
TEDA	Tamil Nadu Energy Development Agency
TFR	total fertility rate
TIDCO	Tamil Nadu Industrial Development Corporation
TMKTPS	Tamil Maanila Kattida Thozhilalar Panchayat Sangam
TNCSC	Tamil Nadu Civil Supplies Corporation
TNHB	Tamil Nadu Housing Board
TNHDR	*Tamil Nadu Human Development Report*
TNMSC	Tamil Nadu Medical Services Corporation
TNPSC	Tamil Nadu Public Service Commission
TNSCB	Tamil Nadu Slum Clearance Board
TNSTC	Tamil Nadu State Transport Corporation
TNUDF	Tamil Nadu Urban Development Fund
TPDS	Targeted Public Distribution System
U5MR	under-five mortality rate
ULB	urban local body
VHN	village health nurse

ACKNOWLEDGEMENTS

Like all scholarly ventures, we too owe a great deal to others. In the course of writing this book, we received invaluable help from many friends and colleagues. While we acknowledge our gratitude to all of them, a special mention must be made of a few. First and foremost, we would like to thank late M. S. S. Pandian. The core ideas for this book evolved from our countless conversations with him. We are intellectually indebted to him in many ways.

There are others whose constructive engagement with our work proved to be crucial. Over several exchanges, Utathya Chattopadhyaya contributed substantially towards chiselling our conceptual framework. Conversations with Patrick Heller sharpened ideas on sub-national development in India. Interactions with S. V. Rajadurai and J. Jeyaranjan have been invaluable and inspiring. S. Anandhi needs special mention for her critical inputs. Discussions with Achin Chakraborty, Karthick Ram Manoharan and Vignesh Rajahmani too were very helpful in revising a couple of chapters.

It was Rob Jenkins who encouraged us to go ahead with the book project on Tamil Nadu though he was wary of locating it within a global canvas. Hope the book does not disappoint him. Loraine Kennedy has been a wonderful source of support all through. The work has also immensely benefitted from the intellectual camaraderie and warmth of K. T. Rammohan, Raman Mahadevan, Judith Heyer, V. M. Subagunarajan, Padmini Swaminathan, K. P. Kannan and Andrew Wyatt over several years. Atul Sood and Mohanan Pillai have been a source of strength for long. We thank them immensely for their generosity.

Colleagues at Madras Institute of Development Studies (MIDS), A. R. Venkatachalapathy and Ajit Menon in particular, have always been supportive. A number of friends including Aarti Kawlra, Serohi Nandan, Suvaid Yaseen,

Shantanu Chakraborty, Ajay Chandra, K. Ezhilarasan, Babu Jayakumar and Vikash Gautam contributed in no small measure towards strengthening key sections of the book. Dennis Rajakumar, Sandeep Sharma and Manoj Jatav were always open to clarify issues on data and methods. Gayathri Balagopal and M. Suresh Babu too provided useful suggestions and inputs. We got to present our early ideas on the theme of the book at conferences hosted by the Indira Gandhi Institute of Development Research (IGIDR), Institute for Human Development (IHD) and another jointly by Dr B. R. Ambedkar University and Ashoka University. We thank the organisers, especially R. Nagaraj, Alakh N. Sharma, Rajan Krishnan and Ravindran Sriramachandran for these opportunities. Three anonymous referees provided useful suggestions for improvement. Several activists, senior bureaucrats, journalists and entrepreneurs spared valuable time to share their insights and personal experiences that were indispensable to this work. We are deeply grateful to all of them.

Meera and Pulari endured our lengthy discussions over the last two years with patience, enthusiasm and hope. Preeti Swarrup enlivened life in Chennai and was a source of eternal optimism. Aparajithan Adhimoolam and Digant Chavan spent countless hours in conceptualising the cover design while Ashok Chandran helped us with preparing the bibliography. Megha Susan Philip and Gopika Kumaran helped collate and analyse some of the data used in the book. We thank them as well.

We owe a lot to Anwesha Rana at Cambridge University Press (CUP) for seeing this work through. Not only did she ensure that we finished things on time through her gentle persuasive skills, but also offered useful tips from start to finish. At CUP, we would also like to place on record our appreciation of Jinia Dasgupta and her team's meticulous copy-editing support.

We thank the United States–India Educational Foundation for the support provided to the first author through the Fulbright–Nehru post-doctoral fellowship.

Finally, we gratefully acknowledge the administrative support provided by Madras Institute of Development Studies and the Watson Institute for International and Public Affairs, Brown University, that made our work a lot easier.

1

THE DRAVIDIAN MODEL[1]

An Introduction

Subnational trajectories of development and sources of divergences increasingly constitute an important dimension of understanding the political economy of global development (Crouch and Streeck 1997; Storper 1997). The literature on subnational variations in the Global South, and institutional sources of their dynamism is, however, recent but expanding (World Bank 2009; Moncada and Snyder 2012; Giraudy, Moncada and Snyder 2019). Given that the fastest growing economies are primarily in the Global South, particularly Asia, an understanding of such processes in the Asian context becomes important at the current conjuncture. In fact, the Asian experience with 'catching up' and economic transformation has contributed substantially to the idea of the 'developmental state' (Evans and Heller 2018). While the Japanese experience highlighted a strong role for state action, recent successes of the East Asian newly industrialising economies (NIEs) reinforced the importance of the 'developmental state' as a conceptual category to understand what makes some countries improve their citizens' capabilities better than others.

Importantly, the relationship between capital accumulation, state and civil society in the Global South is seen to be distinct from the experience of Western capitalist economies. Chatterjee (2004) and Sanyal (2007) for example, have dealt at length with how governmental imperatives in postcolonial countries do not follow that of advanced capitalist economies even as they significantly shape the global capital accumulation dynamic. Chatterjee in his more recent work (2019) also points to the distinctiveness of politics in these regions, arguing that mobilisation in postcolonial democracies like India often draws upon reworked social identities forged through modern print cultures and governmental imperatives. Further, as Harriss-White (2003) has established, capital accumulation tends to rely on social stratification and actually reinforces social hierarchies based on caste and gender identities. Piketty (2020), in fact, argues that status-based inequalities in such countries, for instance based on caste, not only persist but constitute important sources of inequality as they modernise. Mapping the links between accumulation, state acts, political mobilisation around identities and development trajectories in these regions therefore becomes important.

India and China have been two of the fastest growing economies in the world since the early 2000s, contributing substantially to global wealth creation, given the size of their economies (Bardhan 2008). Talking about China's achievements on the growth front, Evans and Heller (2018) reason that it is impossible to understand the Chinese state as a unitary one despite having a centralised apparatus. Rather, they convince us that it should be seen as a multi-tiered system with subnational state institutions responsible for the 'day to day business of China's development' (p. 6). They therefore call for a 'multi-level embedded autonomy'[2] approach to understand the nature of interactions between policy formulation at the national level and implementation at the subnational level. While nature of the bureaucracy and 'embedded autonomy' based explanations account for national-level trajectories in the context of north eastern Asian economies, regional dynamism, variations and their embeddedness are not adequately accounted for. This becomes particularly important in a phase marked by growing divergence between regions in China (Ho and Li 2008) and India (Ghosh 2012), and emergence of regional economic miracles such as Shenzhen (World Bank 2009).

The development experience of India, the fastest growing economy in recent years, is intriguing. Despite being home to a well-entrenched democracy and a robust bureaucracy, it fails to deliver comparable development outcomes (Evans and Heller 2015, 2018). Development parameters for parts of India are closer to sub-Saharan Africa and lower than other South Asian countries like Bangladesh and Sri Lanka. There are, however, regions in India, the development outcomes of which are comparable to that of many Asian economies. Tamil Nadu, the southern-most province in the country is one such region (Drèze and Sen 2013). Comparable in economic output to Vietnam and Laos PDR,[3] the state's human development parameters are better than most states in the country (*Tamil Nadu Human Development Report*, hereafter

TNHDR [Government of Tamil Nadu 2017]). The Indian State is a 'quasi-federal' one with subnational governments given primary responsibility for crucial sectors like agriculture and human development including health and education. Further, given that democratic institutions have a longer history, political regimes at the regional level and the factors enabling them are likely to shape outcomes more than in many other Asian regions. Since the early 1990s, the union government has also sought to rescale governance by devolving crucial resource mobilisation tasks to subnational governments (Kennedy 2014). This 'responsibilisation' of state governments has been accompanied by growing regional disparities (Kar and Sakthivel 2007; Ghosh 2012) and club convergence among the richer and poorer states.

India therefore offers an interesting site to understand the political economy of such subnational development. Our attempt is to address this issue taking the case of Tamil Nadu in southern India, a state that has been noted for its ability to combine relatively high levels of economic growth with human development, particularly in the domains of education and healthcare (Drèze and Sen 2013; Harriss and Wyatt 2019). Arora (2009) classifies the Indian states in line with the stages of development proposed by Rostow (1959), and points out that states like Kerala, Tamil Nadu and Maharashtra have crossed the take-off stage and have entered the maturity phase. He also cites Kochhar et al. (2006) to argue that some of the states including Tamil Nadu resemble developed countries in the way they have diversified the sources of their growth. To quote Kochhar et al.,

> With the caveat that Indian states are enormously large entities and are internally very diverse, it would appear that the fast growing peninsular states are starting to resemble more developed countries in their specialization, while the slow growing hinterland states, with still rapidly growing, less well-educated, populations … may not have the capability to emulate them. (2006: p. 25)

In per capita incomes too they rank much higher than most states in the country. Understanding the sources of the distinctiveness of development trajectories, particularly in a context where states are embedded in a common macro-economic regime, is therefore central to tracking subnational variations.

This book contributes to the growing literature on how regional institutions and political regimes shape global development trajectories by mapping the politics and processes influencing the emergence of Tamil Nadu's fairly unique development path. Not only has the state revealed significant economic dynamism and structural transformation as mentioned above, the state also has better parameters of human development compared to similar economically dynamic states like Maharashtra and Gujarat (Kalaiyarasan 2014; Government of Tamil Nadu 2017). It has been a pioneer in forging a social welfare model based on providing entitlements outside the domain of employment that has since been adopted elsewhere (Vijayabaskar 2017; Kalaiyarasan 2020). Importantly, the state is also known for a distinct mode of political mobilisation that privileged caste-based inequalities over asset-based ones. We therefore ask, how does mobilisation against status-based inequalities transform developmental outcomes? We contend that while a distinct set of processes rooted in regional political mobilisation against caste hierarchies played an important role in the development outcomes in the state, the processes underway at the regional level are also shot through with national and global processes of development and capital accumulation. We therefore adopt a multi-level approach to subnational analysis, and demonstrate how national and supranational factors have also shaped this process. Before moving on to empirically establish a case for a study of the sources of Tamil Nadu's development outcomes, we highlight the set of policy processes that shaped subnational trajectories in India in the post-reform period. To do that, we engage with the emerging literature on regional institutions and regional development processes and how they contribute to shaping global development.

SIGNIFICANCE OF THE SUBNATIONAL SCALE

There are three analytically distinct but interrelated processes that make the subnational scale significant globally. One concerns shifts in economic processes and accumulation dynamics, while the second is rooted in the political imperative to govern the process of growth and the outcome of state action at the national level. Third, as Chatterjee (2019) and Giraudy,

Moncada and Snyder (2019) point out, it is important to understand political mobilisation at subnational scales as they not only shape larger developmental outcomes but are also critical to recover alternate political imaginaries beyond the level of the nation-state. Since the 1990s, the 'region' has re-emerged as a focus of industrial dynamism through innovation processes in the Global North (Krugman 1991; Storper 1997; Malmberg and Maskell 2002). Within mainstream economics, the emergence of the regional has been understood primarily through the new economic geography literature pioneered by Krugman. Economies of agglomeration allow for learning and technological dynamism that lead to concentration of economic activity rather than an evening out of spatial inequalities. This reasoning also has its antecedence within the broad domain of economic geography that has consistently highlighted the persistence of differences across regions, even in a dynamic sense. Starting with Marshall's observations on the tendency of economic activity to agglomerate in specific locales in late 19th-century England, going on to structuralist explanations for persistence of global divisions of labour and on to new economic geography that highlights the importance of learning and its positive spillovers within local geographies, there is overwhelming evidence that economic activity does not tend to develop in homogeneous space or lead to equalisation of returns across space (Harvey 2005; World Bank 2009). As a result, globalisation may undermine the efficacy of several national policy instruments, and proceed through regional integration across borders, drawing upon regional and local institutions to sustain accumulation (Hay 2000). Given the variations in institutional capacity across regions, globalisation is therefore likely to accentuate regional divergence within nation-states. Regional institutions are, however, dynamic entities, and are as much shaped by interactions with national and supranational institutions and economic impulses as they shape the process of globalisation (Coe et al. 2004). The observation that regional institutions are likely to be critical to the shaping of the process of globalisation therefore opens up our attention to the agency of subnational governments[4] and subnational politics in not only responding to globalisation but also in shaping its contours.

The next source of significance of the region or the subnational scale is one of governance. Amidst a perceived shift in the accumulation regime from Fordist to post-Fordist and the regulatory regime from Keynesian to neo-liberal, national governments have initiated a process of state rescaling, allowing greater agency for subnational governments to design and implement policies (Jessop, Brenner and Jones 2008; Kennedy 2014), even as pro-market reforms allow for a greater agency to the global capital accumulation dynamic to shape policies. Keating (2013) for example maps the emerging salience of the 'meso' region in the European Union (EU). Similarly, Lobao, Martin and Rodriguez-Pose (2009) point out how implementation of pro-market reforms and integration with global markets have been often accompanied by national governments devolving more responsibilities to regional and local governments. Regional governments, therefore, have strong incentives to engage in institutional learning and innovation. They are forced to assume the role of 'institutional entrepreneurs' with the aim of promoting regional development, particularly in the context of transition economies (Spencer, Murtha and Lenway 2005).

Further, as Snyder (2001) points out, the approach allows one to move away from giving primary agency to national-level actors, to subnational actors and regimes that have shaped national-level indicators. Importantly, such subnational variations are becoming more visible during a period when older dichotomies between the core and periphery postulated by structuralist geographers are less rigid. Though income inequalities between countries have come down marginally, subnational differences in income, that is, differences across regions within countries have increased globally (Garretsen et al. 2013), pointing to the importance of regional or subnational political regimes and institutions in taking advantage of the new spaces of accumulation. This therefore brings to the forefront, the importance of understanding how subnational politics shapes policy-making at that scale. Jeffery et al. (2014) show how, despite a unitary policy framework, there are growing regional differences in policy outcomes within Germany because of the agency of regional electorates. Fitjar (2010) maps the emergence of regional identities across western Europe, often more pronounced in regions where a different regional language is spoken or located further away from the country's capital.

We, however, know much less about the interactions between processes of development and regional political regimes in the context of the Global

South. There are, however, a few studies that emphasise subnational variations in such countries (Moncada and Snyder 2012; Giraudy, Moncada and Snyder 2019). Eaton (2004) acknowledges the growing salience of subnational actors across the Global South, from Russia and China to India and South Africa, particularly since the 1990s, when several of these countries began to economically integrate with global markets and adopted similar macro-economic policies to facilitate such integration. Efforts to rescale by central governments in these countries imply that subnational actors and political regimes are crucial to outcomes of globalisation. Huang (2015) illustrates this by showing how a combination of subnational policy choices, incentives for political actors and interactions with the national-level policy framework produce variations with regard to the extent of coverage under social health insurance programmes in China. Though there are similar studies on subnational divergence in economic trajectories,[5] there is less literature on political processes at the subnational level. Regional dynamism or otherwise is also accompanied by questions of regional politics around redistribution and welfare. In addition to growth, differences in the ability of regions to provide for social welfare and the sources of such differences are critical to our understanding of variations in subnational development. With the growing recognition of the role of human capital in sustaining growth dynamism, and the re-orientation of development as one aimed at expanding human capabilities (D'Costa and Chakraborty 2019), visibility of politics and policies around investments in human development and social welfare at the subnational level has increased. Since the initiation of economic reforms in the early 1990s, India too has witnessed divergence in terms of both economic growth and human development across states.

POLICY REFORMS AND REGIONAL DIVERGENCE IN INDIA

The Indian economy has experienced one of the fastest growth rates in the world for nearly 15 years, a period during which the state has sought to, and succeeded to an extent, in implementing a set of reforms that can be labelled 'pro-business' (Kohli 2012).[6] This is also a phase when several measures were undertaken to integrate its product and factor markets with the global market, and also devolve more responsibilities to subnational governments. Market-oriented economic reforms were accompanied by the downscaling of resource mobilisation responsibilities to state governments (Kennedy 2014). Until then, the union government had played a key role in mobilising resources for investment and in locating economic activity. Since the 1990s, the union government shifted the onus of resource mobilisation considerably to state governments which were encouraged to attract private investments through various incentives. In fact, as Jain and Maini (2017) point out, subnational governments in India have even begun to shape the nature of foreign relations through their autonomous engagement with other countries for investments and trade. Even as regional governments positioned themselves as active agents shaping growth and private investments, their ability to chart autonomous paths of development is likely to be varied (Jenkins 2004).

This is a period that was also characterised by divergences in regional growth performance (Kar and Sakthivel 2007; Ghosh 2012). The western and southern regions have grown at a much faster rate compared to the rest of the country. This divergence and the emergence of a set of fast-growing states opened up a discursive narrative about the ideal subnational model state to emulate. In post-reform India, it has become commonplace in popular debates to pit one state vis-à-vis another as the appropriate model. If it was Chandrababu Naidu's undivided Andhra Pradesh in the late 1990s (Mooij 2003), it was the Gujarat model in the 2000s, which has, however, been contested (Nagaraj and Pandey 2013; Kalaiyarasan 2014). Such debates also speak to larger debates on the direction of economic development by scholars such as Drèze and Sen (2013) and Bhagwati and Panagariya (2013). The Bhagwati–Sen debate epitomises the differences in developmental priorities at the subnational level. While Bhagwati's proposition makes a case for a trickle-down approach where growth will translate into development as it provides resources for human development, Drèze and Sen make a case for a capability-centred developmental path where investments in human capabilities should be prioritised, which can then translate into economic development. According to them, this path is likely to be more inclusive. Both positions draw empirical support from the experiences of subnational regions.

While Bhagwati and Panagariya (2013) base their arguments on the Gujarat model of rapid economic growth driven by a pro-capital growth policy, Drèze and Sen (2013) draw upon the cases of Kerala and Tamil Nadu to point out how public investments in health and education have led to a more inclusive development trajectory.

Rather than seek models for emulation, scholars also argue that in the post-reform era, regional political regimes critically shape policies of distribution and welfare (Harriss 1999). Using a classificatory scheme drawn from an earlier study, Harriss differentiates political regimes based on the source of political power that ruling parties draw from, and the extent of their stability. He contends that these two factors shape the distributivist policies of subnational governments. Based on this scheme, he classifies Tamil Nadu, Kerala and West Bengal as three states where political power has been drawn from lower-caste and lower-class mobilisation over a long period. This political base, he points out, may explain the emergence of more proactive welfare regimes compared to other states where substantial political power has been drawn more from upper castes and upper classes. However, as Singh (2015) points out, mere sourcing of power from lower castes alone does not adequately explain outcomes. West Bengal, for example, reveals poor human development indicators despite having a regime drawn from the lower classes (Kalaiyarasan 2017b). Moreover, as Witsoe (2013) argues based on his study of Bihar, political regimes that draw their power from lower castes need not necessarily generate human development. Further, it is still not clear whether such differences in political regimes can shape the trajectory of economic growth. It is also for this reason that Kohli (2012) is not able to clearly slot the developmental path of Tamil Nadu within his typology of states. As we argue in the next chapter, it is the distinctive way that power and social justice were conceptualised by populist Dravidian[7] mobilisation in the state that may explain its developmental trajectory.

Subnational trajectories of development and divergences thus constitute an important axis to understand the political economy of Indian development. Importantly, given the size of India's economy, and the fact that it is the fastest growing economy globally, it is imperative to recognise the institutional embedding of one of its most progressive subnational regions as it negotiates national rules and institutions and global market impulses to forge a developmental path. The book therefore contributes to the growing literature on the dynamics of subnational development by mapping the politics and processes that enabled better development outcomes in Tamil Nadu. In the next section, we critically review the existing accounts of the state's development experience.

CURRENT EXPLANATIONS

Most literature on the state's developmental experience deals with the impulses and implications of its welfarist or populist politics. Though their primary focus was on the mobilisational strategies of the Dravidian movement, Narendra Subramanian (1999) and Arun Swamy (1998) attribute the state's welfare interventions to competitive populism in the domain of polity. They identify two strands of populism. One, assertive or empowerment populism, that involved mobilisation based on the Tamil-Dravidian identity, appealed to the intermediate castes, and was characterised by initiation of affirmative action policies that led to a degree of access to higher education and modern jobs among the better off sections among these castes. They also identify a paternalist or protection populist strand in policy-making, aimed at actors or classes (lower castes) that failed to benefit from assertive populist measures. This involved launch of several welfare programmes that are now considered typical of the state's developmental trajectory. Both studies identify the limits of such moves in delivering inclusive development by pointing to the inability of the state to engage substantively with land reforms, and also suggest that the Dravidian movement was biased towards the propertied intermediate castes. While we question this reading at length in the next chapter, neither of them recognise the possibility that interactions between the domain of social welfare policies and the domain of economic incentive structures may shape the trajectory of economic development. There is therefore little engagement with the process of human capital formation or capital accumulation and labour outcomes. Further, given the timing of their studies, they do not account for the state's ability to sustain a relatively more inclusive development path in the post-reform period, characterised by not only registering above average growth rates but also above average reduction in poverty, particularly among the Scheduled Castes (SCs), and below average increases in inequality (as discussed later in this chapter).

More recent explanations by Drèze and Sen (2013), Vivek (2014) and Lakshman (2011) ascribe the success of Tamil Nadu to a long history of collective action, in turn attributed to political mobilisation among the lower castes and classes by the Dravidian and the left movements. Such mobilisations in the past have lent voice to the beneficiaries of public investments in health and education which in turn has ensured that institutions of delivery are rendered accountable. Lakshman (2011) while conceding the limits of this mobilisation in terms of its class and caste character in line with previous studies, admits that it did lead to the development of political patronage for the poor. The studies do not offer a historical perspective or evidence of the processes that made such collective action possible or of what shaped other domains such as labour outcomes or capital accumulation. Vivek (2014), while pointing to the presence of collective action in a set of villages in the state reads the history of past political mobilisations into such action rather than actually mapping the links between the emergence of a historic bloc of subaltern actors making material claims on the state and better delivery. Narayan (2018), on the other hand, sees a different role for political mobilisation in the more efficient delivery of services. First, the entry of lower-caste members into the bureaucracy, and second, the mediation of party cadres between citizens and the bureaucracy ensured better delivery of public services. In all these accounts, however, collective action is reduced to primarily ensuring efficiency of delivery of public services and social welfare programmes. They do not therefore account for the pattern of accumulation and economic transformation in the state, interactions between accumulation processes, social mobilisation and development outcomes.

Singh (2015), makes a case for identity-based mobilisation in delivering subnational development. Countering standard arguments that identity-based mobilisation hinders welfare, Singh argues, based on the experience of Kerala and Tamil Nadu, that it was the formation of a Malayalee and Tamil identity, respectively, in the two states that fostered 'solidaristic' ties across social groups and a collective ethos that made social development possible. In the context of Tamil Nadu, she contends that the initial imagination of a subnational Tamil identity among educated urban elites in the early 20th century was insufficient. It was the diffusion of this subnationalist ethos among the non-elites in the second half of the 20th century that led to better design and implementation of social welfare policies. Apart from the near exclusive focus on interventions in social sectors, Singh does not tell us why such identity formation led to a distinct pattern of development in the state. Sinha (2005), Kennedy (2004) and Harriss and Wyatt (2019) are a few interventions that seek to understand the processes of accumulation and growth, and institutions governing these processes. Sinha attributes the relative lack of industrial development vis-à-vis Gujarat to a lack of emphasis among regional elites to spur industrial growth as they pursued anti-central-government politics. In fact, she sees a link between a greater emphasis on welfare policies and the relative neglect of industrial development. Harriss and Wyatt (2019) posit a 'growth for elites and welfare for the poor' strategy of accumulation in the state, in line with earlier interpretations. According to them, though social welfare policies launched by successive governments in the state do address the issue of poverty, this does not undermine the power of the capitalist class. In other words, they claim maintenance of status quo in the domain of the economy. Such a reading does not allow for possible changes in the modes of capital accumulation nor shifts in the basis of entrepreneurship. None of the studies, in fact, empirically establish how the relations of power are reproduced nor do they offer explanations for the sustained growth process that has made the state's development trajectory unique. It is worth reiterating at this point that in post-reform India, the state has not only managed to reduce poverty levels dramatically through a slew of welfarist interventions, but has also managed to ensure high per capita incomes, and that too consistently higher than all-India average rates (Government of Tamil Nadu 2017).

This phenomenon is particularly striking, given the diverse trajectories of the three states that have drawn political power through mobilisation of lower classes and castes (Harriss 1999). While Kerala's high levels of human development have not been backed by expansion of the productive sectors,[8] West Bengal has not only failed to revive the strong industrial base it inherited from the colonial period, but has also not been able to improve human development indicators significantly despite implementation of land reforms

(Kalaiyarasan 2017b). At the other end, states that have non-social-democratic regimes like Gujarat and Maharashtra have managed to deliver on the growth front, but have not done well in the domain of human development (Kohli 2012). Our study of Tamil Nadu is therefore meant to not only offer a better explanation of outcomes and the development trajectory in the state, but is also meant to open a dialogue on the developmental possibilities at the subnational level. In the remaining chapters, we establish how welfare interventions are linked to the emerging processes of accumulation and growth. We also identify the limits of this process that are rooted not just in populist mobilisation, but also in the mode of economic transformation and the constraints posed by its status as a subnational entity. We use the term 'model', therefore, to open the field of subnational studies and to generate questions on the links between development and caste based mobilisation.

Further, there is no work on Tamil Nadu that compares with works on other states such as on Kerala (Heller 1999), Gujarat (Sud 2012), Uttar Pradesh (Pai 2007), Punjab (Singh 2008) and Bihar (Witsoe 2013). Given the growing recognition of the state's developmental experience, we propose to address this gap by (a) mapping the trajectory of economic development in the state since the 1960s; (b) linking the trajectory to processes in the domain of subnational political mobilisations, public policy and macro-economic shifts at the national level and (c) identifying the limits to such a model of subnational development in the context of a changing macro political–economic environment.

Using a comparative framework, the rest of the chapter establishes the empirical basis of the state's distinct development trajectory. Using data over a 50-year period, the chapter maps the growth and developmental performance of the state in comparison with other economically dynamic states like Gujarat and Maharashtra,[9] and establishes that the state has indeed registered significant accomplishments in terms of growth, income, poverty reduction and structural transformation.[10] Indicators such as gross state domestic product (GSDP), per capita income and employment status are used to map the process. Sectoral shifts in terms of both income and employment are mapped. Next, evolution of the state's achievements in poverty reduction and human development over this time period will be traced through use of indicators in health, education and poverty.

ECONOMIC GROWTH AND STRUCTURAL TRANSFORMATION IN TAMIL NADU

We begin with a comparative mapping of economic growth in the state.

The state has consistently clocked higher growth than the all-India average in the post-reform period. In the 1960s, Tamil Nadu had higher poverty levels than the national average (Drèze and Sen 2013), though it had a relatively higher per capita income. The decadal average per capita income for the state in the 1960s was INR 10,314 (at 2004–05 price) while the corresponding figures for Maharashtra, Gujarat and West Bengal were INR 11,236, INR 10,105 and INR 9,151, respectively (Table 1.1).

Since then, the state's income has risen in comparative terms. While it had a per capita income twice (203 per cent) that of Bihar in the 1960s, it has gone up to four times (420 per cent) in the 2010s. Its ability to increase per capita income much more than that of West Bengal during this period too is notable. Such increase in income is also borne out by a comparison with the all-India average; while the state had an income only marginally (by 14 per cent) higher than India's per capita income in the 1960s, it has gone up to 155 per cent of the all-India average in the 2010s. In terms of position, while the state stood fourth among 12 large states in the 1960s, it occupied the third rank in 1990, and moved up to the second position in 2014 (as per method adopted by Chakravarty and Dehejia 2016). As per our estimates, the state's per capita income has risen in relative terms but is lower than Maharashtra and marginally less than Gujarat.

Table 1.1 Per Capita Income (INR) at Base 2004–05

Year	Tamil Nadu	Maharashtra	Gujarat	West Bengal	Bihar	All India
1960s	10,314	11,236	10,105	9,151	5,091	9,005
1970s	11,474	13,192	11,272	9,229	5,400	9,951
1980s	12,855	16,142	14,565	10,588	6,391	11,754
1990s	20,623	25,704	22,031	14,852	6,571	16,172
2000s	34,050	40,228	34,810	23,784	8,386	25,355
2010s	57,831	63,764	58,193	33,487	13,775	37,333

Source: RBI, *Handbook of Statistics on Indian States*, https://rbi.org.in/Scripts/AnnualPublications.aspx ?head=Handbook+of+Statistics+on+Indian+States (accessed 12 March 2019).

What is also significant is the nature of economic growth. The increase in per capita incomes has been accompanied by structural transformation of a degree that is higher than any other major state in the country. Not only does the state have the second lowest share of population dependent on agriculture, agriculture contributes less than 8 per cent to the state's income which is less than half the all-India average (Government of Tamil Nadu 2017). Importantly, it has the largest share of workers in manufacturing, and has built a vibrant manufacturing base, particularly in labour-intensive sectors like textiles, garments, leather goods and automobile manufacturing. As per the *Annual Survey of Industries* (*ASI*) 2014 (Government of India 2014), Tamil Nadu has the highest share (15.4 per cent) of registered factories in India. The state also has the highest (15.1 per cent) share of persons engaged in Indian registered manufacturing. In other words, it has managed to shift a higher share of population from agriculture to the industrial sector. In terms of gross value added (GVA), the state stands third after Maharashtra and Gujarat despite having the largest share of its labour in manufacturing, indicating the relatively higher labour intensity of its manufacturing base. According to Amirapu and Subramanian (2015), Tamil Nadu's manufacturing output has reached as high as 18 per cent of the GSDP, second only to Gujarat's 22 per cent. Though Gujarat has a higher manufacturing base, it is not as broad based as Tamil Nadu. As Nagaraj and Pandey (2013) show, export-oriented petroleum refining alone accounts for about a quarter of the GVA in registered manufacturing in Gujarat, which may not offer enough by way of employment. The dynamism of Tamil Nadu's manufacturing is also evident when we look at the unorganised sector. Combining the output of both organised and unorganised sectors in employment, as per the National Sample Survey Office (NSSO) 2011–12, the state has the highest share of employment (19.9 per cent) as against 19 per cent in Gujarat, 12.2 per cent in Maharashtra and 12.6 per cent at the all-India level.

After the economic reforms of the early 1990s, the state has sustained its productive dynamism through mobilisation of foreign capital as well. It has managed to attract a number of multinational firms to set up operations, and has also drawn investments into urban infrastructure development through promotion of public–private partnerships (PPPs). Particularly noteworthy is the Sriperumbudur case—an industrial cluster close to Chennai, which has been recognised as a successful instance of state policies enabling the attraction of foreign investments (World Bank 2009). Leading global firms specialising in the production of hardware and electronic goods like Nokia, Samsung, Motorola, Dell and Foxconn have set up productive capacities in the region over the last 15 years, responding to a slew of government incentives. Though it had a production base for automobile manufacturing even earlier, Chennai has emerged as India's leading automobile and auto components exporter, and is often referred to as the 'Detroit of India'. The region accounts for 35 per cent of auto component production in India, and is home to the world's leading automobile producers like Hyundai, Ford, Daimler Benz, Yamaha, BMW and Mitsubishi (Babu 2009). Hyundai has made Chennai the manufacturing and export hub for its small cars, with Chennai being its largest base outside South Korea. In fact, the *World Development Report* (World Bank 2009), with its focus on the importance of new economic geography in understanding growth dynamism, has identified overlaps in the growth processes underway in this region with that of China's Shenzhen province.

Apart from having a strong manufacturing base, the state is also home to vibrant software, medical and educational services industries. In 2016, the state along with Karnataka and Telangana accounted for 60 per cent of the information technology (IT) and information-technology enabled services (ITeS) exports from India (Dubbudu 2017). Given that India is the largest exporter of software services globally, the significance of this phenomenon cannot be understated, as this growth is premised on the build-up of human capabilities. Apart from national players like Infosys, Tata Consultancy Services (TCS) and WIPRO, it also houses software development centres of multinational corporations (MNCs) like IBM, CTS and Oracle. In addition, thanks to a relatively robust public healthcare system, private investments in medical education and emergence of corporatised private healthcare providers, the state has also come to be a leading centre for medical services. Private investments in overall education, in particular, technical education, have led to the state also becoming a major provider of educational services.

Another significant aspect is the spatial dimension of industrialisation in the state. Enterprises are more evenly distributed across sub-regions within the state. Though the western (Coimbatore and Tiruppur regions) and northern (Chennai and Kancheepuram) parts are the most industrialised regions, industrialisation is still spatially diverse if one makes a comparison with Gujarat and Maharashtra. Each sub region has specific industrial clusters dominated by small-scale enterprises and localised entrepreneurship (Damodaran 2016). Such decentralised industrialisation integrates the countryside with urban areas, and is likely to create more diversification options outside of agriculture. The state has one of the highest shares of income from non-farm sector employment among rural households. A steady decline in both the share and absolute number of cultivators since the 1990s suggests a movement of the rural workforce to non-agricultural and urban spaces. The percentage of cultivators in rural Tamil Nadu has come down from 29 per cent in 1981 to just 13 per cent in 2011, which is one of the lowest figures across states in India (Government of Tamil Nadu 2017).

Besides Chennai, most of the regional clusters are known for their agro-commercial-based entrepreneurship drawn from the middle castes. Many of them are from peasant and provincial mercantile castes as opposed to the dominance of elite pan-Indian trading communities in other regions (Chari 2004; Damodaran 2008; Mahadevan and Vijayabaskar 2014). As we demonstrate in Chapter 5, entrepreneurship in the state is also socially broad based. The Dalit Indian Chamber of Commerce and Industry (DICCI) in fact claims that the state is home to one of the highest concentrations of Dalit enterprises in India (Naig 2015). While Tamil Nadu, along with Gujarat and Maharashtra, is among the most industrialised states in the country, what makes it distinct from the other two, is this labour-intensive, spatially and socially inclusive nature of industrialisation, which has drawn a greater share of population out of agriculture.

GOVERNANCE AND PHYSICAL INFRASTRUCTURE

The ability to structurally transform is likely to be tied to better economic governance. The state ranks second after Kerala with regard to public governance indices (Indo Asian News Service 2018). A more robust exercise of constructing a governance index was done by Mundle et al. (2012) to map the quality of governance across states using indicators such as infrastructure, social service delivery, fiscal performance, law and order, judicial service delivery and quality of legislature. According to this ranking, the state falls within the top five for all of these indicators. In the domain of physical infrastructure, it has one of the best sets of combined indices for roads, electricity and telecom, and was ranked third among the major states in India in 2010.[11] Tamil Nadu is particularly known for its transport infrastructure, and ranked the highest in the country. On the energy front, the state is one of the top nine markets globally for renewable power generation (Sushma 2018). Originating primarily in wind energy with the setting up of wind farms, the state has in recent years also diversified into solar power. At present, the state derives close to 15 per cent of its energy requirements from such renewable sources. Having mapped the state's achievements in economic growth, structural transformation and governance, we now highlight its achievements in the realm of distribution by looking at poverty reduction and inequality.

DISTRIBUTION AND POVERTY REDUCTION

As stated earlier, Tamil Nadu was one of the poorer states in India in the 1960s. As per the estimate of Suryanaryana (1986),[12] the incidence of rural poverty in Tamil Nadu was 51.7 per cent in 1960–61—one of the highest as compared to the major states (Gujarat: 37.4 per cent, Maharashtra: 41.4 per cent, and even slightly higher than Bihar: 49.7 per cent), and much higher than the all-India average (38.2 per cent). The state has, however, seen a dramatic decline in poverty in the last 50 years, and has done better than most states with regard to poverty reduction (see Table 1.2).

According to Tendulkar committee metrics,[13] the incidence of rural poverty in Tamil Nadu has come down to 15.8 per cent in 2011–12, which is one of the lowest in the country. The rate of decline in rural poverty between 1960–61 and 2011–12 has been faster than in most states.[14] Urban poverty decline too has been more rapid (Table 1.2). The incidence of poverty in urban Tamil Nadu was as high as 51.8 per cent in 1973–74, comparable to Bihar's 53.9 per cent, and worse than the all-India average. After 50 years, the incidence of poverty has come down to 6.5 per cent in 2011–12, the third lowest among the major states, and also lower than that of Gujarat or Maharashtra.

What is also significant is that the state has done better in poverty reduction across caste groups. The socially marginalised have seen a faster reduction of

Table 1.2 Trends in Incidence of Poverty across Selected States in India

Year		Tamil Nadu	Maharashtra	Gujarat	West Bengal	Bihar	All India
				Rural Poverty			
1960–61	All	51.7	41.4	37.4	61.6	49.7	38.5
1993–94	All	51.2	59.4	43.3	42.6	62.5	50.2
	SC	66.4	74.1	56.6	48.3	76.8	62.4
2004–05	All	37.5	47.9	39.1	38.2	55.7	41.8
	SC	51.2	66.1	49.3	37.1	77.6	53.5
2011–12	All	15.8	24.2	21.5	22.5	34.4	25.7
	SC	23.3	23.8	22.3	22.6	51.7	31.5
				Urban Poverty			
1973–74	All	51.8	45.2	53.9	46.6	53.9	48.9
1993–94	All	33.8	30.5	28.2	31.3	44.8	31.6
	SC	57.1	48.6	49.3	50.3	66.9	51.7
2004–05	All	19.7	25.6	20.1	24.4	43.7	25.6
	SC	40.7	36.0	18.7	40.9	71.2	40.6
2011–12	All	6.5	9.1	10.1	14.7	31.2	13.7
	SC	9.3	15.8	12.7	15.7	43.0	21.7

Source: Authors' estimation from various rounds of NSSO–CES data except for the year 1960–61, which was adapted from Suryanarayana (1986).

poverty compared to others. Since we do not have poverty estimates for caste groups for 1961–62, we track this process from 1993–94 to 2011–12. The gains SCs made in the rate of poverty reduction between 1993–94 and 2011–12 in Tamil Nadu is 43.1 percentage points, which is higher than that in Gujarat (34.3 percentage points) and Bihar (25.1 percentage points), but lower than that in Maharashtra (50.3 percentage points). Urban poverty reduction too is suggestive of this relatively more socially inclusive development process. The incidence of poverty among SCs in urban Tamil Nadu was 66 per cent in 1993–94 which reduced to to 12.7 per cent in 2011–12 (Kalaiyarasan 2014)—one of the highest poverty reductions among the states in the country. In sum, Tamil Nadu has managed to address poverty better than most states. This is particularly significant because the state had inherited no historical advantage

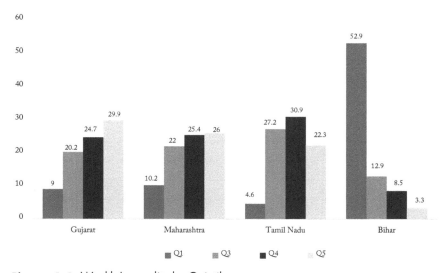

Figure 1.1 Wealth Inequality by Quintile
Source: National Family Health Survey-4 (2015–16).

and had either similar or higher levels of poverty than that of several states in the early 1960s.

Chatterjee (2019) contends that populist regimes tend to be more engaged with issues of absolute poverty than relative poverty. The state has, however, also reduced relative poverty to an extent. As assets are more durable, wealth inequality is a better measure of inequality compared to income and consumption based inequality measures. The recent National Family Health Survey (NFHS-4, 2015–16) offers quintile distribution of households based on their wealth.[15] In Tamil Nadu, as Figure 1.1 shows, the proportion that lies in Q3 and Q4 accounts for close to 60 per cent of the population.

This suggests a relatively better diffusion of economic growth as the corresponding figures for Gujarat and Maharashtra are about 45 per cent and 47 per cent, respectively. On the other hand, the state has relatively less poor—5 per cent in the bottom quintile. A state like Bihar has about 75 per cent of its population in the lowest two quintiles indicating more concentration in the lower spectrum of distribution. We now turn to the gains made by the state in the domains of education and public health.

EDUCATION AND HEALTH

Not only does the state have relatively higher literacy levels, but the improvements are again more inclusive across social groups (Chapter 3). The literacy rate for those above the age of 6 years was 21 per cent in 1951 and has improved to 80 per cent in 2011. The corresponding figures for India are 18 and 74 per cent, respectively. An outcome indicator that captures the spread of literacy is the reduction in gender gap in literacy. Tamil Nadu had a gender gap greater than that at the all-India level until 1981. Since 1981, the gender gap in literacy in Tamil Nadu has recorded significant improvements. Importantly, youth in the state have relatively better access to higher education. According to the 2017–18 report of the All India Survey on Higher Education (AISHE) (Government of India 2018a), 48.6 per cent of Tamil Nadu's youth in the age group of 18–23 years are engaged in some form of higher education or the other which is the highest for major states in the country, and even better than that of some countries in the Global North (Figure 1.2).

Access to tertiary education is also relatively inclusive with about 42 per cent of youth among the SCs being enrolled in higher education as against

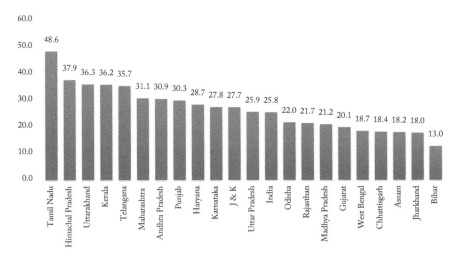

Figure 1.2 Gross Enrolment Ratio in Higher Education for All Groups (18–23 Years)
Source: Government of India (2018a).

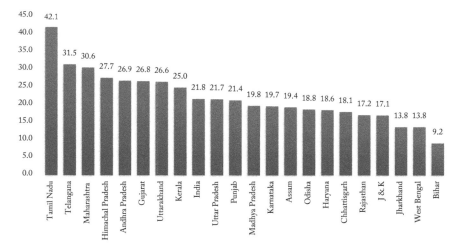

Figure 1.3 Gross Enrolment Ratio in Higher Education for Scheduled Castes (18–23 Years)

Source: Government of India (2018a).

21.8 per cent at the all-India level (Figure 1.3). In fact, this access is also much higher than what all castes could achieve in a state like Uttar Pradesh (only 26 per cent).

Tamil Nadu has performed better in the domain of health as well (Chapter 4). The total fertility rate (TFR) has shown a sharp decline from 3.9 in 1971 to 1.7 in 2013. The corresponding figures for the all-India level are 5.2 and 2.3, respectively. The decline in fertility rate is the fastest in Tamil Nadu, and comparable to many high income countries (less than replacement rate). Similarly, the state has done well in reducing mortality rates too. The infant mortality rate (IMR) has declined from 121 in 1972 to 19 in 2015, while the decline for India was from 139 to 41. The under-five mortality rate (U5MR) is 20 in the state as against 43 for India. The maternal mortality ratio (MMR) too is much better than the all-India average—90 for Tamil Nadu as against 178 at the all-India level. As with overall trends, as we elaborate in Chapter 4, the achievements in health among marginal social groups in the state are much better than most states, and comparable to the health status of the general population in states like Uttar Pradesh. Tamil

Nadu is therefore unique among the major states in India for its ability to combine processes of structural transformation with human development. It is particularly important to note that this process has been sustained during a period of pro-business and pro-market economic reforms initiated by the union government, suggesting an ability to draw upon regional political and economic institutions to negotiate with global economic impulses. That it has managed to do so without undermining the process of human development highlights the salience of the subnational political regime and the factors that shape the regime's actions.

The rest of the book is organised as follows. In the next chapter, drawing upon historical material on the roots of populist mobilisation in the state, we develop an analytical framework to explain the nature of popular demands emerging in the region, and how these demands are institutionalised in policy regimes. Subsequent chapters are devoted to mapping the processes and policy interventions that led to developmental outcomes across different domains. Chapters 3 and 4 address the processes underlying the outcomes in education and health, respectively. We argue that a demand for inclusive modernisation led to a series of interventions in the domains of education and health that translated into better human development outcomes. In particular, we emphasise the emergence of a 'common sense' around affirmative action policies and the importance of technical education. In the domain of health, we map the policy interventions in public health and the role of a socially broad-based bureaucracy in delivering better health outcomes. In Chapter 5, we move on to underscore the processes that enabled capital accumulation and a more broad-based entrepreneurship in the state. We highlight how social justice was imagined in terms of accelerating industrial development, which in turn led to both creation of supportive infrastructure, and direct policy measures. Chapters 6 and 7 engage with labour market outcomes, and policy and political processes that shaped such outcomes. In these chapters, we argue how mobilisation through aggregating subaltern caste identities and subsequent interventions have led to relatively better labour outcomes. While Chapter 6 deals with rural labour regimes, Chapter 7 focusses on urban labour with specific emphasis on industrial labour. The last chapter evaluates the development process in light of the emerging limits.

NOTES

1 By the term 'model', we mean 'a theoretical description that can help you understand how a system or process works ...' See Collins Dictionary for definition. Available at https://www.collinsdictionary.com/dictionary/english/model (accessed 10 December 2020). We, therefore, use it to explain how different parts or variables within a system interact with one another to generate systemic processes. As an interpretative model, it helps to explain development outcomes in the state. But, recognition of some elements of the model are likely to be useful in other contexts. Here, our contention is that mobilisation against caste based inequality can deliver dignity and development simultaneously.

2 'Multi-level' refers to the interactions between processes taking place at the subnational, national and supranational levels. 'Embedded autonomy' speaks to the nature of the links that the State has with local actors. While it is important that the State is embedded enough to respond to the demands of such actors, it should also be autonomous from sectional interests to craft policies that are developmental in nature (Evans 1995).

3 See https://statisticstimes.com/economy/comparing-indian-states-and-countries-by-gdp.php (accessed 20 April 2019).

4 Throughout the book, we use the terms 'region', 'subnational' and 'state' interchangeably. We use 'State' to refer to the state apparatus at the national level.

5 De Silva and Sumarto (2015) highlight variations in poverty and health outcomes across subnational units in Indonesia. Yelery (2014) in the context of China, and Mykhnenko and Swain (2010) in the case of Ukraine, map such subnational divergences.

6 While Jenkins (2004) suggests that the Indian state did attempt to initiate pro-market reforms by stealth, Kohli argues that the reforms have been more 'pro-business' than pro-market, with evidence of cronyism.

7 We elaborate on the nature of this mobilisation in the next chapter.

8 While Kerala has the best indices of human development parameters, we would also like to point out that Kerala's development experience is an exception. Despite not having a dynamic productive base, the state has

relied on its human capital and geographic location to generate remittances and drive growth. Consequently, we prefer to draw comparisons with states like Maharashtra and Gujarat that have developed a dynamic industrial base like Tamil Nadu.

9   While we use secondary data to compare Tamil Nadu's development outcomes with that of Gujarat and Maharashtra, we do not engage with a comparative analysis of the political and policy processes in the two states.

10 Throughout the book, we compare the growth and development outcomes of Tamil Nadu primarily with these two states, and the all-India average.

11 See http://www.idfc.com/images/news_release/infra-index-131210-pres-sent-to-mint.pdf (accessed 15 June 2019).

12 Suryanarayana (1986) constructs poverty lines based on methods provided by Bardhan (1973) and Ahluwalia (1978) at 1961–62 prices across states, and updates these poverty lines from 1961–62 (17th round of NSSO) to 1977–78 (32nd round of NSSO).

13 The Tendulkar methodology requires a mixed reference period (MRP) series of expenditure to calculate the incidence of poverty. The method used to construct the MRP series is the following—MRP = 30 days reference period data for all other items + 365 days reference period for low frequency items (cloth, footwear, durable goods, education and medical) − 30 days reference period for low frequency items.

14 The computations of Suryanarayana and Tendulkar are not strictly comparable as the bases of poverty lines differ, but they still give us an idea of the distance that different states have travelled since the 1960s in poverty reduction.

15 The quintiles are compiled by assigning a household score in an index of assets ranging from TV and car to housing characteristics to each household member, ranking each person in the household population by their score, and then dividing the distribution into five equal categories.

2

CONCEPTUALISING POWER IN CASTE SOCIETY

If subnational political regimes can shape development trajectories, the constituents of such a regime, and the factors enabling this, require explanation. Towards this, in this chapter, we develop a framework to understand the factors and processes contributing to the state's developmental achievements. We emphasise the primary role played by Dravidian mobilisation against upper-caste hegemony and its vision of social justice in shaping this regime (Pandian 2007; Rajadurai and Geetha 2009; Krishnan and Sriramachandran 2018a and 2018b). We highlight the political labour involved in the formation of a historic bloc or a 'people' comprising of a range of subaltern groups under a transitive 'Dravidian'–'Tamil'–'non-Brahmin' identity against this hegemony. We argue that this mobilisation articulated a demand for 'self-respect' and 'social justice' which has shaped the development trajectory of the state as political regimes sought to respond to this demand. Social justice was to be secured through a process of inclusive modernisation that will undermine the caste-based division of labour. The mobilisation thus demanded, and sought to ensure, equality of opportunity in the expanding modern domain. We draw upon Laclau's (2005) interpretation of populist mobilisation to understand how such demands coalesced to become a 'Dravidian common-sense' (Forgacs 2000)[1] in the state, and shaped its subsequent development.

Following Pandian (1994, 2007), Rajadurai and Geetha (1996) and Geetha and Rajadurai (2008), we show how leaders of the Justice party, the political precursor to the Dravidian movement, and subsequently Periyar, founder of the Dravidian movement and the Self-Respect Movement (SRM) distinguished the 'productive' 'non-Brahmin' castes from those who survived off rentierism and/or through labour that did not contribute to the well-being of the region.[2] Their mobilisation made visible the contours of caste-based social injustice, constituting in turn what we refer to as 'Dravidian common-sense' that comprised of securing justice through *caste-based reservation, faith in a productivist ethos, need for greater state autonomy and forging an inclusive modernity*. Importantly, as Pandian and more recently Sriramachandran (2018) point out, mobilisation was not founded on essentialised identities, but through forging of Dravidian 'people' based on an aggregation of disparate subaltern 'social' demands. We propose that the Dravidian movement approximates to what Mouffe (2018) calls left populism that effectively created a chain of equivalence between caste oppression and Dravidian-Tamil identity. We rely on Laclau's understanding of populism to refer to the political ability to forge and appeal to a 'people' consisting of heterogeneous groups with different 'social demands', and mobilising them on the basis of a 'popular' Dravidian-Tamil demand.

Before turning to mobilisation by the Dravidian movement and its vision of social justice and implications for developmental imagination, we outline the context and the set of historical contingencies that led to a specific conceptualisation of power in the Madras Presidency[3] under colonial rule. We then track the evolution of the conception of social justice within the Dravidian movement, and mark its distinctiveness. Drawing upon the works of Periyar, the founding ideologue of the movement, we show how the movement conceptualised caste-based power to be more systemic than that of economic class in the Indian context. This in turn translated into an imagination of social justice that saw abolishing caste-based hierarchies and injustice as fundamental to building an egalitarian socioeconomic system. Broad basing access to opportunities in the modern economy, administration and public sphere was in turn a small step towards this process, and more critical to the project than redistribution of rural assets like land. We also make a case for how a critique of Brahminical Hindusim[4] and the nationalist movement was crucial to the imagination of an alternate and inclusive 'Dravidian-Tamil' identity. If political mobilisation based on a Dravidian-Tamil identity enabled the coalescence of diverse demands into a set of rights for all Dravidians-Tamils, what were the factors that led to the emergence of a specific form of popular demand that managed to assume a hegemonic role in the state? The reason of populism as put forward by Laclau (2005), and elaborated more recently by Mouffe (2018) and Chatterjee (2019) helps us to not only understand what made this identity-based mobilisation advance substantive democracy but also to understand fissures and possibilities within such a populist project.

POPULISM, TAMIL STYLE

Contrary to dominant readings of the emergence of populism as an aberrant outcome of liberal democracy, the Laclauian argument is that it can be a distinct political reason operating in the 'field of democracy' (Chatterjee 2019: p. 82). Making 'people' sovereign implies that construction of a 'people' becomes important. He also sees this political constitution of a 'people' as offering a way of advancing the project of radical democracy in a context where capitalist development has not led to the anticipated emergence of a homogenous working class capable of acting for itself and consequently against the capitalist system. The multiplicity of sources of power and marginalisation is even more so in the context of postcolonial societies. That power in such societies is inter-sectional, involving multiple configurations of ethnicity, language, religion, caste, gender and class, is well acknowledged (Radcliffe 2015; Banerjee and Ghosh 2019). Under such conditions, especially with the strong embedding of capitalist accumulation in these identities (Harriss-White 2003), political mobilisation of subaltern groups subject to multiple axes of exploitation, subordination and discrimination under a politico-cultural identity opens new democratic possibilities. It, however, also runs the risk of a dominant elite exercising hegemonic control over such marginalised groups through claims of representing the 'people'. It is therefore important that mobilisation of subaltern groups should also be accompanied by establishing ideological hegemony such that it actually advances the interests of subaltern groups.

Laclau (2005: p. 77) identifies the following to be essential to populist mobilisation:

1. Unification of a plurality of demands.
2. Constitution of the 'people' and 'enemy' by building an internal frontier.

3. Construction of a popular identity around which the chain of equivalence across particularistic (social) demands can be consolidated.

Typically, populism is built by investing signifiers without precise meanings such as 'people', 'justice' or 'order' with an array of accumulated particularistic grievances or demands. When a particular or 'social' demand is not addressed as such, there is potential for political imagination to link up this demand with other particularistic demands coming from other groups, and show how they are being denied by a common actor such as the state or a socioeconomic oligarchy. Relationships among these diverse grievances can then be built by establishing equivalence across these particularistic demands. This requires creation of a political enemy against which this chain of equivalence gets established. In doing so, the struggle for each demand implies not just a struggle for that demand but also stands in for the universal equivalent. Political labour makes this possible through consolidation of these multiple demands around a popular identity such as the 'Dravidian' or 'Tamil people'. Such an identity can not only help aggregate demands of a heterogeneous population but also appeals to them on a register of affect. The popular demand is denied by the powerful elite or the state—who constitute the enemy of the people. An internal border is built between 'the people'— community of the oppressed—and the elite or the state—the oppressor. The ability of a term like 'justice' to represent a chain of equivalence across several social demands and animate political action in a particular direction depends on the historical context as well as the nature of political labour (Howarth 2015).

Dravidian mobilisation, we demonstrate in this chapter, managed to essentially build such a 'people', articulating a popular demand, and against an elite oligarchy. We suggest that a 'Dravidian-Tamil' identity was used by the movement to build a Gramscian 'national–popular' project (Forgacs 2000: pp. 364–70) in the region. This mobilisation led to the emergence of a common sense that in turn translated into a policy regime that comprises elements of the *economic–popular* and *social–popular* that we elaborate later. This common-sense informed claim-making and policy-making in the state not only after the coming to power of the Dravidian parties, but even during previous political regimes. To begin with, we would like to highlight the complex configurations of social and economic power in the region that led to the construction of a specific frontier of demands.

BUILDING A SUBALTERN HISTORIC BLOC[5]

Though our concern in this book is primarily the domain of the material, it is critical to understand how scriptural sanction of caste hierarchy constituted an important axis for establishing the Dravidian identity and mobilisation that also spoke to the material domain. Suntharalingam (1980) points to the hegemonic position occupied by members of Brahmin communities in south and western India, unlike in other parts of the country. The colonial state not only opened up new spaces of mobility for local elites in the Madras Presidency but also generated a field for certain kinds of engagement with the state and constitution of a thin civil society confined to those with exposure to modern education. Colonialism also brought along with it ideas of modernity that allowed for contestations of the terms on which colonial power was being exercised. We follow Pandian (2007) in identifying four broad strands that constituted the political logic of the SRM: the Christian missionaries and the Orientalists' interpretation of the 'Indian' past, the emergence of rationalist associations and dissemination of their critiques of religion, the Dalit and Saivaite narratives of alternate social imaginaries and finally, the formation of a political outfit to represent non-Brahmin interests, namely, the Justice Party.

Pandian highlights the critical role played by Christian missionaries in the constitution of native identities in colonial south India as well as in setting the terms of engagement with caste and the 'Hindu' religion by caste elites, Brahmins in particular. To begin with, while the natives did not see themselves as 'Hindus' and observed a plurality of rituals and practices, the missionary and colonial discourse sought to enfold all these practices within 'Hinduism'. But they also recognised the heterogeneity of 'Hindu' practices, with missionary-scholar G. U. Pope holding that the Saiva Sidhantha tradition, unique to south India, was the most sophisticated and also noting that the caste system is intrinsic to the Vedic Hindu tradition. The missionaries, based on a hyper-literal reading of myths, pointed out the dubious claims of native religion, and the ideas propagated through these myths. However, as Suntharalingam and Pandian observe, their efforts were not always successful in enlisting converts.

The next strand of critique of social power came through the rationalist route. Native elites increasingly began to use the anti-clerical and rationalist literature that found its way into the Madras Presidency from the West to counter such manoeuvres by the missionaries. The elites also drew support from Theosophists like Annie Besant who saw Eastern spiritual traditions to be more sophisticated, and went on to promote and actually privilege native religious traditions that upheld caste hierarchies and the caste-based division of labour over other strands. Rationalist readings, however, opened up avenues for criticising the validity of such practices that justified inequality or unscientific beliefs. Arasu (2012) sheds light on the emergence of such rationalist movements in the second half of the 19th century. A Hindu Freethought Union, later renamed the Madras Secular Society, brought out journals in English and Tamil (*The Thinker* and *Thathuva Vivesini*, respectively) during 1882–88 that carried news and discussions on the latest scientific discoveries and implications for religious beliefs and practices. Among the six volumes published, many articles engaged with what was seen as the irrational basis of both Christianity and the 'Hindu' religion. Frontal attacks on what was seen as immoral in the 'Hindu' religion were published. Many articles questioned restrictions on women, the validity of child marriage, ban on widow remarriage, caste hierarchies and exploitative relations between the upper and lower castes. They called for a new ethics based on principles of liberty, equality and modern rational thought rather than reliance on scriptures that upheld unethical practices. One of the leading intellectuals of the Madras Secular Society, Attippakkam Venkatacala Nayakar wrote the *Hindumata Achara Abhasa Darshini* in 1882, a critique of Vedic Hinduism and its social practices (Arasu 2013; Kaali 2019). Kaali notes how Nayakar's work anticipates subsequent 20th century critiques in this domain.

In a context where claims of religion were beginning to be evaluated through rationalist parameters, the terrain could no longer be secured through faith alone. It had become a turf of multiple contestations. Such contestations posed dilemmas for the caste elites whose claim to their position within the traditional caste hierarchy was accompanied by their entry into positions of power in the colonial bureaucracy where they had to give up on certain orthodox practices. They had to therefore secure their traditional source of power even as they became 'modern'. In response, Pandian points out how they began to validate their practices through scientific logic. Untouchability, for example, was justified on the basis of hygiene. The caste system was validated in terms of a natural division of labour that aided the social organisation of production and promoted skill development through specialisation. There were also constructions of the innate supremacy of caste elites through the use of eugenics (Pandian 2007: pp. 158–59). Simultaneously, Pandian charts the efforts to establish equivalence between the culture of the caste elites and 'Indian' nationalist culture. Given the dominance of upper caste among the professional and administrative elites, efforts to imagine a tradition and culture that is 'Indian' were by default traditions that upheld their caste privileges.

As Rajadurai and Geetha (2009) demonstrate, such constructions critically drew upon material produced by Orientalists like Max Muller, apart from Theosophists like Annie Besant. The Orientalists saw in the Vedas and other Sanskrit texts, the essence of Indian civilisation, and this was crucial to the caste elites' imagination of what was authentically Indian and 'national'. According to Muller, threats to this culture came from a set of inferior people inhabiting the subcontinent who corresponded to the non-Aryans. It was this combination of Orientalist and Theosophist constructions of authentic Indian culture that reinforced the Brahmins' claim for superiority in the caste hierarchy. This was also crucial in elevating the scriptural sanction of their privileges as well as their social practices to be the core constitutive elements of an Indian national tradition. The elevation of Sanskrit and Vedic traditions was seen to simultaneously emaciate other cultural traditions and languages— Tamil in the particular context of the Madras Presidency.

This power in the cultural-ideological domain was combined with securing of power in the material domain as well. At the turn of the 20th century, as several scholars document (Irschick 1969; Arooran 1980; Suntharalingam 1980), upper castes held a disproportionately large share of seats in higher education and jobs in the colonial bureaucracy, with their share increasing as one moved up the job hierarchy. Access to English education also helped caste elites to enter other modern professions like law. Since recourse to modern law was emerging as a major means of arbitration of claims over property, lawyers amassed considerable wealth and power. This monopoly also helped them reinforce the idea of the natural superiority of their intelligence over that of other castes, and of their caste status. Since they could also exercise disproportionate control over the domain of formal politics by virtue of their ability to engage on terms set by colonialism, they could effectively combine hegemony over the cultural and the material domains. They thus inscribed their authority by forging links between a 'Hindu' past and 'national' culture and combining it with power in the material domain through control over the bureaucracy and judiciary. They used the courts and the legislature to preserve 'Hindu' practices, and hence perpetuate their dominance across domains. It is this context that set the terms of mobilisation by the Dravidian movement in Tamil country.

The chain of equivalence across the Hindu-India-Sanskrit spheres that sustained the caste elites' dominance in the material and social domains was precisely what the Dravidian movement sought to undermine. In response, a new chain of equivalence began to be established: Dravidian-Tamil. As stated earlier, the movement was not the first to do so. Christian missionaries and native scholars (Kaali 2018) had already highlighted the oppressive dimensions of the caste system, and recovered a rich source of ancient Tamil literature that was suggestive of a history very different from that claimed by the caste elites and the Theosophists. The discovery of the Dravidian languages and their origins independent of Sanskrit by another school of Orientalists (Trautmann 2006) provided further means to build such a counternarrative. Before it assumed a political form, the hegemony of this narrative was also questioned by intellectuals like Pundit Iyothee Thoss, a Dalit Buddhist scholar, and Maraimalai Adigal, a Saivaite scholar.

In the material domain, the colonial sphere opened up opportunities, albeit unequal, for non-Brahmin elites as well (Suntharalingam 1980). The Brahmin dominance in this sphere was beginning to be questioned and countered by these elites by the turn of the 20th century. Their claims were primarily around a greater share of opportunities opened up by colonialism. A Madras Dravidian Association was formed in 1912 by C. Natesa Mudaliar, who also built a hostel called the Dravidian Home, for non-Brahmin students to avail modern education.[6] This was followed by the formation of a joint stock company, the South Indian People's Association, to start a newspaper, and also the South Indian Liberal Federation in 1916, a political association that was transformed into the Justice Party in 1917. The Association issued a non-Brahmin manifesto that demanded justice and equality of opportunity as enshrined in British law (Naidu 2010). The Manifesto, while questioning the oligarchic control over education and employment in public administration by the Brahmins, demanded a rightful share of employment and education for all communities. They also formed the government when limited franchise elections were held in the Presidency following the Montagu–Chelmsford reforms from 1921 to 1926, and then after a break, again until 1930. They passed some landmark pieces of legislation such as on communal representation in employment, supply of noon meals to children in government schools in Madras city and government control of temple funds. As we shall see later, such legislation emphasising primary education, health and communal representation resonated strongly with subsequent developmental interventions.

Ideologues of the Justice Party and subsequently, the SRM under Periyar's leadership, also worked the productive versus unproductive castes dichotomy to reveal the exploitative basis of caste relations and hierarchies. They pointed out that despite wealth being generated by non-Brahmin 'productive' castes, it was appropriated by the Brahmins via temples or when they had to rely on them for legal counsel and support. The fact that Brahmins also controlled vast tracts of fertile lands through temples furthered this sense of domination. They also called for an education that will help improve industrial development rather than an education that produces clerks who are seen to add little of value to society.[7] Pandian uses this to highlight the difference between the productivist imagination of the nationalists and the Justice Party; while the former used it to form a historic bloc to unite against colonial rule, the Justice Party used it to expose the fault lines within this 'national' community and imagine a historic bloc of a community of producers being exploited by an elite living off this community. Hence, domination was seen as being exerted more through the construction of a hegemonic ideology with foundations in religion rather than control over the means of production. While the Justice Party continued to represent elite non-Brahmin interests, a few members began to engage in mass campaigns that paved the way for intersections between the elite and subaltern domains.

THE SELF-RESPECT MOVEMENT

Though the SRM was appreciative of the efforts of the Justice Party, Periyar pointed out that the domination of the Brahmin becomes visible to the ideologues of the Party only when they occupy positions of power in the colonial administration. They do not recognise Brahminical power that pervades the cultural and the social domains, and are often willing to concede their privileged role in religious rituals and practices. In other words, they wanted to replace Brahmin elites with another set of elites or broad base the social composition of elites. Criticising their primary focus on getting a share of government jobs, he asks what does such an agenda mean for the common people who continue to labour through their lives and supplicate for material and spiritual favours because of their religious beliefs (Rajadurai and Geetha 2009: pp. 64–65). Referring to the upper-class status of many of the Justice Party leaders, he also pointed out that non-Brahmins actually comprise more than 90 per cent of the population and cannot be confined only to the 5 per cent who are kings and zamindars (p. 66). Importantly, as Pandian (2007) notes, the Justice Party did not see caste in relational terms but as a separate non-Brahmin group that is trying to compete with the Brahmins. Such an approach fails to recognise that the claim to Brahminhood simultaneously produces *shudra*hood and *panchama*hood. Claims to superiority simultaneously inferiorise others, and this claim was being made through religion.

Periyar held that the most important dimension of being human, and which distinguishes them from other animals, is the sense of dignity (*maanam*) that can come only through self-respect (*suyamariyadhai*) (Anaimuthu 1974: Vol. 1, pp. 3–8). Taking issue with Tilak's 'Swaraj is my birthright' slogan, he argues that this addressed only the political and the material domain, but does not speak about the dignity of individuals and their social being. By asserting that 'self-respect' should be our birthright, and not self-rule, Periyar revises the meaning of freedom and independence vis-à-vis the nationalists. He also emphasises experiential equality as fundamental to the idea of equality. Only when people share a similar experience can they develop a sense of fraternity and belonging. By interlocking the domain of the material and the cultural–ideological, upper-caste hegemony denies the possibility of both experiential and material equality, and hence any degree of self-respect. In the absence of such equality within a community, self-rule can only be an empty slogan that conceals the necessity of securing self-respect. He therefore articulated a demand for 'equal rights' that can be claimed by all. This was the basis on which democracy ought to be imagined. It is the upper castes' valorisation of Sanskrit and construction of practices and traditions that privileged their status, which has managed to sustain a hierarchical society and deny self-respect to the subaltern castes.

Unlike the Justice Party, the SRM was clear that the demand for communal representation is not merely about redistribution of jobs and power in the modern economy. This demand is meant to help erode the power of caste elites, and therefore to make way for democratisation of social values and realisation of self-respect. Access to jobs will be helpful, but they are not an end in itself. For him, access to the English language for example, was important because it was a language of modernity rather than one of colonial governance. To quote Periyar,

> … it is no exaggeration to say that it is the knowledge of English which kindled the spirit of freedom in our people … which gave us the knowledge to say 'no' to monarchy and 'yes' to a republic; to say 'yes' to socialism and 'no' to *Sanathanam*. It gave us the knowledge that men and women are equals … (Anaimuthu 1974: Vol. 2, pp. 970–71, cited in Pandian 1996)

Agitations against Hindi were thus as much a demand for inclusive modernity as a demand for restoring to Tamil its status.

Another important shift is the terrain on which politics began to be carried out by the SRM. As Geetha and Rajadurai (2008) point out, the SRM transformed into a mass movement that began to draw in various subaltern communities and caste groups over a period of time. The radical critique of hegemonic power and the ability to draw in a range of social groups marked a decisive shift from previous critiques or modes of claim making. The Dravidian movement could link the diverse critiques of the caste system and traditions upholding caste hierarchies and division of labour including Saivite (Venkatachalapathy 1995), Dalit (Aloysius 1999), socialist and rationalist critiques into a common frontier, and imagine a politics that could aggregate these demands. Based on an elaboration of the movement's understanding of domination and power, in the next section, we outline the elements of a programme of emancipation envisioned by the SRM.

THE DRAVIDIAN DEMAND

Ideologues of the Dravidian movement held that the caste-based division of labour not only generated social inequalities but importantly denied economic opportunities to the lower castes as it tied them to traditional occupations that were deemed inferior. They drew upon the Enlightenment premise of social transformation, and held ideas of modernity and modernisation of education and economy to be critical to undermine social and economic hierarchies. We already hinted at this in the previous section through Periyar's support for the English language. This premise, it must be remembered, was forged in a context of socioeconomic opportunities being generated by an emerging modern colonial economy and bureaucracy and being appropriated disproportionately by the caste elites. The ideologues saw the source of upper-caste power in both the religious domain and in its ability to monopolise modern education and hence premium jobs in the modern economy. Periyar held that the caste-based division of labour perpetuated systemic discrimination against lower castes, incarcerating them in the world of physical labour. He was also aware of the control wielded by the north Indian merchant capital within the Congress and its collusion with the caste elite in driving the nationalist movement. He was particularly critical of Gandhi's efforts to cast the village accompanied by its artisanal craft traditions as the authentic site of Indian regeneration and made a strong case for liberation of lower castes through escape from such spaces and occupations. As Aloysius points out, Periyar critiqued village reconstruction programmes promoted by Gandhi, arguing that it is a political strategy to arrest the masses within traditional, caste-bound geographical spaces (Aloysius 2013). He invokes the caste metaphor to talk of rural–urban hierarchies. To him, the village is a geographical lower caste destined to serve the 'upper caste towns' and its revival may only reinforce the monopoly over intellectual capital and mental labour by the upper castes. A move away from demeaning physical labour marked by inferiorised caste identities, and entry into modern occupations that were less marked by caste, was therefore seen as important. Social justice was therefore tied to spatial mobility as well. He also pointed to the inefficiencies inherent in traditional artisanal production and called for incorporation of modern production technologies that can render menial, ritually marked labour, redundant.

Taking up the question of exploitation of labour, he makes a distinction between the 'caste-labourer' and the 'wage-labourer' even as he seeks to bring them together under the Dravidian fold (Vidiyal 2017: pp. 743–44). In India, people are born as labourers but into different castes that are all invested with ritually low and impure status. Such caste workers are divided by caste and made to believe that they are antagonistic to one another, when in fact they are all denied access to the returns of their labour because of the caste system. He therefore calls for unity among caste workers and wage workers and insists that the cadres of the movement communicate the importance of this unity. This emphasis on the dual identity of the worker, in terms of both class and caste, also finds resonance in Annadurai's appeal to the cadres of the political party Dravida Munnetra Kazhagam (DMK hereafter, formed in 1949 by C. N. Annadurai to extend the Dravidian political agenda into the electoral domain) in his book *Panathottam*.[8] In the wake of a strike by textile-mill workers, he calls upon the cadres to communicate to other poor people, the reasons why the mill workers are striking and struggling. They are Dravidians too like the rest of Tamils, he says, and hence it is important that people realise how their fellow men are being oppressed. He further points out that for the worker,

> all that he knows is the struggle that he is going through in his life. To him, all talk about the Aryan–Dravidian divide may seem like a lot of noise. But we [meaning cadres of the Dravidian movement] know both. It is therefore understandable that they may forget us. But it is an unpardonable crime if we forget them. (Annadurai 2017 [1949]: p. 61)

His simultaneous appeal on two registers, as a fellow Dravidian and a fellow labourer, thus establishes an equivalence between their class and caste identities.

Democratising access to modern education and employment in the modern economy therefore becomes key to undermine caste relations of hierarchy, as it opens up possibilities to move away from caste-inscribed labour. Movement from rural to urban too, was seen as a movement from 'pre-modern' time–spaces ridden with caste and gender hierarchies, where work and labour only serve to reproduce identities, to spaces that potentially allow for new mobilities, economic and social. While the movement did recognise the importance of economic-asset-based inequality and economic exploitation of labouring classes by capitalists and the landowning classes (Rajadurai and Geetha 2009; Rajadurai 2012), emphasis was placed more on relations of power emanating from the caste-based division of labour.

To Periyar, redistribution of propery without abolition of caste-based privileges is unlikely to lead to an egalitarian system because of the entrenched power of caste elites (Rajadurai 2012; Manoharan 2017). Distribution of economic assets at one point in time without abolishing caste privilege and ensuring a sense of self-respect, will only lead to assets going back to the hands of the upper castes. He used the example of lawyers appropriating lands from traditional landowners to drive home this point. This vision of social justice is thus tied to inclusive modernisation, and to the developmental logic of structural transformation. Justice is therefore linked to the ability to transform the economy from a predominantly agrarian economy marked by poor returns, low productivity and caste rigidities to a structurally diversified and a modernised one. It is also important to elaborate the approach the movement had towards capital accumulation. Since structural transformation and modernisation cannot take place without capital accumulation, the Dravidian ideologues were not antagonistic to it though there was a call for a strong public sector as well as for strengthening cooperatives. They envisioned a democratisation of the accumulation process and privileged the role of regional capital in opposition to the mercantile big business groups from the north that wielded control in the Presidency and also wrested most concessions from the government. Annadurai lays out this idea clearly in his *Panathottam*. Asserting that manufacturing is the lifeline of any country, he contends that the reason for the state's backwardness was essentially the absence of state support for modern industrialisation.[9] He goes on to accuse the Congress government (then in power in Tamil Nadu) of not being able to tap into the region's geo-economic potential by failing to establish any economic links with South East Asia (1949: p. 25). He further laments the siphoning of savings from the state through the banking system to fund the accumulation of elite north indian business communities. This position against north Indian big business was accompanied by a demand for public ownership of industries, and encouragement of local capital.

Another significant aspect of the Dravidian vision is therefore the regional dimension, and freedom from domination exercised through networks of pan-Indian power (Manoharan 2020a). Since caste elites sought legitimacy through the nationalist movement by inscribing their culture into the national, the Dravidian movement sought to build on the critique of this tradition through a call for an alternate society characterised by mutual respect and brotherhood. Given the interlocking of the socio-material domination of the upper castes with the domination of capital accumulation by mercantile elite at the pan-Indian level, this alternate society could be realised only at the subnational level. Importantly, as Pandian evocatively maps (1993), this imagined community was not based on an appeal to ethnicity but to a community of the oppressed, be it in terms of caste, gender, language, race, ethnicity or religion. While Periyar did not believe in territorial nationalism, the Dravidian movement did hold that its vision of social justice can only be secured through regional autonomy which became a major agenda ever since the Dravidian parties have been in power.

The Dravidian movement, through its appeal to the Dravidian-Tamil identity thus managed to build a Dravidian common-sense that spoke to these groups simultaneously even though some groups may have adversarial relations with others. The components of that common-sense may be identified as the necessity for caste-based reservation, recognition of the importance of a productivist ethos, broad basing of mobility into the modern economy, regional autonomy and an anti-Hindi stance because of its links with the scriptural sanction of caste and gender hierarchies and hence its association with a denial of substantive democracy. Before we highlight the issues that underlie such a transformative agenda, we take a brief detour to provide an illustration of how this common-sense worked and works in the state using the example of affirmative action, and the recent protests against ban of *jallikattu*, a traditional bull-taming sport in the state.

DRAVIDIAN COMMON-SENSE: TWO ILLUSTRATIONS

Affirmative action policies not only enable equality of opportunity but are also redistributive measures given the scarcity of public goods such as higher education or secure, well-paid employment. Commenting on affirmative action policies in India, Piketty (2020) argues that such redistributive measures have contributed to reducing inequalities between lower castes and the rest of population. To him, status–based inequality is as durable as that originating from property. Unlike traditional left mobilisation that saw land reform as the axis of redistributive politics, Dravidian mobilisation privileged undermining of status-based power by broad-basing access to education and non-farm jobs as important pathways to mobility without discounting the role of landed power.

At the all-India level, however, there is considerable evidence on how provisions on reservation have been consistently subverted (Balagopal 2009). Courts too, have interpreted laws pertaining to caste-based reservation in ways that have weakened the effectiveness of such policies (Galanter 1984). As Galanter points out, 'the Indian courts ... have done little directly to offer remedies for the deficiencies of implementation of existing schemes ... In part, this is due to the posture of the Constitution, which provides no explicit authorization for affirmative judicial action' (1984: p. 544). Caste elites also often misused the court's ambiguous interpretation to curtail their effectiveness. In other words, elites who govern public institutions have subverted the provisions on reservation using the tacit support rendered by the arbitrariness of the judiciary. The burden of ensuring the effectiveness of affirmative action has therefore fallen on the potential beneficiaries from lower castes, who are forced to appeal to the judiciary at their own risk to enforce the implementation of reservation.

Tamil Nadu, however, offers a different history. State institutions have not only provided resources for such cases but have even fought in the courts.[10] Civil society too was not hostile to the idea of social justice unlike in several other states. When the reservation policy (both Mandal I in the 1990s, and Mandal II in the 2000s) was introduced at the national level, several pro-reservation rallies were carried out, unlike in north India, which witnessed huge protests on the streets against it that forced the union government to a compromise in 2006.[11] This support in the state indexes the horizontal solidarities that populist mobilisation managed to sustain. The recent spate of protests against the introduction of a national-level entrance exam for admission to medical colleges too, was against the elite bias of this move.[12] A resonance was built across demands for affirmative action, the language question and regional autonomy to mobilise against the union government. This trajectory of mobilisation also is unlike what happened to lower-caste mobilisation in Bihar (Witsoe 2013). Witsoe reads the emergence of lower-caste politics in Bihar as populist mobilisation against the upper castes, but the Tamil case differs on at least two accounts. First, unlike populism in Bihar, it delivered better economic and social outcomes. Second, populist mobilisation could sustain the horizontal coalition of disparate caste groups despite differences across them, whereas backward-caste and Scheduled-Caste (SC) mobilisations in Bihar and Uttar Pradesh (UP) were dominated by specific castes within each of these categories. The Dravidian-Tamil identity worked to build solidarities by muting internal caste divisions among the intermediate and lower castes. On the contrary, lower-caste mobilisation in the north was carried out more through valorising individual castes based on mythological stories of origin within the dominant Hindu fold rather than forging a cohesive alternative identity like the Dravidian one (Jaffrelot 2000).

In early 2017, the state witnessed mass protests against the ban on *jallikattu*, a bull-taming sport with an ancient lineage in the region, by the Supreme Court (Himakiran and Nirmala 2020). The ban order was in response to a case filed by PETA (People for the Ethical Treatment of Animals), and this was met with the biggest mass protests in the state ever since the anti-Hindi agitation of the mid-1960s. It was led by youth, cutting across political and social divides. Once again a discursive link was made between the upper-caste dominated PETA and the union government's support for the ban. While PETA was seen to ignore other kinds of animal cruelty indulged in by the elite such as horse racing and use of exotic pets, the union government's support for the ban was seen as an infringement of the rights of Tamils. In the globalising Tamil region, this ban was also read as a move by global corporates to take over the livestock economy and decimate local economies and livelihoods dependent on indigenous livestock. *Jallikattu* came to stand for 'Tamilness' just as it also stood for destruction of agrarian livelihoods and domination of the union government in policy-setting. Importantly, this Tamilness appealed to several linguistic and ethnic groups in the state, who participated in the protests (A. Kannan 2017). A particularly suggestive instance is that of a Sikh actively participating in the protests in Coimbatore because he identified with this tradition! Sriramachandran (2018), similarly points out how the non-Brahmin–Dravidian equivalence enabled the non-Brahmin Telugu-speaking community to identify with the movement' just as Tamil-speaking Muslims have also been closely associated with it (Anwar 2018). It is this encompassing non-essentialising mode of constructing the Dravidian-Tamil identity that allowed for the building of such horizontal solidarities.

To sum up, the movement succeeded in aggregating a range of social groups marked by class, caste, linguistic, religious and ethnic diversity, by establishing a chain of equivalence across these groups, and communicating a political logic of difference vis-à-vis elite nationalism and caste elites. Laclau (2005) argues that it is the very impreciseness or vagueness of populism that many see as problematic that makes populist mobilisation possible. According to him, the imprecise nature of the political appeal made by 'populist' leaders or movements allows them to aggregate a range of interest groups or classes that may otherwise be antagonistic to each other. However, the building of such horizontal solidarities around a signifier like the Dravidian-Tamil identity also has implications for particularistic demands as well as for political possibilities after populism gets institutionalised within a state apparatus.

LIMITS: EQUIVALENCES TO DIFFERENCES

As we stated earlier, populist mobilisation in Tamil Nadu subsumed particularistic demands by sub-groups around other identities like Adi Dravidar, Shudra, Christian or Muslim, agricultural or industrial worker, small farmer or woman, under a universalist Tamil/Dravidian political frontier against caste elites and those who upheld caste hierarchies, and those who wielded pan Indian political and economic power. While discrete demands can only be addressed through demand-specific interventions, it is through political labour that one can build an array of equivalences among several demands. This is done through what Chatterjee describes as 'rhetorical and performative and other modes of representation of grievances' (2019: p. 83). Political parties and popular leaders rhetorically tie together the various unfulfilled demands of these heterogeneous populations into chains of equivalence.

Building of equivalence implies a partial surrender of a particularistic demand. The process happens, as Laclau writes, 'through a partial surrender of particularity, stressing what all particularities have, equivalentially, in common' (2005: p. 78). For Laclau, entry of any particular demand in an equivalential chain is therefore a mixed blessing (p. 88). While its incorporation within a larger political frontier makes this particularistic demand legible by becoming part of an 'institutional ensemble', it does not, however, guarantee that this equivalential chain—the constructed people and its populist demand— necessarily addresses all individual or particular group demands. It may therefore generate possibilities of new political frontiers and enemies. Further, such a populist project can also take a resilient form by making the divide permanent. As Pierre Rosanvallon points out, it often 'becomes a compulsive and permanent stigmatization of the ruling authorities, to the point where these authorities are seen as radically alien enemy powers' (p. 268).[13] This freezing and essentialising of identities, and of the political enemy, is a distinct possibility as many right populist mobilisations suggest.

Another problem with such a construction of a popular community is that some would gain more than others. The relationship among many of these groups is also still hierarchical. As Chatterjee (2019) argues, 'the people' can become a floating signifier—changing over time—that can exclude some and include others. Once power gets institutionalised within administrative structures, the logic of difference takes over that of equivalence. It is in this context that one has to visit Dalit critiques of the Dravidian-Tamil identity, which are premised on the contention that intermediate castes have used the Dravidian identity only to marginalise their demands. Successful populism is one which can change its strategies to accommodate emerging demands and contradictions in response to particularistic demands and yet maintain the relation of equivalence. Such populist politics need not also be transformative always. It might ensure a degree of inclusion and participation in the power structures but may not necessarily address the demands of specific groups, say that of specific sub-castes or women. Recent attempts by Hindutva groups to delink 'Tamil' from 'non-Brahmin' are suggestive of this possibility (Pandian 2012).

The degree of radicalisation of demands decides the level of transformation of institutions and the degree of responsiveness of those institutions. However, over time, when some of these claims get institutionalised, they generate limits to further radicalisation of demands. The trajectory of contemporary Tamil polity and its contradictions needs to be therefore understood as emerging from the exhaustion of institutionalisation of claims as well as an outcome of shifts taking place in the larger macro-environment. Importantly, there are also limits posed by the process of modernisation itself, which in turn feeds into the trajectory that populist regimes can assume.

INSTITUTIONALISING POPULISM

Gramsci articulated the importance of building a 'national popular' will by a political force so as to forge a common vision of social change by incorporating subaltern sections into the political process (Forgacs 2000: pp. 364–70). The emergence of this popular will was crucial to him for substantive social transformation. The emergence of a Dravidian common-sense that we elaborated above approximates such a 'national popular' will. How does that translate into specific interventions when populist forces are institutionalised within structures of state power? We analytically divide the history of populist policy-making in the state into two broad domains, the 'social popular' and the 'economic popular'. While both share certain common characteristics, this distinction helps us to analytically organise different policy processes and interventions in the state. Let us begin with the social popular. We define the social popular as a distinct set of policy interventions that are rights-based interventions such as ensuring inclusive access to modern sectors and public goods such as health and education, the bureaucracy and organised-sector employment. The process ensures the rights of the excluded such as lower castes and women, and tends to undermine the underlying social basis for generating unequal outcomes through claim-making in the long run. Such interventions have a long-term programmatic commitment, and seek to address the basis of social backwardness such as caste and gender hierarchies.

While policies in the social popular are rooted in the desire for democratisation of power and access, 'economic popular' policies are rooted in patronage and emanate from governmental imperatives. Introducing welfare provisions or economic benefits for specific groups of the population falls under this domain. Here, policy interventions are meant to address specific grievances of specific groups, and therefore work on the logic of difference and not equivalence. The social and the economic popular are therefore differentiated based on both their intent and content. While the social popular seeks to enable the social basis for change, the latter tends to be status quoist. They also differ in terms of temporality. Social popular interventions imagine and adopt a longer timescale as they engage with factors that reproduce social domination. The economic popular follows the temporality of the election cycle, and tends to generate interventions that depoliticise poverty. The outcomes are likely to overlap between the two domains with the economic popular helping groups to be mobilised on a social popular agenda. We suggest that when populism was institutionalised through capture of state power, three broad domains were transformed. One, it laid certain basic foundations for structural transformation through investments in economic and social infrastructure. Second, it democratised state institutions including the bureaucracy and access to the modern economy. Third, it managed to build a confident people with a broad-based 'capacity to aspire' (Appadurai 2004). However, over time, the potential for such social popular interventions reaches a limit, and hence loses the capacity to build electoral support. Privatisation of higher education and decline in the role of the public sector, for example, implies a reduced role for affirmative action. Universalisation of primary education loses electoral appeal once it is achieved. When the social popular exhausts its potential for further intervention, the economic popular assumes importance. Wyatt's contention (2013a) that the state has managed to combine universal programmatic policies with clientelist ones indicates the working of the combined logic of the social and the economic popular.

We illustrate this distinction with concrete examples. After the DMK came to power in 1967, it constituted the first Backward Classes Commission to ensure adequate representation for the excluded and marginalised in the bureaucracy and equal opportunities for them in modern sectors. Following this, the state implemented a constantly reworked affirmative action policy to address caste-based inequalities. It also tried to bring in a policy of reservation to address rural–urban and class-based disparities—by offering preferences to rural students and first-generation graduates, respectively, in higher education (Pandian 2012). It validated self-respect marriages[14] and then passed the Equal Inheritance Act in 1989 for daughters. It also legislated to weaken the power of landlords and enabled tenants to claim titles, and further, undermined rural power structures by abolishing hereditary posts in villages and appointing village administrative officers recruited through the state public service commission. These interventions helped transform social hierarchies based on caste and gender, and broad based aspirations among the lower castes.

We now turn to the economic popular. While policies formulated under the DMK laid the foundation for economic transformations that became visible in the 1990s, such policies of transformation were not always helpful electorally. As a result, both Dravidian parties moved into the economic popular—welfare interventions such as provision of loan waivers and household assets like television sets, laptops, bicycles, mixies and grinders. While social popular interventions can translate into redistribution of assets like human capital, economic popular interventions can be socially empowering such as provision free noon meals for school children or of bicycles for high-school attending girl children. While both parties adopted economic popular strategies, the All India Anna Dravida Munnetra Kazhagam (AIADMK) has been proactive in this regard. We offer an illustration of how similar interventions can be distinguished by their popular logic.

The DMK brought an amendment[15] to the Hindu Succession Act, 1956 to ensure equal shares for women in ancestral property. Along with this, the party also brought in many schemes including the Anjugam Ammaiyar inter-caste marriage assistance scheme and the Dr Dharmambal Ammaiyar Memorial Widow Remarriage Scheme, which were meant to be incentives to undermine caste and gender hierarchies, in line with the interpretation of the women's question by the SRM (Anandhi 1991). While these schemes are rooted in normative ideals of social justice and located in the domain of the social popular, they did not translate into electoral dividends. As a result, many of the schemes introduced in the post-1990 period fall under the category of the economic popular. For example, one of the existing schemes was reworked by the AIADMK as Thalikku Thangam Thittam(Gold for Marriage) which was hugely popular among women. Named after the social activist Moovalur

Ramamirtham, the scheme offers four grams of gold and cash of up to INR 50,000 to poor women for marriage if they have completed a degree or a diploma. Though it was meant to incentivise girl students to pursue higher education before marriage, it is designed more as a clientelist scheme.

While both types of schemes share welfare content, the former is still located within a narrative of gender and caste justice whereas the latter assumes the form of patronage. The legislation on equal property share for women for instance, was an outcome of a long-term narrative around ensuring women equal access to property. The 'gold for marriage' scheme, on the other hand, was not rooted within such a mobilisational logic. The economic popular is contingent and driven by immediate electoral compulsions, while the social popular is programmatic and guided by certain normative ideals. In Laclau's (2005) words, while the social popular works on a populist logic of equivalence, the economic popular largely operates on the differential logic of governmentality. This is, however, not to suggest that there has to be necessarily a sequential logic to this process. Economic popular policies may be implemented in conjunction with social popular policies though the latter's exhaustion drives the former more intensely. The electoral appeal of economic popular interventions becomes particularly important in a context where modernisation, however inclusive, fails to deliver on its promises.

The logic of economic popular interventions is therefore also implicated in another imperative. A major variable that is seldom taken into account to explain the limits of populist regimes is the limits inherent to the logic of modernisation and structural transformation. A standard assumption that informed political support for modernisation is that an expansion of the modern non-agricultural domain, capitalist or otherwise, ensures the transition of a substantial share of households from agriculture into this domain. In other words, once this sector expands, it should be able to absorb the labour force being released from agriculture. Recent studies, however, point out that such a transition is increasingly becoming impossible in the Global South due to a variety of factors (Sanyal 2007; Ferguson 2015). Populations are rendered irrelevant to the process of capital accumulation. A populist regime that has sought to generate inclusive modernisation has to therefore confront and respond to the emerging limits of this process. We argue that this factor, which has not been recognised adequately, actually plays an important role in shaping policies of populist regimes in the state.

IMPLICATIONS

The outline of our framework thus helps to identify our analytical departures from previous interpretations of the state's trajectory and also some earlier readings of the nature of mobilisation. In Subramanian's understanding of the Dravidian, for example there was no space for the Brahmin or for the Dalit (1999: p. 105). The latter assertion that the movement was essentially meant to represent the interests of elite segments of the backward castes has a longer history and continues to be assumed by many subsequent scholars of Tamil Nadu (Lakshman 2011; Gorringe 2017; Harriss and Wyatt 2019). Subramanian also claims that it was because of electoral politics that the Dravidian parties had to accommodate the interests of the Dalits by offering them a series of welfare measures.[16] In class terms, the Dravidian movement represented the propertied, the small producers and educated unemployed youth (Barnett 1976) and did not represent the working classes. Failing to address the interests of the working classes and the lower castes, they were outdone in this regard by the AIADMK, which split from the DMK in the mid-1970s.

This interpretation of the Dravidian mobilisation as we delineate earlier is, however, incorrect. Subramanian's account of the history of the SRM as one working with essentialised racial categories or marginalising Dalits has been countered by scholars like Pandian (2000), Rajadurai and Geetha (2009), Punitha Pandian (2017a and 2017b), Subagunarajan (2018), Thirumavelan (2018) and most recently, by Manoharan (2020b), among others. His reading of the factors driving the two sets of policies also therefore does not resonate with the political logic of Dravidian mobilisation or with the structural factors that circumscribe its politics. Our study of Tamil Nadu is therefore meant to not only offer a better explanation of outcomes and the development trajectory in the state, but also meant to open up a conversation on mobilisation against status based inequalities and the limits of its institutionalisation within a framework of inclusive modernisation.

NOTES

1   Defined as 'empirically prevailing states of consciousness of ordinary people' (Chatterjee 2011: 146)

2   Different phases of the emergence and evolution of the Dravidian movement can be distinguished (Anandhi 1991). For the purpose of this book, we use the term 'Dravidian movement' or 'mobilisation' to refer to all the following movements and parties: the Self-Respect Movement and the Dravidar Kazhagam (DK) initiated by Periyar, and the Dravida Munnetra Kazhagam (DMK) started by C.N Annadurai. Though the Justice Party articulated issues of caste-based discrimination and inclusive modernisation, it is the SRM and then the DK and the DMK that radicalised and broad based mobilisation against caste. The DMK went on to capture power in 1967 after which its splinter, the AIADMK and the DMK have alternated in power in the state. We use the term 'Dravidian parties' to refer to the DMK and the AIADMK.

3   Today's Tamil Nadu was named as such in 1968 and constitutes much of erstwhile Madras presidency. The presidency was divided mostly among three states- Andhra Pradesh in 1953, Kerala and Karnataka in 1956.

4   We use Brahminical Hinduism as a religious practice that sanctions caste hierarchy—pan-Indian and rooted in Sanskrit. While this term is close to M.N. Srinivas' conception of Sanskritic Hinduism, we treat its sanctity of caste hierarchy as its core. For Srinivas' conception, see Fuller and Narashimhan (2014).

5   By subaltern historic bloc, we refer to the emergence of a new articulated relationship between subaltern classes and intellectual practices as part of a political mobilisation, whereby members of the subaltern classes themselves constitute the leadership (drawn from Sotiris 2018). Though Gramsci refers to this formation in the context of imagining and mobilising alternatives to capitalism, here we use it to refer to the emergence of a bloc that envisions a politics against caste hierarchies.

6   As Pandian (2007) observes, it shows how the ideas put forward by the Madras School of Orientalists, who proposed a distinct set of Dravidian languages, began to be assimilated. While the Brahmins were comfortable in their Aryan identity, this allowed for a coalescence of the rest.

7   We address this in more detail in Chapter 5 in this volume.

8   Published originally in 1949, it can be translated as 'Garden of Money'.

9   'Manufacturing is the lifeline (*uyirnaadi*) of any country' (Annadurai 2017 [1949]: p. 44).

10   For instance, besides filing a petition in the Supreme Court seeking exception from the court ceiling that reservation shall not exceed 50 per cent in India, the state was the first to move a constitutional amendment to protect its reservation of 69 per cent. In the state assembly, it also unanimously passed an act, The Tamil Nadu Backward Classes, Scheduled Castes and Scheduled Tribes (Reservation of Seats in Educational Institutions and of Appointments or Posts in the Services under the State) Act, 1993, and appealed to the union government to place it under the ninth schedule of the Indian Constitution to protect it from judicial review.

11   The union government introduced a constitutional amendment—the Central Educational Institutions (Reservation and Admission) Act, 2006— providing for 27 per cent reservation for Other Backward Classes (OBCs) in institutions of higher education; the elites opposed this across north India forcing the union government to expand the educational infrastructure in these institutions and increase the number of seats by 54 per cent so that the number of open quota seats for elites will remain the same.

12   This is discussed in greater detail in Chapter 3 in this volume.

13   Elite stigmatisation, alien and not Tamil enough.

14   The Amendment Act (Number 21 of 1967) made self-respect marriages an option for couples who did not want to go through with the rituals and sanctions of traditional Hindu marriages.

15   Tamil Nadu Act 1 of 1990, section 2 with effect from March 25, 1989.

16   This understanding of the material basis of political mobilisation in the state draws partly from earlier characterisations of the movement by Cambridge school historians (Baker 1976; Washbrook 1977 cited by Pandian 1995). To them, the non-Brahmin mobilisation in the state was essentially in terms of a political faction vying for space with other factions in colonial India. In this narrative, non-Brahmin elites essentially mobilised to demand a greater share of the spoils of the colonial economy, which was otherwise monopolised by the Brahmins. They were seen as a faction supported by a dominant elite whose interests it sought to protect rather than a movement based on horizontal solidarities questioning the dominant order.

3

DEMOCRATISING EDUCATION

In September 2018, a Dalit family in Kuzhumur, a village in the backward district of Ariyalur, built a library housing 2,500 books and computers with online access (*TNM* 2018). Making a case for the initiative, members of the family said that this will help rural children access educational materials that are normally available only to children from urban elite households. Supported by various political parties, the library was to commemorate the memory of their daughter Anitha, who had committed suicide a year earlier when she failed to get admission into a medical college despite scoring 1,176 marks out of 1,200 in her school final exams. These marks were the sole basis for admission into medical colleges in the state before introduction of the National Eligibility Cum Entrance Test (NEET), a national-level eligibility-cum-entrance exam for admissions, overturned the basis for eligibility, and rendered such high marks irrelevant. Anitha's death fuelled large-scale protests all over the state and constituted an important moral axis for subsequent agitations around this issue. Since then, a couple of more teens committed suicide following their failure to clear NEET (Ranjan 2019). This raises important questions about aspirations and access to education in the state: What made such aspirations the norm for many lower-caste youth? When NEET failed to evoke similar resistance in other parts of the country, why did it become a major concern in Tamil Nadu?

Such aspiration, we argue, is rooted in a Dravidian common-sense that made access to modern education a key pathway to mobility and social justice. This chapter explains the forging of this common-sense and such aspirations among lower-caste groups, and the policy response in this domain. We draw upon Arjun Appadurai's (2004) conceptualisation of the 'capacity to aspire' to map the constitution of aspirations among subaltern groups in the state. Appadurai defines the 'capacity to aspire' as the cultural capacity of the poor to find the resources required to contest and alter or improve the course of their destiny. For him, such a capacity comprises of two domains of freedom. First it requires removal of material deprivation rooted in backwardness in education and poverty. The second involves securing dignity and respect that are denied by low status aspirations vis a vis the elites. While we address the issue of poverty and employment in Chapters 6 and 7, here we argue that the Dravidian demand for self-respect through access to modern education was critical in generating such capacities to aspire. This milieu in turn incentivised a series of policy measures aimed at creating educational infrastructure as well as broad-basing access. This has led to not only high levels of literacy in the state across social groups but has also enabled the entry of nearly 50 per cent of youth finishing school into tertiary education. We point out that while 'social popular' policies towards universalising primary education, and affirmative action policies in higher education played an important role in this regard, they were supplemented by 'economic popular' policies like the free noon-meals scheme for school children and group-specific economic incentives and subsidies that reduced the cost of education.

We begin with mapping school educational outcomes and demonstrate how the state has done better not just in terms of educational levels but also in the rate of change in outcomes. We then relate the outcomes to certain deliberate institutional interventions. The chapter traces the policy processes that generated intermediate outcomes such as creating school infrastructures and initiatives to retain students in schools. We highlight the political roots of such policies, and establish continuity in processes and interventions in broad-basing access to education since the formation of the Justice Party. We then focus on the state's achievements in higher education. As education is a subject in the concurrent list, we point out how the state-level higher education policy evolved and interacted with that of the union government. We demonstrate how the state used caste-based reservation to democratise education. We also draw attention to how this led to broad-based human capital formation, even as it fed into collective aspirations for democratising access to education that in turn shaped subsequent policy response. Importantly, the emergence of such a common-sense ensured that lower-caste groups saw reservation policies as their rightful entitlement and forced institutions to respond to their demands unlike in most parts of the country.

EDUCATIONAL OUTCOMES

In terms of literacy, Tamil Nadu ranked fourth among the major states in 2017–18, a marginal improvement from its fifth position in 1993–94 (Table 3.1). Tamil Nadu fares slightly better compared to Gujarat and Maharashtra. In fact, the literacy rate in Tamil Nadu was slightly lower (67 per cent) than that of Maharashtra (68 per cent) in 1993–94. The state has therefore, over time, improved its relative position. Another important measure in educational outcomes is current attendance, which indicates the current participation of the population in various educational institutions. The state again performs better in comparison to most states and the all-India average. By 1993–94, about 83 per cent of children in the age group of 6–14 years were in school in Tamil Nadu compared to just 71 per cent at the all-India level. The corresponding figures for Gujarat and Maharashtra were 78 per cent and 85 per cent, respectively. It improved to 99 per cent in 2017–18 compared to 97 per cent for both Gujarat and Maharashtra, and the all-India average of 95 per cent. Importantly, such outcomes are caste and class-inclusive.

Caste-based division of labour hierarchised intellectual over manual work, and resulted in exclusion of lower castes from formal education (Omvedt 2011). The extent to which lower-caste groups have been able to access education therefore becomes an important yardstick in understanding the role and nature of state intervention in democratising education. Caste groups which have historically been denied or had restricted access to education have performed better in educational outcomes in Tamil Nadu (Table 3.2). The literacy rate for Scheduled Castes (SCs) and Scheduled Tribes (STs) was 77 per cent in 2017–18 for the age of 6 and above in Tamil Nadu against 75 per cent in Gujarat and Maharashtra, and 70 per cent at the all-India level. As the table indicates, the state has done better than the other two states despite having similar or lower rates in the early 1990s. As

Table 3.1 Basic Educational Outcome

States	Literacy for Age 6 and Above				Current Enrolment for Age 6–14	
	1993–94	Rank	2017–18	Rank	1993–94	2017–18
Andhra Pradesh	47.6	14	65.8	16	66.5	96.7
Assam	70.9	2	87.0	2	80.8	98.3
Bihar	43.2	16	72.7	13	56.5	93.0
Gujarat	64.5	6	82.6	5	78.2	96.9
Haryana	61.3	9	79.0	9	81.1	97.2
Himachal Pradesh	68.6	3	86.0	3	91.0	98.6
Karnataka	57.5	10	75.7	11	75.4	98.0
Kerala	91.7	1	94.2	1	95.2	99.7
Madhya Pradesh	49.6	12	74.0	12	64.8	94.9
Maharashtra	68.3	4	81.7	7	84.8	97.4
Orissa	51.2	11	76.1	10	66.7	99.0
Punjab	63.3	8	82.0	6	82.2	97.6
Rajasthan	44.5	15	70.5	15	60.5	94.3
Tamil Nadu	67.2	5	82.8	4	82.5	99.3
Uttar Pradesh	48.7	13	71.7	14	63.7	91.4
West Bengal	63.5	7	79.7	8	71.3	96.0
All-India	57.2		76.8		71.2	95.3

Source: Estimated from NSSO– Employment-Unemployment Survey (EUS) 50th round and Periodic Labour Force Survey, Ministry of Statistics and Programme Implementation (PLFS) 2017–18.

the Other Backward Classes (OBCs) were not enumerated as a separate category in surveys conducted in the 1990s, we do not have data to compare shifts over time. But the latest data (2017–18) shows that the literacy rate among OBCs in the state is 84 per cent, compared to 81 per cent, 82 per cent and 77 per cent for Maharashtra, Gujarat and the all-India level, respectively. The state once again ranks fourth with regard to literacy levels of OBCs, among the major states.

The state performs better in terms of current attendance among lower-caste groups as well. In 2017–18, it retained 99 per cent of children between the ages of 6 and 14 years among SCs/STs as against 97 per cent in Maharashtra and 94 per cent in Gujarat and at the all-India level. Twenty years earlier, such attendance for children of the same age among SCs/STs was 77 per cent in

Table 3.2 Educational Indicators by Caste Groups

| | Literacy for Age 6 and Above | | | | | Current Enrolment for Age 6–14 | | | | |
| | 1993–94 | | 2017–18 | | | 1993–94 | | 2017–18 | | |
States	SC/STs	Non-SCs	SC/STs	Non-SCs	OBCs	SC/STs	Non-SCs	SC/STs	Non-SCs	OBCs
Andhra Pradesh	32.2	52.1	64.2	66.4	61.7	53.9	70.5	93.9	97.8	97.7
Assam	69.8	71.1	88.2	86.6	86.6	83.8	80.0	99.0	98.1	96.9
Bihar	27.0	49.4	60.8	76.2	73.9	41.8	61.9	89.9	94.0	93.2
Gujarat	52.6	68.9	74.8	85.5	81.9	73.6	80.0	93.7	98.2	98.4
Haryana	48.0	65.7	72.3	81.5	79.9	71.6	85.0	96.4	97.5	97.5
Himachal Pradesh	62.2	70.7	82.3	87.8	89.1	88.7	91.8	99.3	98.3	99.4
Karnataka	40.1	62.8	66.3	78.6	76.0	65.0	78.8	96.1	98.7	98.7
Kerala	82.3	92.7	84.7	95.2	94.7	93.6	95.4	99.1	99.7	99.8
Madhya Pradesh	34.8	59.6	64.5	80.3	77.3	52.2	73.3	92.2	96.8	96.1
Maharashtra	52.3	71.5	74.5	83.9	80.7	72.9	87.5	96.9	97.6	98.0
Orissa	33.1	63.3	68.6	81.6	78.1	52.0	77.0	98.9	99.0	98.7
Punjab	46.8	71.5	74.1	86.3	81.4	69.0	89.8	96.9	98.1	97.2
Rajasthan	29.3	51.0	64.5	73.9	70.4	43.2	67.9	91.4	96.2	95.6
Tamil Nadu	52.0	71.6	76.9	84.7	84.2	77.2	84.1	99.3	99.1	99.0
Uttar Pradesh	33.1	53.1	66.1	73.6	71.0	52.2	66.9	90.2	91.9	91.4
West Bengal	51.3	69.9	72.7	83.3	81.4	63.6	75.8	95.5	96.3	96.4
All-India	41.4	62.9	69.8	79.7	76.5	59.6	75.5	93.9	96.0	95.4

Source: Estimated from NSSO–EUS 50th round and PLFS 2017–18.

Tamil Nadu as against 73 per cent in Maharashtra and 74 per cent in Gujarat, while at the all-India level, it was 60 per cent. The state has thus achieved universal coverage in retaining children in schools across caste groups. However, indicators such as dropout rates and the extent to which different caste groups enter into higher education are equally important in this regard. Caste gap in educational attainment in Tamil Nadu is almost zero in school education among the current generation unlike among previous generations, showing that inter-caste differences in attainment of school education are eroding over time. Both micro and macro studies affirm this trend in the state.[1]

Tamil Nadu does well in most other educational indicators as well. It ranks first in terms of gross enrolment ratio in middle school, and third in terms of the composite index of elementary education. As per the last educational development index (averages of access, infrastructure, teachers and outcomes) computed by the National University of Educational Planning and Administration (NUEPA), Tamil Nadu tops among the major states.[2] The latest report on the performance grading index (PGI), released by the Ministry of Human Resource Development (MHRD) (2017–18), also places the state at the top in terms of access and equity, and in fifth place in infrastructure.[3] The learning outcome has, however, been a source of concern. Though Tamil Nadu is one of the two states where learning outcomes in public schools are better than in private schools (Balagopal and Vijayabaskar 2018), overall learning outcomes are relatively poor with the report placing the state in the seventeenth position. We now move on to map how improvements in infrastructure made educational attainments possible.

SCHOOL INFRASTRUCTURE

Though there has been an increase in enrolment of children in private schools in recent years (Government of Tamil Nadu 2017), government schools continue to dominate provisioning of education in the state. As per the *Annual Status of Education Report (ASER)* 2018, about 68 per cent of school children (age 6–14) are still enroled in goverment and government-aided schools in Tamil Nadu.[4] Currently, the government runs 66 per cent of elementary schools and

52 per cent of secondary schools in the state. As per the *TNHDR* (Government of Tamil Nadu 2017), the state not only has one of the best indices of infrastructure for primary schools such as availability of drinking water, separate toilets for girls and electricity, it has also ensured better human resources (also see Table 3.3).

The average pupil–teacher ratio and pupil–classroom ratio is lower in Tamil Nadu as compared to the all-India average. The NITI (National Institution for Transforming India) Aayog's school education quality index (SEQI) for the year 2016–17 classifies Tamil Nadu and Kerala as the best in school education in India. The ranking is based on 30 indicators including single-teacher schools, percentage of schools meeting teacher norms, transition rates of students from one level to another, schools with libraries or reading rooms, and so on. This emphasis on primary education goes against the argument that Weiner (1990) makes that India's education policy has been historically biased towards elites.

Myron Weiner points out in his landmark study, *The Child and the State in India* (1990), that though the Indian Constitution guaranteed free and compulsory education under its directive principles, it was hardly translated into practice. Attention was instead given to higher education for elites.[5] Inequality in access to education got translated into inequality in other economic domains including wage differentials. Indian elites in fact sustained

Table 3.3 Basic Infrastructure in Primary Schools (2015)

States	Percentage of schools with:				
	Kitchen shed for cooking	Drinking water	Urinal for boys	Separate toilet for girls	Schools having electricity
Andhra Pradesh	55.6	93.9	99.6	99.6	91.7
Karnataka	94.8	100	98.9	99.5	96.8
Kerala	92.9	99.5	96.9	98.5	95.6
Gujarat	96.1	100	99.9	99.9	99.2
Maharashtra	90.2	99.6	98.8	99.1	90.6
Tamil Nadu	96.6	100	99.6	99.8	98.6
India	79.8	95.8	96.5	97.0	52.4

Source: National University of Educational Planning and Administration (2017): U-DISE 2015–16, School Education in India: Flash Statistics.

their position at the top by denying education to a substantial proportion of the population. Based on his fieldwork, Weiner notes:

> Many orthodox high-caste Hindus regard it as sacrilegious that members of the lower castes should read sacred texts, or that girls should learn to master writing. The notion that it is unnecessary (and even undesirable) for lower castes to acquire education is not easily shaken by schools [*sic*] teachers, many of whom regard lower-caste children as unfit for studies. (1990: 139)

If the orthodox elites used a religious basis to deny education to the majority, the modern elite thought '… bookish learning in the schools might lead the lower castes and classes to give up menial work and seek white-collar positions …' (p. 139). Such caste elitism, according to Weiner, gets reflected in schools operating in India. Further, for Weiner, this elitism also translated into low regard for and ascription of low value to school teaching. Moreover, according to him, the divide between mental and manual labour gets re-enacted through the modern education system.

> The Indian position rests on deeply held beliefs that there is a division between people who work with their minds and rule and people who work with their hands and are ruled, and that education should reinforce rather than break down this division. (Weiner 1990: p. 5)

The low level of public expenditure, particularly in primary education, can therefore be explained by such elitism. Though recent efforts at the national level have sought to counter this elitism (Harriss 2017), Tamil Nadu has a longer history of addressing this bias.

PUBLIC EXPENDITURE ON EDUCATION

Though the state ranks only eighth in terms of per capita expenditure on education, the quality and composition of expenditure has made a difference. Over time, the state has steadily shifted its priority from primary to higher levels of education to match the growing demand. In 2015–16, the state's social expenditure was around 39 per cent of its total expenditure, out of which expenditure on education has been around 46 per cent, and accounted for 2.3 per cent of the gross state domestic product (GSDP) (Shanmugam 2018). Of the total expenditure on education, school education alone accounts for about 84 per cent, with a shift in emphasis from primary to secondary education over time. About 70 per cent of its educational expenditure (revenue) was on primary education in 1955–56, which came down to 52 per cent in 1980–81. During this period, the share of secondary education has gone up from 20 per cent to 29 per cent, and the share of higher education has gone up from 11 per cent to 19 per cent (Madras Institute of Development Studies 1988). The state has thus gradually diversified its resources to secondary and higher education once primary education infrastructure was deemed sufficient. It was also one of the first states to have a separate directorate for primary education (Madras Institute of Development Studies 1988).

Efficient public expenditure also implies lesser expenses for households. As per the National Sample Survey (NSS) 71st round (2014), the average expenditure of a higher secondary student in a government school in Tamil Nadu is INR 2,862, which is less than half the all-India average of INR 6,916 (2016: pp. 103–04). The corresponding expenditure in Maharashtra is as high as INR 8,788, while it is INR 9,179 in Gujarat, amounting to three times what a student in Tamil Nadu has to spend. Even the expenditure that an upper-primary or a secondary student incurs in a government school in Tamil Nadu, of INR 1,518 and INR 2,171, respectively, is again lower than that of the two states or the all-India average. The lower expenditure is a consequence of several financial incentives that have improved over time to ensure that children from less privileged backgrounds enter schools. While we dicuss some of the schemes in a later section, we locate these interventions as an imperative of a century-long mobilisation, in the next section.

MOBILISING TO DEMOCRATISE

As we establish in Chapter 2, political mobilisation in the state was primarily against caste-based discrimination in access to various domains, and towards abolition of caste. The pre-history of the Dravidian movement (Arasu 2012;

Kaali 2018) combined with the monopoly of upper castes in the domain of modern education and employment laid the foundations for a strong political premise that broad basing of education is critical to securing social justice. We must also mention here the role played by Christian missionaries in introducing education in the Presidency. The Presidency in fact accounted for the largest number of schools in the country (Narayan 2018). The idea of modern education as a key resource also permeated in Tamil society, with a number of caste associations and prominent leaders from non-Brahmin castes building schools in different parts of the region. This awareness about the importance of modern education and consequent demand for education also translated into the government expanding the scope of public schooling in the Presidency. As early as in the 1930s, compulsory primary education became a component of the fourteen-point programme that Periyar made for the Justice Party (Arooran 1980: p. 181). While the Justice Party saw that access to education was access to power, Periyar's interpretation laid an even more persuasive basis for democratisation of power through educational mobility.

Even before the Justice Party came to power in 1920, mobilisation by lower-caste groups and representations to the colonial government through their associations led to the passing of a government order (GO) in 1919 (Home: Education No. 329; cited in Rasathurai 2009: pp. 79–82). The order pointed out that separate schools for *panchama* students cannot be a long-term solution to bringing more and more students from untouchable communities into schools. Based on reports submitted by officials from various parts of the Presidency, it goes on to highlight how discriminatory practices among upper-caste students and their families prevent low-caste students from enrolling in common schools. Importantly the GO points to the micro geographies of caste power that constituted and enabled such discrimination and exclusion. Articulating the importance of subverting the basis of such spatial control wielded by the upper castes, the GO suggests the following, among others, to end such discrimination. To begin with, it says that wherever schools are located in upper-caste neighbourhoods, efforts should be made by school authorities to move the school to locations which are less infused with caste power. Further, wherever schools are run on rented premises owned by landowners who do not want *panchama* children in their schools, local education authorities should make efforts to move the schools out of such premises. The GO also insists that any new school that will be set up ought to get a certificate stating that it is located in a place that can be accessed by people from all castes before it can claim public money for setting up or running. Finally, it insists that the Director of Education and the heads of zilla parishads and urban local bodies submit annual reports on activities undertaken on these aspects to the government (Rasathurai 2009: pp. 79–82).

LINKING MEAL PROVISIONING TO EDUCATION

Apart from an increase in the number of schools, one of the earliest moves to broad base access was made by the Justice Party when it formed the government in 1920. It was found that in several schools in the Chennai Corporation, located in depressed-class areas, the students were neither in a position to afford their noon meal nor in a position to go home and eat. They also observed lower rates of enrolment in these schools as a result. In response to representations by the Justice Party leader P. Theagaraya Chetty, the government allotted one anna per student to provide a noon meal in select schools in the Chennai Corporation through a GO in 1922 (Rasathurai 2009: pp 168–69, 203–04). This proved to be the beginning of a long history of linking food provisioning with access to education that the state has come to be known for. Schemes like scholarships and financial aid for students from lower castes were also introduced, apart from hostels for lower-caste students (Rasathurai 2009). While such efforts improved access to education, P. T. R. Dr Palanivel Thiagarajan,[6] currently a DMK member of the legislative assembly (MLA), also remarks that this in turn led to an enhanced basis for political mobilisation around caste discrimination. He points out that children often lived in caste-based settlements where discrimination may not be particularly evident. When they come and sit together in a classroom, their encounter with caste discrimination becomes acute. Normally two pots for drinking water will be kept in a classroom, one for the Brahmins and another for non-Brahmins. Since the latter outnumber the former, the pot meant for them is likely to be emptied much faster, but they will never be allowed to drink from the pot allotted for Brahmin students. Such awareness in turn fed into the anti-caste movement.

While the Justice Party pioneered the free mid-day meal scheme to improve the enrolment of lower-caste students in schools, the scheme was re-introduced by the Congress government in 1956 under the chief ministership of Kamaraj, who also hailed from a lower-caste background. Kamaraj's role in promoting primary education also illustrates the embedding of the importance of modern education and its ties to social power in the political narrative of the state, which no political party could afford to ignore. Earlier in 1953, the Congress government under the Chief Ministership of Rajagopalachari had tried to introduce modifications to primary schooling with a vocational component (Anandhi 2018). This initiative meant that while students from all caste backgrounds can attend common schools in the mornings, the students were supposed to go back to their households in the afternoon and spend time with family members learning their family vocation. Given that the family vocation was strongly tied to caste-determined occupations, this was seen as a way to reinforce caste hierarchies by not only leaders of the Dravidian movement but importantly, even among non-Brahmin leaders within the Congress party. Rajagopalachari also oversaw the closure of over 6,000 schools citing lack of finances. Following massive protests all over the state, Rajagopalachari had to resign and the scheme was withdrawn. After coming to power in 1954, Kamaraj not only reopened the closed schools, but also started new schools in rural and remote areas, increasing the percentage of school-going children in the age group of 6–11 years from 45 to 75 in a span of seven years (Kumaradoss 2004). He also introduced a mid-day meal programme in elementary schools with contributions from the government and the community.

As cooking of food was found to increase the work burden on schoolteachers, the DMK government introduced a centralised kitchen with dedicated staff, soon after coming to power in 1967 (Rajivan 2006). The biggest improvement in this regard was clearly the Puratchi Thalaivar (PT) MGR Nutritious Meal Programme introduced in 1982, which initially covered children in the age group 2–5 years in pre-school noon meal centres, and primary school children in rural areas. Over time, it was expanded to include both urban areas and children in higher grades of schools. The pre-school noon meal programme (NMP) centres were later merged with the integrated child development services (ICDS) (Government of Tamil Nadu 2017). Narayan (2018) maps a series of institutional interventions that could not have been possible without political commitment that ensured the successful implementation of the programme. Subsequent governments have sought to improve upon this not only by enhancing the quality of nutrition (supply of eggs, for example) but also by attempting to make the food tastier and varied by roping in leading chefs to design the menu for the meals. Since 2013, the state government has introduced a variety of meals within the programme on a pilot basis in one block in each district, with a different menu on each day, keeping in mind nutritional requirements as well as taste.

Another intervention with links to the Justice Party was the provisioning of infrastructure like hostel facilities for students from socially backward sections, besides incentives like subsidised transport.

IMPROVING INFRASTRUCTURE

Like the mid-day meals, the idea of hostels for lower castes also goes back to the Justice Party days. As we pointed out in Chapter 2, it was Natesa Mudaliar—a founder member of the Justice Party—who was the first to run *Dravidian Home*, a hostel for students from non-Brahmin communities pursuing education in Chennai. This was a much-needed facility as students from many communities did not have access to hostel and mess facilities, owing to caste discrimination (Arooran 1980). While such efforts were supported by Justice Party ministries in the 1920s, school infrastructures were also expanded by civil society initiatives among different non-Brahmin castes along with sections of Christian missionaries and the British colonial bureaucracy (Arooran 1980). This process was considerably expanded when the DMK government opened a number of hostels across the state, which enhanced the enrolment of students (Spratt 1970). When the DMK assumed power in 1967, one of the poll promises they fulfilled was to waive tuition fees for poor students of all castes in the pre-university and pre-technical courses. They also opened up hostels for SCs and OBCs (see Table 3.4).

Table 3.4 Number of Residential Hostels for Scheduled Castes, Scheduled Tribes, Backward Classes, Most Backward Classes, Denotified Communities and Minority School Children in Tamil Nadu, 2013

S. no.	Classification of Hostels	Number of Hostels	Number of Students
1	Adi Dravidar Welfare Hostels	1,143	82,130
2	Tribal Hostels	42	2,782
3	Government Tribal Residential Schools	301	31,594
4	Hostels for Backward Classes	611	34,325
5	Hostels for Most Backward Classes	360	19,485
6	Hostels for Denotified Communities	136	10,534
7	Hostels for Minorities	11	900
	Total	2604	181,750

Source: Government of Tamil Nadu, Department of AdiDravidar and Tribal Welfare, Performance budget 2014–15; Government of Tamil Nadu, Department of Backward Classes, Most Backward Classes, Denotified Communities and Minority Welfare, Performance budget 2014–15.

In addition to such empowering policies that made sustained broad-basing of entry into modern education possible, governments have also used 'economic popular' policies to reduce the cost of accessing education. The state provides several educational resources like slates, notebooks, stationery and textbooks (1st–12th standard) to students from lower castes. In 2011–12, it introduced distribution of free bicycles for students from SCs, backward classes (BCs), most backward classes (MBCs) and minority communities pursuing the 11th standard in government or government-aided or partly-aided schools, and a free laptop scheme for children in higher secondary and tertiary education. The government has further introduced a Special Cash Incentive Scheme from 2011–12 to reduce dropouts at the secondary level. An amount of INR 1,500 for students studying in the 10th and 11th standards and INR 2,000 for students studying in the 12th standard in government or government-aided schools is deposited in the Tamil Nadu Power Finance Corporation, and is handed over to them on the completion of their higher secondary education. In the case of students studying in government or government-aided schools (classes 1–12), whose income earning parent passes away or becomes permanently incapacitated in an accident, the government provides financial assistance of INR 50,000 deposited in the name of the student in a public sector undertaking so that children do not drop out of school. As the Sarva Shiksha Abhiyan promotes inclusive education, the state government has allocated INR 2.37 crores for 149,214 CWSN (children with special needs) in 2013–14 (Government of Tamil Nadu 2014). In order to enhance enrolment of SC and/or ST girls and to reduce dropouts, the government has been providing a cash transfer since 1994–95 (Government of Tamil Nadu 2014).[7]

In addition, the government has one of the most subsidised transport systems for students using public transport. This allows poor students to commute from rural areas to schools in urban areas as well as children from urban slums and low-income neighborhoods to more distant schools or colleges. In 2016, more than 70 per cent of upper-primary, secondary and higher-secondary students had availed of such subsidised transport facilities (Balagopal and Vijayabaskar 2018). Once again, such financial incentives to increase enrolment of lower-caste children go back to efforts by the Justice Party. In response to their demands, a GO passed in 1919 (No. 1189) offered scholarships for *panchama* students in upper-primary education so as to prevent them from dropping out (Rasathurai 2009: pp. 87–88). This was also linked to the need to create teachers from the lower castes so that the issue of lack of adequate teaching resources in schools for *panchama* students can be tackled. Rasathurai also documents the role of political voices, both within the legislature and outside, in rendering visible some gaps in information critical to policy-making, and also in pushing policy formulation towards democratising access. We now turn our attention to the domain of higher education.

SOCIAL INCLUSION IN HIGHER EDUCATION

While modern school education was meant to ensure greater awareness of their social position and that of the larger world, an awareness denied to lower castes for centuries, higher education was seen as a means to redistribute power emanating from participation in the modern economy. As per the All India Survey on Higher Education (AISHE) 2017–18 (Government of India 2018a),[8] the gross enrolment ratio (GER) for Tamil Nadu is the highest among the major states. Nearly 50 per cent of the youth in the age-group 18–23 years are in some form of higher education compared to the all-India average of 26 per cent. The levels are much higher even compared to the second best performing state. Importantly, it is more evenly distributed across gender, caste, class and space. The enrolment ratios for women are 48 per cent in Tamil Nadu as against 25 per cent at the all-India level. Though lower than that of the overall population, the GER is relatively higher for SC youth suggesting a more broad-based increase in investments in education and access across castes (Government of Tamil Nadu 2017). The state's attainments in higher education is more inclusive in class terms as well.

The 71st round of the NSS (2013–14) allows us to look at the variations in accessing higher education across economic classes (Table 3.5). In 2013–14, the gross attendance ratio as proxy for enrolment (for age 18–23) in higher education in Tamil Nadu was 31 per cent compared to the all-India figure of 20 per cent. Even the poorest economic class in the state—the bottom quintile— had about 15 per cent gross attendance ratio in higher education, which is close to what Gujarat exhibited as a whole. The gross attendance ratio among the bottom quintile was 6 per cent in Gujarat, 10 per cent in Maharashtra and 7 per cent at the all-India level. Not just in absolute terms, inequality between the richest and the poorest strata in higher education attainment in the state is also one of the lowest in the country. The top quintile had 3.6 times (Q5/Q1) higher education attendance than the bottom quintile in Tamil Nadu

Table 3.5 Inequalities in Access to Higher Education (Gross Attendance Ratio for Age 18–23)

Quintiles	Tamil Nadu	Gujarat	Maharashtra	All-India
Q1	14.8	5.9	10.4	6.7
Q2	21.7	5.9	15.2	12.6
Q3	23.4	10.4	16.1	18.3
Q4	35.6	22.9	30.4	27.8
Q5	53.5	43.3	46.3	48.3
All	31.4	15.9	21.9	20.3
Q5/Q1	3.6	7.3	4.4	7.2
Rural	28	10.6	16.3	16.3
Urban	34.6	24.5	29	29.2
Urban/Rural	1.2	2.3	1.8	1.8

Source: Estimated from NSS 71st round (2014).

compared to 7.3 times in Gujarat, 4.4 times in Maharashtra and 7.2 times at the all-India level.

The state has also made higher education accessible to its rural youth. The gross attendance ratio for rural youth in Tamil Nadu is as high as 28 per cent compared to 11 per cent in Gujarat and 16 per cent in Maharashtra and at the all-India level. Thus, the inequality between rural and urban areas is the lowest in the state. The urban to rural ratio in accessing higher education is 1.2 and lower than Gujarat (2.3), Maharashtra and the all-India average (1.8). While the state has ensured more broad-based access to higher education, this penetration of higher education is particularly high for technical or professional education. As per the National Sample Survey Office (NSSO 2014–15), 32 per cent graduates who are enrolled in higher education are in technical or professional courses in Tamil Nadu compared to 15 per cent at the all-India level, 21 per cent for Maharashtra and 20 per cent for Gujarat. Apart from enrolment, there is also a convergence in terms of student performance across caste groups over time. Afirmative action over a long period has reduced the gap in performance in school final examinations across caste groups. Noted educationist M. Anandakrishnan, a long-term observer of higher education in the state, remarks that over time, the cut off marks for admission into engineering and medical colleges have tended to converge across caste groups.[9] For instance, the cut-off marks for medical admission (undergraduate) in 2012 for SCs (198.75) was just one point less than that of the general category (199.75) and 0.75 points less than that of the BCs (199.5). Another study indicates that OBC students in Tamil Nadu also tend to perform better compared to backward caste students in other states (Goyal and Singh 2014).

An equally significant dimension of attainments in education is its contribution to the productive economy, an aspect that has gained importance particularly after the rise to prominence of human capital in development theory. If we compare the levels and the extent of education among its workforce, a cumulative outcome, Tamil Nadu does better than most states in the country (Figure 3.1).

Tamil Nadu has the most educated workforce in the country, second only to Kerala. Workers who are graduates and above in the total workforce are about 20 per cent in Tamil Nadu as against 18 per cent in Maharashtra and 14 per

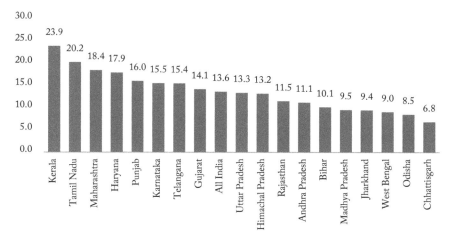

Figure 3.1 Percentage of Workers Who Are Graduates across States in India
Source: PLFS 2017–18.

cent in Gujarat, with the all-India average, too, being only about 14 per cent. This achievement in ensuring access to higher education becomes possible owing to its innovative reservation policies and various policy interventions encouraging students from marginalised sections. This broad-basing cannot be merely due to the availability of infrastructure but is also an outcome of a social and political milieu that allows the lower castes to not only aspire but also equips them with the means to meet their aspirations. We first relate the attainments to investments in infrastructure.

INFRASTRUCTURE FOR HIGHER EDUCATION

Higher educational institutions in the public and of late, increasingly in the private sector, have had a critical role in improving access. The state ranks first among all states with regard to the total of number of universities (it has 59 universities), ranks second in the number of state public universities and has 9.5 per cent of all the universities in the country (Government of Tamil Nadu 2017). The state also ranks first in the number of technical universities. Though technical education is skewed with a higher share of students in undergraduate engineering education, the state also has the highest share of polytechnic students in the country. This growth was made possible largely by opening up avenues for entry of private investments in higher education in the mid-1980s, a move that was inspired by similar initiatives in states like Karnataka. Resource constraints at the state level and a perceived market opportunity for private actors drove this process of expansion of private provisioning of higher education. To reduce the burden of the central government, the centre shifted the provisioning of higher education to the state governments while continuing to maintain regulatory control (Agarwal 2006). Left with limited resources to fund such expansion, privatisation of higher education was seen as a way out. This opened up spaces for subnational elites to invest in higher education for profits. At present, the private sector has a dominant presence in engineering education in the state, accounting for more than 95 per cent of the total engineering colleges.

Despite the enhanced role of the private sector, the state has continued to set up higher education institutions in the public domain (Government of Tamil Nadu 2017). The enrolment ratios in colleges are also better. For instance, the average enrolment per college is 919 in Tamil Nadu as against 678 in Maharashtra and 519 in Gujarat, while the all-India average stands at 698. At 15, the state also has a better pupil–teacher ratio in higher education compared to 25 at the all-India level and those in states like Maharashtra and Gujarat (22 and 26, respectively) (Government of India 2018). Apart from such infrastructure, the state has also provided incentives to enhance student enrolment ratios.

INCENTIVISING ENTRY INTO HIGHER EDUCATION

Several categories of students from less privileged socioeconomic backgrounds are exempted from various expenses incurred for higher education. As a result, on an average, students in the state tend to spend relatively less as in the case of school education. As per the NSS 71st round, the average expenditure incurred by a student pursuing a technical or professional course in government institutions in Tamil Nadu was INR 35,084 as against INR 46,316 in Gujarat, and was a little over half that in Maharashtra (INR 60,047). The all-India average was INR 42,069 (p. 130). Such low expenditures became possible because payment of tuition fees and/or examination fees is waived or subsidised for students from lower-caste groups, Tamil-medium students for different levels of higher education and for girl students in postgraduate degree courses. The same survey (p. 398) notes that out of the total students who received scholarships, SCs alone constituted about 44 per cent in Tamil Nadu as against 16 per cent in Gujarat and 30 per cent in Maharashtra, while the all-India average was about 25 per cent. Beside financial incentives for SCs, the state also introduced a series of schemes for encouraging women. Despite increasing privatisation, such initiatives, among others, have countered the elite bias in higher education visible at the national level.

ADDRESSING ELITE BIAS

Higher education in India has been elitist for a long period. It began as a small enclave under colonialism and continued to be under elite control even in post-independence India. As Balakrishnan (2008) argues, higher and technical education throughout the Nehruvian era up to the 1980s developed at the cost of basic education. This bias meant that higher education continued to be the preserve of upper classes and castes, perpetuating the divide in access to higher education. In fact, a substantial proportion of the increase in economic inequality in India is linked with the increase in returns to education and low level of inter-generational mobility. Higher education in India is thus trapped in a vicious circle; barriers to access higher education widen economic inequality, which in turn widens inequality in access to higher education (Bardhan 2013). This has been further aggravated by privatisation of higher education. Though studies indicate that the quality of training is inadequate in private institutions (Kapur and Mehta 2011), returns on investments in higher education are still high. Further, those who graduate in elite institutions continue to migrate to the West. An estimate shows that the rate of emigration of those with tertiary education is 42 times of those with primary and 14 times of those with secondary education (Kapur 2011). As a result, inequality in higher education continues to be higher than in physical capital in India. Inequality in adult schooling years among people in India is in fact much higher than that in Sri Lanka, China, Vietnam or Indonesia, and even most Latin American countries including Brazil and Mexico (Bardhan 2008).

Tamil Nadu, while following several other states in adopting the privatisation route, has managed to democratise access to higher education. It has ensured participation of different socioeconomic groups of the population. Inequities in access across gender, caste and between rural and urban areas have fallen thanks to the wide spread of colleges in rural areas. About 78 per cent of colleges are located in rural Tamil Nadu as against 57 per cent in Maharashtra and 52 per cent in Gujarat. While location decisions may be guided by availability of cheap land, it does impact access to higher education. Even in income terms, the poor have better access to higher education in the state compared to other states in India, as pointed out earlier. A long history of affirmative action policies in the state has contributed substantially to counter this elite control over higher education.

DEMOCRATISING HUMAN CAPITAL

The passing and implementation of the first communal GO by the Justice Party marks the beginning of the history of democratisation of higher education in the state. While the GO was for communal representation in administrative power in the colonial government, it nonetheless paved the way for the entry of lower castes into the educational sphere (Irschick 1969: p. 218).[10] Another GO proposed in 1922 was also specifically meant for reservation in government posts for non-Brahmins. As a Justice Party member articulated, 'given the social and educational backwardness that the non-Brahman community was steeped in, it was impossible to adapt itself to the changing conditions of the country' without adequate modern education (Irschick 1969: p. 227). Seeking reservation in education was therefore seen as an indirect demand for redistribution of power derived from access to modern education and jobs as well as a requirement to exercise citizenship.

Importantly, the party also sought to privilege a certain kind of modern education that can nurture scientific temper and enable one to participate in the modern economy. Education was therefore seen as a pathway to participate in the process of modern economic development and industrialisation (Geetha and Rajadurai 2008). Making a case for modern education and against the traditional emphasis on scriptural learning, Theagaraya Chetty, a founding member of the Justice Party, wrote,

> We all know that Bombay is the premier city of India! What was the cause of this greatness? It is not the Sanskrit literature, it is not the world-admired Shankara's philosophy, and it is not the political greatness that we are hankering after, which has made Bombay so great. It is enterprise—the enterprise of a small community of settlers, the Parsees (cited in Pandian 2007: p. 163).

Chetty argued that the colonial education system was only fitted to make 'automatic quill-drivers, indifferent school-masters and petty-fogging lawyers … there is no such thing as education suitable to the development of industries' (Pandian 2007: pp. 163–64). This emphasis probably explains the fact that the expenditure on technical education alone constitutes about 35 per cent (Government of Tamil Nadu 2017: p. 111) of the total higher education budget in the state at present. Another important intervention made by the Justice Party was addressing barriers to enter medical education. In the early 20th century, knowledge of Sanskrit was compulsory for admission into medical education. The government overturned the rule, paving the way for non-Brahmins to enter into medical education (Thirunavukkarasu 2013: p. 235).[11]

Importantly, the emphasis on education as the route to self-respect translated into a broad-based aspiration for access. This 'pressure from below' translated into a slew of measures over time that ensured broad basing. While we have highlighted some of the measures earlier, in the section below, we map the role of affirmative action policies, a domain that the state has virtually made its own in the country.

INNOVATIONS IN AFFIRMATIVE ACTION

The state has constantly reworked the categories of reservation to meet the changing demands of social justice by identifying beneficiaries and non-beneficiaries of the system. If the communal GOs during the Justice Party rule facilitated the initial entry of backward castes into the education system, protests from the state and pressure from the state government led to the first constitutional amendment in post-independent India to reintroduce reservation in education on a new pattern with 25 per cent reserved for OBCs and 15 per cent for SCs. This was made possible through large-scale agitations in the then Madras state during the 1950s led by the DK of Periyar E.V. Ramasamy and the DMK of C.N. Annadurai. This resulted in the first amendment to the Indian Constitution which legally validated caste-based reservations. The amendment led to the insertion of article 15 (4) to include the words 'socially and educationally backward' which became the basis for the introduction of reservation policies in most states in India. The coming into power of the Dravidian parties since 1967 led to a further expansion and deepening of the terrain of affirmative action. The DMK government set up a backward classes commission, which recommended increasing the existing reservation to 33 per cent for backward classes, identification of the most backward castes (MBC) and making of special provisions for them. Though not complying with the recommendations entirely, the government increased the reservation for OBCs from 25 per cent to 31 per cent in 1971, but also added two percentage points to the quota for SCs and STs increasing it from 16 per cent to 18 per cent. The AIADMK government led by M.G. Ramachandran increased the OBC reservation further to 50 per cent in 1984, pushing the quantum of reservation in the state to 69 per cent including a 1 per cent separate quota for STs, the highest in any state in India.

This broadening of the domain of affirmative action was accompanied by a deepening of such affirmative action within lower-caste groups. There was a consistent effort, particularly on the part of the DMK, to address differences within castes under each category. A new category, MBC, was created in 1989 within the BC category to ensure that backward castes and denotified communities that were not getting adequate representation within the backward class quota could be adequately represented. They were allotted 20 per cent from within the overall BC reservation of 50 per cent. As a result, these groups have increased their admission to professional courses five- to six-fold (Pandian 2011). Further in 2009, the DMK legislated a separate quota of 3 per cent for Arunthathiyar[12] within the 18 per cent quota for SCs as the latter's socioeconomic condition was worse off than that of other SCs. The DMK was thus responding to emerging differences within the backward classes and the Dalits in their ability to access higher education.

The DMK also tried to address non-caste based sources of inequality. For instance, in 1990, the DMK government introduced the scheme of awarding five extra marks to those applying for professional courses and hailing from families where none had had access to tertiary education before. Again, when the DMK returned to power in 1996, it introduced quotas for students from rural areas (Pandian 2011). Neither of the schemes had any reference to caste, but both were struck down by the Madras High Court. The DMK also introduced quotas for backward sections of Muslims who are socially underprivileged but are excluded from reservation because of their religious identity. Tamil Nadu, in fact, tops in educational attainment among Muslims in India. The percentage of Muslims who have completed graduation is 36 in Tamil Nadu as against 13 per cent in Gujarat and 16 per cent in Maharashtra, while the all-India average is 14 per cent (Jaffrelot and Kalaiyarasan 2019). The relatively better position of Muslims in the state is not only an outcome of inclusive social policies but also of targeted policies of affirmative action. While Muslims were included in the OBC category historically, they were given 3.5 per cent reservation in higher education and government jobs in 2007. All these innovative forms of reservation worked to ensure the relatively better representation of marginal social groups in the higher education system.

Another important initiative undertaken by the Dravidian parties pertains to the recognition of elite bias in clearing entrance examinations to enter professional education. Until 1984, the criteria for admission into professional courses was a combination of school-leaving marks and marks scored in an interview, with the later accounting for only a small share. Sensing the potential for corruption in allotting marks during an interview, an entrance test was introduced which, however, accounted for only 1/5th of the total marks in the admission process. Perceiving that even this creates a bias towards residents in larger cities with access to tuition centres and also towards households who are in a position to invest additional time for their children to prepare and take the entrance test, the AIADMK government abolished the entrance test completely in 2005 (Menon 2006). This narrative and argument against entrance tests clearly had a role in the state's subsequent opposition to the introduction of NEET.

The recent data on admission in engineering and technology courses reveals the democratisation of technical education in the state. Of the total 1,82,255 seats in engineering and technology courses in Tamil Nadu in 2013–14, the share of BCs was 45 per cent, followed by 22 per cent MBCs, 22 per cent SCs and 4 per cent Muslims (Government of Tamil Nadu 2017). Even the Arunthathiyars, a marginalised group within the SCs, had a share of 2 per cent in higher education in the state adding up to 89 per cent. This share is 20 percentage points more than what they are legally entitled to, but almost commensurate with their population. Such redistribution of access to higher education is unique in the history of Indian states. Contrary to popular perceptions, even in private colleges, marginal caste groups do find a degree of representation. Out of a total 1,70,013 seats, BCs have a share of 46 per cent, MBCs 22 per cent, SCs 16 per cent, Muslims about 4 per cent and Arunthathiyars, 2 per cent. It therefore appears that privatisation has not entirely excluded the entry of caste groups in higher education. Notably, 50 per cent of the seats in private colleges too are subject to selection based on affirmative action. In engineering colleges affiliated to Anna University, about 65 per cent of the total seats in non-minority institutions and 50 per cent seats in minority institutions are allotted through a single window system of counselling—a method which is governed by fee regulation and reservation policies. As a result, the state has been able to maintain social diversity in private colleges too. Together, such measures have ensured the generation of a relatively more inclusive pool of educated labour able to gain a foothold in the modern economy. More importantly, the narrative of social justice through affirmative action became a part of Dravidian common-sense that ensures much better functioning of institutions governing implementation of affirmative action policies unlike in other states.

While the Left movement which saw land reform as key to redistributive justice, Dravidian common-sense privileged access to education and jobs as important pathways to social justice in India. Cumulative inequalities cannot be addressed by land reform alone. When modern economic growth is driven by service and industry, education acquires significance in availing opportunities. When the central government led by V. P. Singh

(National Front government) implemented the Mandal Commission's recommendations in the 1990s, Tamil Nadu not only approved it but also passed a resolution on August 21, 1990 in the state assembly welcoming the announcement. Political parties had a series of hall meeting and rallies in the state (Pandian 2007). Looking back at the implementation of the Mandal Commission recommendations, Karunanidhi observes that 'The National Front government in 1989 (of which the DMK was a part) remains my best contribution to national politics. Though the government was short-lived, it implemented the Mandal Commission report [recommendations]' (cited in Panneerselvam 2017).

If Karunanidhi took pride in supporting Mandal I in the 1990s, it was because of a long legacy built by Dravidian mobilisation in the state. Periyar set the precedent when he resigned from the Indian National Congress in November 1925 after his resolution demanding caste-based reservation in government institutions was disallowed in the Kancheepuram conference of the Tamil Nadu Congress (Pandian 2007). He took this defeat to the streets across Tamil Nadu. Since then, social justice through affirmative action acquired significance in all political conferences of the SRM in the state (Pandian 1994). The significance of reservation in the political life of the state became evident in the large-scale agitations following the striking down of the provisions for reservation by the Supreme Court in 1951 forcing the constitutional amendment referred to earlier. Even political parties that oppose reservation at the national level support it in the state. Elites in Tamil Nadu who historically opposed it had to embrace it if they were to be politically relevant (Pandian 2007: p. 6). Reservation thus, not only became common-sense, but also an accepted means to socioeconomic mobility in Tamil Nadu.

The other event that we would like to use to illustrate this path dependence is what followed after the *Indira Sawhney and Others* v. *Union of India and Others*[13] judgement, when the Supreme Court put a ceiling of 50 per cent on the quantum of reservation that can be provided. Tamil Nadu was the first state to move a constitutional amendment to protect its 69 per cent reservation. The AIADMK government led by J. Jayalalithaa unanimously passed The Tamil Nadu Backward Classes, Scheduled Castes and Scheduled Tribes (Reservation of Seats in Educational Institutions and of Appointments or Posts in the Services under the State) Act, 1993 and appealed to the central government to place it under the ninth schedule of the Indian Constitution to protect it from judicial review.

EMERGING LIMITS

Viewing access to modern education as a pathway to substantive democracy in a caste society was not confined to the Dravidian movement alone. Anti-caste leaders like Mahatma Jyotirao Phule and Babasaheb B. R. Ambedkar, too, held similar positions. In the absence of adequate resources to avail opportunities, mere grant of formal freedom to lower castes cannot ensure social justice. Freedom therefore involves the power to act and the capacity to do things.[14] This simultaneity of freedom and endowing the deprived with material resources to act has substantially informed the Dravidian imagination of development in the state. By way of concluding this chapter, we would like to draw from the personal memoirs of Sattanathan, an accomplished bureaucrat, who went on to become the Chairman of the first Tamil Nadu Backward Classes Commission. Hailing from one of the lowest 'touchable' Tamil castes, he narrates his life's trajectory from one of utter poverty to becoming a successful, high-level bureaucrat. The memoir offers a first-hand account of how caste worked in every sphere during the early 20th century. Talking about his mother who happened to be an illegitimate child, he says that when she was asked by her biological father who was fairly wealthy if she wanted anything from him, she didn't know what to ask. He narrates:

> She had neither the imagination nor the courage to ask for anything substantial … He might have given more if he was asked. In poverty one does not even know how and what to ask. (Sattanathan 2007: p. 19)

This telling observation directly speaks to the importance given by Charles Taylor to the terms of recognition (1992). Taylor points out that members of marginalised groups often live in a life-world where they see themselves as inferior beings, which is reinforced when members of that community hold similar opinions. As a result, even when real barriers to improve their lives are broken down, they still may not be in a position to take advantage of this opportunity. Sattanathan's mother's inability to ask is precisely an outcome of such 'mis-recognition'. Changing the terms of recognition that can enable the capacity to aspire is a political process. As the tragic story of Anitha illustrates, political processes and mobilisation in the state made possible a change in the terms of recognition. Entering into the portals of modern education and subsequently modern higher education not only made children from lower-caste backgrounds equip themselves with the skills required to enter the modern economy but also be aware of the cultural norms that render them inferior. It therefore allowed them to simultaneously question dominant norms and also aspire for social and economic mobilities that were not possible earlier. Anitha's aspirations clearly reflect this accumulation of capabilities to aspire, a far cry from the predilection that Sattanathan's mother faced when confronted with choices. The fact that there were no protests among lower-caste youth in other parts of the country against the introduction of NEET indexes the role played by the Dravidian movement in fostering such aspirations.

However, there are limits emerging to this process. Apart from the relatively poor learning outcomes, there has also been a growing shift from public schooling at the primary level to reliance on private schools in recent years (Balagopal and Vijayabaskar 2018). Importantly, this shift corresponds to a spatial–caste–gender divide with lower castes and girl children from rural areas more likely to rely on government schools. With increasing privatisation of higher education, this divide at the primary level is likely to feed into differences that emanate due to differential access and quality of tertiary education. Private institutions are of uneven quality with a large number of them incapable of imparting skills useful in the labour market (Mukherjee 2011). A few institutions are, however, able to place students in better paying jobs and command a higher premium for entry. This difference between elites who are able to enter such institutions and the rest is likely to translate into labour market inequalities that we highlight in Chapter 7. While we take up the implications of this phenomenon in greater detail in Chapter 8, we would like to highlight one important dimension of this emerging dualistic structure of education. While social popular policies enabled reduction in relative differences between caste elites and lower castes with regard to entry, of late, interventions have been more in the economic popular domain, like support through subsidised inputs for education and scholarships. The latter, while they definitely contribute to continued broad-based entry, do not address the entry barriers to access such high-cost education and therefore do not engage with the issue of relative differences.

NOTES

1 The recent study by Asher, Novosad and Rafkin (2020) shows that upward educational mobility is highest in Tamil Nadu and Kerala.

2 See http://schoolreportcards.in/Media/m188.html (accessed 4 January 2019).

3 See https://mhrd.gov.in/sites/upload_files/mhrd/files/PGI_2017-18.pdf (accessed 4 January 2019).

4 District Information System for Education DISE data for 2015–16 puts the figure for primary education at 60 per cent in Tamil Nadu while it is 64 per cent at the all-India level.

5 India's experience suggests that the spread of mass education need not correlate with the levels in per capita income. It is state commitment that ensures universal basic education. For instance, several East Asian countries have shown that low incomes need not deter democratising access to education. Countries such as China and South Korea have not only attained higher rates of literacy than India, but have done so starting from a lower base; they have also been able to provide better access to tertiary education.

6 Personal interview on January 2, 2018.

7 The *TNHDR* (Government of Tamil Nadu 2017), highlights the multiple dimensions along which the state has sought to intervene to ensure access, and also importantly, to reduce drop outs among lower-caste and girl students.

8 The survey defines higher education as education which is obtained after completing 12 years of schooling or an equivalent. This may be of the nature of general, vocational, professional or technical education.

9 Interview dated 3 January 2019.

10 The first communal GO which came into effect on 16 September 1921 included a government instruction extending reservation from the revenue to all departments; a circular was also issued to all heads of departments, collectors and district judges to classify each new recruit to the public services

into one of six categories: Brahmin, non-Brahmin Hindu, Indian Christian, Muslim, European and Anglo Indian (Irschick 1969: p. 236).

11 The story of democratising education in the state would, however, be incomplete without mention of the role of Christian missionaries in education (Hardgrave 1969; Ingleby 1998). Many institutions of higher education as well as schools for the masses were opened by Christian missionaries.

12 Arunthathiyars are located at the bottom of the caste pyramid and are socially and economically much worse off compared to other Dalit communities in the state. They undertake bulk of degrading work like manual scavenging.

13 AIR 1993 SC 477, https://indiankanoon.org/doc/1363234/ (accessed 16 November 2019).

14 On this, John Dewey (1993) says,

> Liberty is not just an idea, an abstract principle. It is power, effective power to do specific things. There is no such thing as liberty in general, liberty, so to speak, at large; if one wants to know what the condition of liberty is at a given time, one has to examine what persons can do and what they cannot do. The moment one examines the question from the standpoint of effective action, it becomes evident that the demand for liberty is a demand for power, either for possession of powers of action not already possessed or for retention and expansion of powers already possessed. (p. 158)

4

DEMOCRATISING CARE

India compares poorly with other developing countries on health parameters despite being among the fastest growing economies in the world (Balarajan, Selvaraj, and Subramanian 2011). In fact, compared to other developing countries, India has one of the lowest expenditures on health as a proportion of its gross domestic product (GDP) (A. Chakraborty 2019). As a result, citizens incur one of the highest out-of-pocket expenditures on health among countries with similar levels of income. Importantly, the increase in economic growth has not been matched by corresponding increases in human development in India. This is a paradox in a country where democratic practices have been better institutionalised as Evans and Heller (2018) point out. Countries with such democratic institutions are expected to invest additional resources towards welfare interventions in education and health compared to more authoritarian regimes that may emphasise growth at the expense of investments in human development.

As in the case of education, scholars use the elite bias hypothesis to explain this paradox (Das Gupta 2005). The Indian health system is biased in favour of elites as it focussed on curative health more than public health. Elites relied on curative medicines to insulate themselves from communicable diseases while neglecting public health, that is, to prevent exposure to such diseases for the rich and poor alike. Tamil Nadu is one of the few states that has, however, managed to work against this bias and build a robust public health infrastructure. The state for example, has already achieved the Millennium Development Goals (MDGs) of reduction in infant mortality rate (IMR) and maternal mortality ratio (MMR) (Vaidyanathan 2014). Given the macro-bias against healthcare, the state's achievements that we map in the next section clearly stand out. What made such outcomes possible?

This chapter traces a set of interventions in this regard, starting with the creation of a separate department for public health in the early-20th century. It goes on to identify factors contributing to the dramatic decline in fertility rate in the state including interventions focusing on maternity and early child care. The state, as mentioned in the previous chapter, is known for launching the nutritious noon meal scheme, a forerunner to similar schemes launched at the all-India level. The chapter also therefore discusses the history of processes instituted and the health implications of the nutritious noon meal scheme. Given the growing out-of-pocket expenses incurred by the public on healthcare (Balarajan, Selvaraj and Subramanian 2011) due to reliance on private providers and the rising cost of medicines, we also highlight the emergence of a robust primary healthcare system coupled with the creation and expansion of a corporation to centralise drug procurement and distribute them at subsidised rates. Importantly, the chapter argues that rather than higher expenditure on health, it is the efficient utilisation of available resources that has been critical to the state's achievements in health outcomes. We also demonstrate how the state's strategic allocation of resources towards primary healthcare made such efficiency gains possible. Finally, we point out how the formation of a bureaucracy inclusive of marginalised social groups is critical to the process.

We therefore emphasise the iterative nature of processes across sectors such as education and affirmative action, and democratisation of governance. If forming the first state planning commission in India with a taskforce constituted specifically for healthcare, investments in public health infrastructure, democratisation of the social profile of health personnel and innovative drug procurement fall under social popular policies, ensuring socially inclusive access to health through subsidised health insurance schemes, noon meal schemes, expansion of its content and coverage and maternity benefits would fall under economic popular interventions. If social popular policies helped build public health infrastructure and democratised health governance, economic popular policies enhanced its coverage and added new schemes to its content.

To begin with, we establish that in terms of health outcomes, the state has done better not just in terms of levels but also in the rate of change in outcomes compared to most states in the country. We then relate the outcomes of certain deliberate institutional interventions. The chapter traces the motivation and processes that translated into intermediary outcomes such as public health infrastructure. Such outcomes are a result of attention to primary healthcare, bucking national trends (Vaidyanathan 2014). Next, we emphasise the state's attention to effective preventive care rather than curative hospital care, especially by sustaining a vibrant public health department. We then highlight how affirmative action and the generation of a pool of healthcare professionals drawn from socially diverse backgrounds ensured an incentive to cater better to socially marginalised groups. Next, we draw attention to the Tamil Nadu Medical Services Corporation (TNMSC), an institutional innovation through which the state has provided essential drugs and diagnostics at public healthcare facilities. In the domain of nutrition enhancement, we discuss the pioneering noon meal scheme in schools. Moving to the domain of claim-making, we argue that changes in the social composition of the bureaucracy also contributed to the broad-basing of 'weak ties' that enabled better information dissemination and helped generate demand-side pressure. Finally, we hint at how the state has negotiated with macro policy reforms to address the issue of tertiary care. But first, the outcomes.

THE OUTCOMES

On most standard health indicators, Tamil Nadu does better than most states. The state's fertility rate has been below replacement rates, comparable to those of developed countries, and is the lowest in the country among the major states (UNFPA 2018). The total fertility rate (TFR) has shown a sharp decline from 3.7 in 1973 to 1.7 in 2013 (see Figure 4.1). The corresponding figures for India are 4.9 and 2.3, respectively. The state attained the replacement rate by the late 1990s while most other states are yet to do so (Government of Tamil Nadu 2017). The state has also addressed the issue of mortality better. The IMR has shown a sharp decline from 121 in 1972 to 19 in 2015 while the decline at the all-India level is from 139 to 41 (see Figure 4.2 and Table 4.1). The under-five mortality rate (U5MR) is 20 in the state as against 39 in Gujarat and 24 in Maharashtra, while it is 43 at the all-India level.

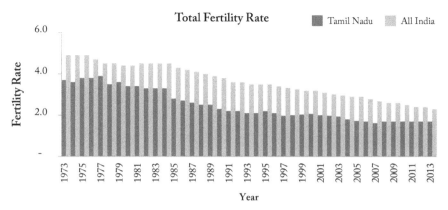

Figure 4.1 Trend in Total Fertility Rate

Source: Sample Registration System (SRS), 'Compendium of India's Fertility and Mortality Indicators, 1971–2013' (SRS n.d.).

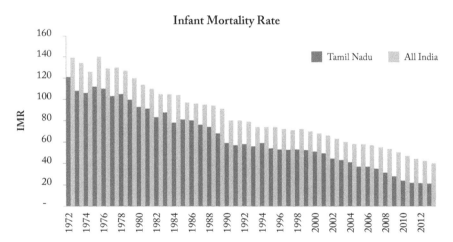

Figure 4.2 Trend in Infant Mortality Rate

Source: Sample Registration System ((SRS), 'Compendium of India's Fertility and Mortality Indicators, 1971–2013' (SRS n.d.).

The MMR, too, is much better than in comparable states and the all-India average—60 for Tamil Nadu as against 75 in Gujarat and 113 for India; Maharashtra fares slightly better at 46 (see Figure 4A.2). The percentage of

Table 4.1 Key Health Indicators for Caste Groups in Tamil Nadu and
All-India

States	1992–93			2015–16		
	SCs	Non-SCs	All	SCs	Non-SCs	All
IMR						
Tamil Nadu	90	65	71	23.6	18.4	20.3
Maharashtra	85	52	56	31.7	19.1	23.9
Gujarat	70	70	74	43.9	28.3	34.2
All-India	107	82	86	31.1	22.6	28.5
U5MR						
Tamil Nadu	127	85	95	31	24.8	26.9
Maharashtra	124	69	76	35.3	24.4	29.1
Gujarat	119	98	104	51.3	36.6	43.5
All-India	149	112	119	38.9	27.8	34.4
Under-nutrition of Children across Caste Groups (in per cent)						
Tamil Nadu	53	45	49	32.1	22.5	27.1
Maharashtra	57	51	54	40.3	29.2	34.4
Gujarat	59	41	50	37.6	29.3	38.5
All-India	58	52	53	42.8	31.2	38.4
Child Immunisation among Caste Groups (in per cent)						
Tamil Nadu	59	67	65	70.8	71.1	69.7
Maharashtra	61	65	64	50.6	56.2	56.3
Gujarat	N/A	52	50	50.8	49.3	50.4
All-India	27	38	35	63.2	64.5	62
Mothers' Antenatal Care (in per cent)						
Tamil Nadu	92	95	94	91.2	94.3	91.7
Maharashtra	90	89	82	93.7	90.6	91
Gujarat	85	77	75	78.4	87.6	80.5
All-India	58	66	53	77.5	85.6	79.3

Source: National Family Health Survey (NFHS) 1 and 4.

pregnant women who deliver their children at a health facility is 99 in Tamil Nadu, which is among the highest in the country (see Figure 4A.3). In fact, there has been an increase in the share of institutional deliveries in public hospitals in recent years (Government of Tamil Nadu 2017). Aggregate indicators may, however, mask the extent to which outcomes vary across different social groups.

Providing an inter-state comparative map of outcomes across caste groups in the next section, we establish that the health status of Scheduled Castes (SCs) too, is better than in either Gujarat or Maharashtra, and even better than that of caste elites in states like Uttar Pradesh (UP).

CASTE AND HEALTH

As in the case of the overall trends, health indicators for SC groups in Tamil Nadu are better than the all-India average. In 1992–93, the IMR for SCs in Tamil Nadu was 90 points and it has come down to 23.6 points in 2015–16. While the IMR came down from 85 to 32 in Maharashtra and 70 to 44 in Gujarat in the same period, the corresponding figures for India stand at 107 and 31.1 points, respectively. The U5MR among SCs has fallen from 127 to 31 during this period and is again better than the national average (see Table 4.1). The percentage of undernourished children among SCs too has fallen during this period, and is lower than at the all-India level (see table 4.1). Such a trend holds for child immunisation and mothers' antenatal care as well (see Table 4.1).[1] In fact, across many health indicators, deprived caste groups in Tamil Nadu enjoyed better health status than even dominant caste groups in the northern states. As per data from the fourth National Family Health Survey (NFHS-4) for (2015–16), the IMR for upper castes (non-SC/OBC) in UP is 60.2 which is much higher than that for SCs (23.6 points) and OBCs (18.4 points) in Tamil Nadu. Such outcomes among lower-caste groups hold true for other indicators such as child immunisation and mothers' antenatal care too.

About 99.1 per cent of pregnant women among SCs in Tamil Nadu delivered their children at a health facility as against 88.6 per cent in Gujarat and 93 per cent in Maharashtra, while only 75.9 per cent of even upper-caste women avail such facilities in UP. A supporting indicator of health among women and children is the proportion of births that are assisted by a health professional (that is, a doctor, nurse, or midwife). The delivery assistance given to pregnant SC women by such health personnel is about 99 per cent in Tamil Nadu while it is just 77.8 per cent even for upper-caste women in UP. The relevant indicators for SC women in UP are much worse. Tamil Nadu has therefore managed to not only provide overall healthcare but has made sure that the system is inclusive of lower-caste groups as well. Studies also affirm that the state has one of the best reproductive health and childcare systems in this country, with better contraceptive prevalence rates and extent of antenatal check-up coverage than most states (Mehrotra 2006).

We would like to point out that the reproductive health outcomes that we have mapped for the state are also a result of demand-side interventions in domains such as literacy and efforts to increase the age at marriage for women (Sinha 2016). The state's ability to reduce the gender gap in literacy over time that we discussed in the previous chapter has therefore been critical in this regard. This reduction in literacy gender gap has been accompanied by a considerable decline in TFR. The declining fertility rate also has a close relationship with the marrying age of women. As per NFHS-4, the average age at first marriages (the median age) among women in the age group 25–49 in Tamil Nadu is 20.1 as against 19.7 in Gujarat and 19.9 in Maharashtra, while the corresponding figure for India is 18.6. The age at marriage determines the extent to which women are exposed to the risk of pregnancy and also influences fertility levels. Both the increase in age at marriage and the reduced gender gap in literacy, while driven by larger socioeconomic changes have also been incentivised by specific interventions that we discuss later. Mere expenditure does not translate into a robust health infrastructure (A. Chakroborty 2019). Similarly, mere generation of intermediate outcomes such as creation of health infrastructure need not translate into health outcomes. We therefore emphasise the role of intermediary processes between these stages of healthcare interventions.

THE PROCESSES AND INTERMEDIATE OUTCOMES

Sen and Drèze (2011) point out that the state has seen a gradual consolidation of *universalistic social policies* and built an extensive network of 'lively and effective healthcare centres' offering access to people from across social groups. In this section, we map the processes that have contributed to such access as well as better health outcomes.

POLITICAL COMMITMENT TO HEALTH INFRASTRUCTURE

As we demonstrate later, the state has generated better health infrastructure and outcomes with no marked difference in the quantum of health expenditure compared to many other states. Further, the state has focused on creating a primary healthcare infrastructure that is one of the best in the country. As a senior bureaucrat observed, 'about 50 per cent [of the] state buildings are associated with the health and education sectors'.[2] Not only did the state make effective use of the limited assistance occasionally offered by the central government to build infrastructure, it has also used its resources very strategically towards primary healthcare. The political regime's commitment to health can be seen in the many committees the state constituted on health. As a senior public health expert observes:

> The government of Tamil Nadu was the first to constitute a state planning commission with a task force on health ... presided over by Malcolm Adiseshiah ... [It] divided itself into working parties to consider in depth the problems of health services, medical education, family planning, nutrition, sanitation, the role of voluntary organisations and indigenous medicines, including homeopathy. It handed over its report to the Chief Minister of Tamil Nadu, M Karunanidhi, in 1972. (Sanjivi 1973)

The state has more primary health centre (PHC) density than at the all-India level, a key infrastructural intermediary in ensuring public health. A circular from the health department[3] outlines the role of PHCs in addressing maternal, infant and child mortality in the state. The PHCs through their village health nurses (VHNs) monitor registration of each pregnant woman since 8–12 weeks of pregnancy and also enumerate all children of the ages of 0–5 for vaccination, ensuring adequate nutrition and other medical check-ups. The PHCs are also responsible for antenatal, intra-natal and postnatal care of mothers, as well as infant and child care in their jurisdictions. The population covered by a PHC in Tamil Nadu is 27,215 whereas the corresponding figure for India is 32,884 (see Table 4.2). The wider coverage of PHCs in the state becomes clearer when we look at the extent of coverage of villages. On average, a PHC covers 12 villages in Tamil Nadu while the all-India average stands at

25 in 2015. The state also has a well-functioning network of health sub-centres. One sub-centre caters to two villages compared to the national average of four villages. Even the community health centre (CHC), which operates at the taluk (block) level, has more density as compared to most states in India. Each CHC covers 42 villages in the state, while the national average stands at 116 villages.

The health centres are also better functioning and equipped on an average compared to Gujarat or Maharashtra. More than 89 per cent of the PHCs function 24 × 7 in the state while the all-India figure is just 39 per cent (see Table 4.3). Establishing a PHC does not guarantee the functioning of the unit. Several intermediary parameters for Tamil Nadu have translated expenditure

Table 4.2 Health Infrastructure across States in India

States	Average Rural Population Covered by a			Average Number of Villages Covered by a		
	Sub-centre	PHC	CHC	Sub-centre	PHC	CHC
Andhra Pradesh	4,541	32,350	1,80,189	2	16	88
Bihar	9,491	51,244	623,929	5	25	303
Chhattisgarh	3,781	24,820	126,503	4	25	130
Gujarat	3,942	26,404	107,747	2	14	57
Haryana	6,409	34,830	150,085	3	14	62
Himachal Pradesh	2,982	11,923	78,178	10	40	262
Jharkhand	6,338	76,621	133,272	8	99	172
Karnataka	4,015	15,924	181,890	3	12	142
Kerala	3,819	21,203	77,649	0	1	5
Madhya Pradesh	5,718	44,882	157,357	6	47	164
Maharashtra	5,818	33,990	170,989	4	24	121
Odisha	5,229	26,797	92,760	8	39	136
Punjab	5,877	40,619	115,628	4	29	84
Rajasthan	3,574	24,760	90,193	3	21	78
Tamil Nadu	4,273	27,215	96,700	2	12	42
Telangana	4,439	32,313	189,345	2	16	94
Uttarakhand	3,810	27,381	119,270	9	65	285
Uttar Pradesh	7,569	44,414	200,928	5	31	138
West Bengal	5,997	68,408	178,175	4	44	115
All-India	5,377	32,884	151,316	4	25	116

Source: Rural Health Statistics 2015, Ministry of Health and Family Welfare.

Table 4.3 Facilities at Primary Health Centres (PHCs)

States	PHC with Two Doctors (%)	PHC with Lady Doctor (%)	PHCs Functioning on 24x7 Basis (%)	PHCs with Labour Room (%)
Andhra Pradesh	36.6	50.1	44.8	85.4
Bihar	3.1	8.7	41.9	41.9
Chhattisgarh	12.9	8.4	28.8	88.3
Gujarat	23.6	29.7	22.6	80
Haryana	28.3	25.3	64.2	78.4
Himachal Pradesh	3.9	18.3	0.7	34.8
Jammu & Kashmir	28.1	44.1	32	54.5
Jharkhand	24.8	10.7	33.7	75.8
Karnataka	6.9	26.5	43.2	71.1
Kerala	80.5	55.5	25	7.5
Madhya Pradesh	11.4	11.9	71.2	63.7
Maharashtra	76.3	37.9	55	93.3
Odisha	54.3	40.2	9.8	45.6
Punjab	27.6	43.6	49.5	63
Rajasthan	15.3	9	47.1	80
Tamil Nadu	73.5	72.7	89.3	95.4
Telangana	41.2	58.4	49.3	100
Uttarakhand	23.7	22.6	33.5	63.8
Uttar Pradesh	21	9.1	12.1	54.6
West Bengal	22.1	15.6	25.6	99.5
All-India	26.9	27	39.2	69

Source: Rural Health Statistics 2015, Ministry of Health and Family Welfare.

into functioning infrastructure. On an average, only 27 per cent PHCs have doctors (mandatory two doctors at each unit) at the all-India level while in Tamil Nadu it is as high as 74 per cent. More than 72 per cent of PHCs in the state have a lady doctor while the corresponding all-India figure is only 27 per cent. The percentage of PHCs, which have an attached labour room, is as high as 95, while it is 69 per cent in the country. Field-based studies also endorse such a vibrant health infrastructure in the state (Drèze and Khera 2012). The state, thus, not only has a wider network of PHCs but also well-functioning ones with modern equipment. If the state used the assistance provided by the rural health component of the Minimum Needs Programme during the Fifth

Five Year Plan (1974–78) to build PHCs in rural Tamil Nadu earlier, it used the recent assistance under the National Rural Health Mission (NRHM) to equip PHCs with better equipment and infrastructure, upgrade 385 of them into CHCs and open 197 new PHCs in areas previously not covered (Vaidyanathan 2014).

Healthcare functioning has also been aided by better density of the total health workforce (doctors, nurses and midwives, dentists, pharmacists and other medical staff). This better density is a cumulative outcome of medical colleges established in both the public and the private domain. The state stands second in generating healthcare personnel in the country with a larger number of medical colleges than the official norm in India.[4] By 2014, the state had 45 medical colleges against the recommended norm of 14, and was again ahead of most states (Choudhury 2016).[5] Of the total 385 colleges in India, Tamil Nadu alone accounts for about 12 per cent, and also 12 per cent of the total intake of students in the country (Choudhury 2016). Importantly, even as it encouraged private-sector entry, the state has made efforts to set up medical colleges in the public domain in different parts to ensure equitable access (Government of Tamil Nadu 2017). Even in terms of allopathic doctors registered with the Medical Council of India per million population, the state ranks second. According to the National Health Profile (2019), it has 17.7 registered doctors per 10000 population, as against 8.7 at the all- India level. Similarly, in the case of nurses and auxiliary nurse midwives (ANMs), the state has 44.4 per 10,000 population as against the national average of 22' (National Health Profile, 2019). According to the NSSO-EUS, the state has 9.07 doctors per 10,000 population, much more than the national average of 4.28. Similarly, in the case of nurses and auxiliary nurse midwives (ANMs), the state has 10.4 per 10,000 population as against the national average of 7.4.

Importantly, the state has also built a cadre of medical officers dedicated to PHCs with incentives to work in remote and underserved areas. As a result, it has retained doctors within the public health system. Only 7.6 per cent of medical officers' posts in PHCs are vacant in Tamil Nadu, while in a state like Bihar, the corresponding figure is as high as 63 per cent (Alexander 2018). Similarly, the state has also built a network of VHNs who receive performance-based compensation to administer vaccinations, medicines and contraceptives, and to offer counselling, referral and other services for reproductive and child health. These VHNs are trained for 18 months both in-house and in the field before they are certified (Alexander 2018). Such infrastructure has been made possible through an emphasis not just on the effective use of available resources but by also ensuring that the composition of such expenditure is skewed towards primary healthcare.

PUBLIC EXPENDITURE: COMPOSITION MATTERS

Comparative studies often establish a weak link between public expenditure and health outcomes across lower-income countries, suggesting that how well money is spent is at least as important as how much is spent (Berman and Ahuja 2008). Similarly, Dipa Sinha (2016) shows that one per cent increase in per capita public health spending (average per year) over a period of five years has been associated with only 0.35 per cent reduction in IMR. Dholakia and Dholakia (2004) too show a limited but positive relationship between public expenditure and indicators of health, education and nutrition.[6] Our contention is that the extent to which the composition of expenditure is biased towards primary health or otherwise plays an important role in shaping certain key health outcomes. The percentage of social sector expenditure to the total expenditure has been around 40 per cent since the 1990s except during the phase—2002–08 (see Table 4.4). This ratio is quite similar to many states such as Andhra Pradesh, Bihar, Orissa, Madhya Pradesh and West Bengal. In terms of per-capita expenditure, Tamil Nadu ranks third after Kerala and Punjab. The average per-capita expenditure during 2005–10 at 1999–2000 prices for the state was INR 383 as against INR 309 in Maharashtra and INR 266 in Gujarat (see Table 4.5). Nevertheless, it is the expenditure bias towards primary healthcare that stands out.

Apart from the relatively low levels of public expenditure on health at the all-India level, Das Gupta (2005) also argues that there has been a tendency towards elite capture of the health sector by funnelling resources to high-end tertiary sectors rather than concentrating on primary health. Not only does India spend very little on the health sector, but even that limited amount is spent on expanding subsidised medical training and high-end tertiary

Table 4.4 Proportion of Social Expenditure to Total Expenditure

States	1990–93	1993–96	1996–99	1999–2002	2002–05	2005–08	2008–11
Andhra Pradesh	40.9	36.6	39.1	36.5	31.7	33.4	38.4
Bihar	41.4	40.7	43.2	41.8	34.5	40	42.4
Gujarat	33.7	34.1	33.4	35.4	28.9	33.3	37.8
Haryana	31.1	24.4	24.3	34	23.1	31.5	39.7
Himachal Pradesh	33.6	36.9	37	35.6	29.3	33.4	36.1
Karnataka	36.6	38.4	38.6	37.1	29.4	34.3	39.2
Kerala	41.5	39.7	42.5	39.9	34.5	33.1	34
Madhya Pradesh	40.3	40.9	40.9	39.7	30.3	34.9	37.2
Maharashtra	37.7	37.2	37.6	35.5	30.8	37	39.9
Orissa	36.9	38.6	38.4	39.8	29.5	33.3	41.7
Punjab	25	23.9	22.6	24.7	17.4	19.8	24.6
Rajasthan	37.4	37.5	39.3	40.4	35.7	39.7	44.2
Tamil Nadu	40.4	41	39.9	38.5	33	35.5	40.2
Uttar Pradesh	35.5	30.6	33.6	33	26.1	33.8	38.3
West Bengal	44	40.6	38.4	37.1	27.7	31.8	38.2
All-India Average	37.4	36	36.7	36.3	30.2	34.6	38.8

Source: Adapted from D. Sinha (2016).

medical services at the cost of essential public health services. Therefore, the effectiveness of public spending rests both on the composition of spending (reflecting political priorities), as well as efficiency, that is, to what extent the services are actually reaching the people. These in turn are seen to depend on political will and how accountable the government is to the people, whether there is 'public action' on these issues and so on. On the face of it, the fact that primary health accounts for about 45 per cent of the total budget, which is much higher than that of many other states in India, testifies to the direction of political priorities in the state.

INVERSION OF MYRON WEINER'S THESIS

Like education, health too is held to have been subject to elite capture in India.[7] Based on surveys of official planning reports of the 1970s, Jeffery remarks that the Indian '... model of health services is top-heavy,

Table 4.5 Average Per Capita Real Public Expenditure on Health (at 1993–94 Price)

States	1980–81 to 1987–88	1988–89 to 1991–92	1992–93 to 1997–98	1998–99 to 2002–03	2005–10*
Andhra Pradesh	63	73	75	103	224
Bihar	34	44	47	57	155
Gujarat	75	87	89	121	266
Haryana	75	74	71	90	323
Karnataka	65	77	86	118	343
Kerala	75	90	97	116	438
Madhya Pradesh	51	57	58	75	242
Maharashtra	76	83	85	101	309
Orissa	55	60	58	77	251
Punjab	92	117	107	162	324
Rajasthan	62	78	88	107	332
Tamil Nadu	71	90	101	124	383
Uttar Pradesh	41	59	58	57	282
West Bengal	58	67	71	104	277

*Post the NRHM period, it includes health expenditures under the NRHM. The figure is in constant 1999–2000 prices.

Source: Reserve Bank of India Bulletin for various years. The data for previous years until 2002–03 is adapted from Seeta Prabhu and Selvaraju (2006).

over-centralized, heavily curative in its approach, urban and elite oriented, costly and dependency creating' (1994: p. 116; see also Jeffery 1988). Cassen too argues that India's 'health system shares several features of the pattern of health services in other developing countries including a large share of health budgets devoted to major hospitals in urban centres and a consequent relative neglect of rural health infrastructure' (1978: 201). Tamil Nadu seems to have bucked this all-India trend. This commitment to primary healthcare is evident since the days of the Justice Party in the Madras Presidency. The Justice Party fought the election in 1921 on two major planks: the enactment of affirmative action for non-Brahmins in state employment and the promotion of health and education for all. Keeping its promises, the government introduced a scheme in 1924 to deliver healthcare to the rural population of the Presidency (Muraleedharan 1992). Incentives were designed to attract health professionals to go and stay in rural areas. The creation of an effectively working primary health infrastructure along with attention to nutrition through the noon meal scheme alludes to this process of inversion of priorities. The inversion of priorities is also visible in the state's emphasis on public health.

PUBLIC HEALTH

The elite bias in policy-making meant that the focus shifted from improving public health systems to supporting curative technologies and methods of healthcare financing. As a result, medical doctors acquired more status and power than public health professionals, particularly with the growing corporatisation of tertiary care. Acquiring qualifications in specialised curative skills therefore became more attractive than pursuing public health (Das Gupta 2005). Tamil Nadu, on the other hand, took a different route. It retained its separate cadre of public health personnel when public health services were merged with the medical services in the 1950s in the rest of India (Das Gupta et al. 2010).

It is important to note here that health is a state subject in the Indian Constitution. As in the domain of education, the state has a track record of effective public health policies since the Justice Party's rule in the 1920s. The Madras Presidency was the first province in British India to pass a Public Health Act in 1939 which placed the responsibility for provision of public health services, including maternal and child health, in the hands of the state. The Act has seen many amendments according to the changing needs of the state. Public health professionals have to secure a public health qualification in addition to their medical degree. The Public Health Act[8] assigns responsibilities to different layers of the government and agencies, sets standards of food hygiene, water quality and so on and mandates regulation and inspection of agencies and establishments. Tamil Nadu has been successful in maintaining anticipatory/preventive health planning. The deputy director of health services (DDHS), who is responsible for the health of the district as a whole, conducts regular inspections that include assuring sanitary conditions and vector control. The DDHS also prepares the district's Epidemic Contingency Plan, including plans for responding to natural disasters, controlling diarrhoeal diseases during floods and so on (Das Gupta et al. 2010). A recent example was the intervention made in the aftermath of the 2016 floods in Chennai city. Amidst concerns raised in several quarters over the possible outbreak of such diseases once the flood waters recede, the preventive intervention undertaken by public health authorities ensured that no such outbreaks occurred. In other words, the state is able to respond proactively to avert potential health threats.

This success story of public health administration in Tamil Nadu is usually attributed to smooth coordination between the public health managers and technical staff. Sujatha Rao (2017), the former union health secretary in the Government of India, argues that the health secretary, particularly at the state level, is accountable for better health outcomes. She further asserts that Tamil Nadu's success lies in keeping its health secretary unchanged for at least three years. This certainly makes a contribution, but there are other significant factors at play. Importantly, she does not quite tell us why such accountability mechanisms have been generated to begin with. In other words, she does not explain why relatively more effective institutional practices emerged in the state. Santosh Mehrotra (2006) argues that the real explanation for such performance has to be located in the set of incentives emanating from social mobilisation. One outcome of such mobilisation is the emergence of a socially inclusive pool of healthcare professionals who are incentivised to serve in the public health system.

SOCIAL INCLUSION AND INCENTIVISATION

Apart from its ability to generate a pool of skilled healthcare professionals, Tamil Nadu has an incentive structure in place to retain professionals in the public healthcare system. Medical colleges are spatially distributed, ensuring that every district headquarters has at least one public medical college in the state. While this production of health personnel ensures the adequate supply of doctors for the public health system, an incentive structure developed over time allows the state to retain doctors even as other states are witnessing brain drain due to the exodus of doctors to the private sector or their leaving the country for better prospects. Rao et al. (2011) in fact suggest that many states fail to retain doctors in rural areas due to the inability of the public sector to attract them accompanied by the disinclination of qualified private providers to work there. We provide two extreme examples of Karnataka and UP to illustrate this. While Karnataka produces marginally more health and medical personnel than Tamil Nadu, it has not been able to retain them in the public health system. The state has a poor doctor–patient ratio in the public health system with one doctor for every 13,556 people as against the national average of a doctor per 11,082 people while Tamil Nadu has a much better ratio with one doctor for every 9,544 people (National Health Profile 2018). The other example is UP which lacks in both production of health personnel as well as in retaining them within the public health system. With only 31 medical colleges, less than the official norm of 42, the doctor–patient ratio in the public health system is only 19,962.[9] Tamil Nadu, on the other hand, not only generates more health personnel but also retains them in the public health system.

A related aspect is the social composition of medical officers. If the 69 per cent reservation policy in education has ensured the production of doctors across caste groups, reservation in public employment has ensured the presence of doctors and other medical professionals across communities in the public health system. The results of a medical entrance exam for MBBS/BDS held in 2015–16 illustrate this pluralisation of representation in the medical profession in the state. Of the 31,525 total seats, OBC candidates secured 67.9 per cent, which is higher than their reserved quota of 50 per cent, while SCs accounted for 26 per cent of the total seats which is eight per cent more than what they are entitled to.[10] In other words, at least sections of the SCs and OBCs are in a position to compete for a share in the open quota. This ability to generate a pool of skilled healthcare professionals from a range of caste locations is important for several reasons. While it generates a relatively inclusive opportunity structure and diffuses aspirations among marginalised youth, it also makes possible a communally representative healthcare bureaucracy. Such a bureaucracy is crucial in incentivising more democratic access. They are likely to appreciate the importance of delivering healthcare to marginal groups and are hence more responsive to demands emanating from these groups (Mehrotra 2006). Healthcare professionals also constitute a voice that could resist incursions of privatisation. For instance, when the AIADMK-led government introduced a policy of hiring doctors on a contractual basis in 2005, the Tamil Nadu Government

Doctors' Association launched a series of protests and ensured the reversal of the policy. When the DMK came to power in 2006, the then governor had to mention the policy stance of regularisation of appointments of medical personnel in his speech.[11]

Another important incentive is the 'in-service quota' in postgraduate admissions to all branches of medicine, including super-speciality courses, for doctors who complete a minimum of two years of service in PHCs or district hospitals. The state has a 50 per cent in-service quota for postgraduate courses in all medical colleges run by the government as well as seats[12] reserved for the government in private colleges (Kalaiyarasan 2017a). In addition, students completing post-graduation and super-speciality courses availing the in-service quota need to work in public hospitals for a minimum of three years. Such rules for the admission process at both undergraduate and postgraduate levels in all branches of medicine have ensured the retention of specialist doctors who are incentivised to work in rural areas.

Moreover, the state has a separate public health cadre with distinct qualification requirements, service conditions and pay scales. The public health cadres are recruited as health officers through the Tamil Nadu Public Service Commission (TNPSC). While the minimum qualification at the entry level is an MBBS, they are also required to obtain a Diploma in Public Health within four years of their appointment for regularisation as health officers (Datta 2010). Since there is no lateral entry, these health officers can retire as Director of Public Health and Preventive Medicine in the state. A significant portion of health personnel are thus allotted to the public health department in Tamil Nadu. The department alone comprises of an almost 36,000-strong workforce, which is about 42 per cent of the total health workforce in the state (Datta 2010). Unlike in other states where a general doctor or a surgeon can become the director of the public health department, a public health professional alone can become the director of the department in the state. The department also has its own incentive structure for internal promotion. As a result, a health officer can become DDHS by the age of 45, whereas his clinician counterpart may need to wait until the age of 55 to reach an equivalent salary and status in the health system (Datta 2010). Many of these health personnel also opt for teaching assignments to share their experiences as the system provides inter-transferability with medical colleges. The state also has similar pathways for paramedical personnel. The VHN who manages sub-centres is recruited from the anganwadi workers of the Integrated Child Development Services (ICDS), and is sponsored for an 18-month training programme. Based on their seniority, the VHNs are appointed as sector health nurses (SHNs) with six months of training. They also get promoted to community health nurses (CHNs), and can retire as a district maternal and child health officer (DMCHO) having started as an anganwadi worker after finishing their class 10 education.

We now turn our attention to the interventions designed to improve access to the health system.

RATE OF UTILISATION

Better health outcomes are not merely based on spending and the creation of intermediary outcomes like effective infrastructure. On the demand side, it is important that citizens recognise the importance of accessing healthcare, particularly of the preventive kind. Incentivising and ensuring access through such awareness creation is therefore an important component of this process. Its excellent record of immunisation, among other achievements, illustrates this (Government of Tamil Nadu 2017). Once again, the rate of utilisation of health services in Tamil Nadu is not only higher than in most states but is also pro-poor in nature (Acharya et al. 2011). Looking at access to the public health system across income quintiles, Acharya et al.'s study finds that in Tamil Nadu, unlike in other states, the bottom 20 per cent of the income quintiles use public healthcare more than the top quintile. In other states, the richer income groups are held to disproportionately use public facilities, marginalising the poor. The study also observes that the state has a better drug distribution system. It goes on to suggest that apart from supply-side factors like better infrastructure for healthcare, the state has also devised a range of incentives for effective access to such services and for increasing institutional deliveries. This takes us to the dimension of creating demand for healthcare.

The Dr Muthulakhmi Reddy Maternity Benefit Scheme, named after one of the first female Indian doctors under colonial rule and an activist who fought for women's rights, illustrates this process. The scheme offers INR 18,000 in five instalments for the first two pregnancies of every woman in the state. Within three months of the pregnancy, based on her registration at the local PHC, a pregnant woman gets INR 2,000 along with a box of nutrition enhancing products worth an additional INR 2,000. After the first four months of pregnancy, she gets a similar incentive. Immediately after her delivery, she gets a third instalment of INR 4,000. The fourth instalment of INR 4,000 is given after the first vaccination of the child. The fifth instalment of INR 2,000 is given after the MMR vaccination at any time during 9 to 12 months after childbirth.

A novel approach that combines maternal health with infant healthcare, this phased out process not only improved health outcomes but also made health personnel at PHCs more accountable to the people. As a result, the delivery of antenatal and postnatal services improved in the state. For instance, the NFHS-4 (2015–16) shows that a woman receiving antenatal care from any skilled provider in the state is 92 per cent as against 79 per cent at the all-India level. Similarly, 67 per cent of women use a public facility for child delivery as compared to the all-India figure of 52 per cent. The data shows that the average out-of-pocket cost paid for delivery at a public facility for the most recent live birth is lowest in the state. The phased instalments of the scheme also made child immunisation compulsory.

Yet another slew of schemes that have contributed to improving both age at marriage and the educational attainment of girls before marriage are marriage assistance schemes like the Moovalur Ramamirtham Ammaiyar Ninaivu Marriage Assistance Scheme. This scheme is a conditional transfer scheme for girls from poor households at the time of marriage. The government provides a fixed amount of cash and gold if the girl has completed 10 years of schooling and is above the age of 18. The amount transferred is doubled if the girl has completed a bachelor's degree or a diploma (Balagopal and Vijayabaskar 2018). While such schemes are expected to help the daughters of poor and vulnerable households, they also work to increase both the age at marriage and the levels of educational attainment.[13] Together, they are likely to have contributed to better awareness and hence an ability to take advantage of maternal and antenatal care provided by the public health system. A more immediate factor in facilitating access is the public procurement and distribution of drugs at subsidised rates.

DRUG POLICY

A key measure of well-being is reduction in the out-of-pocket expenditure on health of households. Drugs and diagnostics alone account for 70 per cent of out-of-pocket expenditure (Rao 2017). Tamil Nadu has pioneered free provision of essential drugs and diagnostics at public healthcare facilities (Reddy 2016). Kumar et al. (2011) also observe that the state allocates more resources towards drugs and medical research when compared to other states in India. As a result, it has been able to bring down the burden of out-of-pocket expenses on healthcare more than most states. It has set up an elaborate network consisting of a pharmaceutical corporation, the Tamil Nadu Medical Services Corporation (TNMSC) and a well-developed supply chain with computerised records (Lalitha 2008; Narayan 2018). The TNMSC has a transparent process of drug procurement based on the Tamil Nadu Transparency Tenders Act 1998.[14] The process allows only a 15 per cent price rise from the previous year's rate for the medicine it buys. The corporation also follows the two-bid system, one for technical specifications and the other for prices. This dual-tier process ensures that the procurement of drugs is cheaper and the drugs are of good quality. The corporation also has drug warehouses and health facilities which are linked electronically to ensure adequate inventories and continuous flow of medicines to its PHCs.[15] As a result, TNMSC prices are several times lower than market prices (Selvaraj et al. 2014), and this has also ensured the highest percentage of availability of free drugs in public health facilities. The result of such measures is reflected in secondary data as well. The NSS (71st round 2014–15) indicates that the average expenditure a household incurs for hospitalisation in a government health facility is lower in Tamil Nadu in both rural and urban areas (see Table 4.6). Since this difference in average expenditure is accounted through provision of free medicine at government hospitals in Tamil Nadu, state interventions have managed to insulate the poor from the negative effects of increases in drug prices. We now turn our attention to the nutritional aspects of healthcare, a dimension that has been well recognised in literature on social welfare in the state.

Table 4.6 Average Medical and Non-medical Expenditure Per Hospitalisation Case in Public and Private Facilities (INR)

	Tamil Nadu			All-India		
Public	Rural	Urban	Total	Rural	Urban	Total
Medical	459	780	600	5,512	7,592	6,120
Non-medical	1,986	1,598	1,816	1,682	1,451	1,614
Total	2,445	2,378	2,416	7,193	9,043	7,734
Private						
Medical	19,554	33,261	27,228	21,726	32,375	25,850
Non-medical	2,221	2,641	2,456	2,266	2,287	2,275
Total	21,775	35,902	29,684	23,992	34,662	28,124
Public + Private						
Medical	11,842	23,757	18,006	14,935	24,436	18,268
Non-medical	2,126	2,336	2,234	2,021	2,019	2,021
Total	13,968	26,092	20,240	16,956	26,455	20,288

Source: NSSO 71st round (2014).

THE NOON MEAL SCHEME

Child nutrition rates in particular show that the state has been doing well as compared to the all-India average thanks to the ICDS and the 'noon meal' programme. Tamil Nadu has the distinction of being the first state in post-independence India to introduce free mid-day meals for school children.[16] The scheme, however, has its antecedents in the Justice Party rule in the Madras Presidency during the colonial period as pointed out in the previous chapter. The scheme acquired new life again under the chief ministership of K. Kamaraj, through the slogan of 'combating classroom hunger' in the 1950s (Rajivan 2006). The programme retained children in schools and effectively reduced dropouts, especially children coming from a lower-caste and class background. The programme was expanded from 1982 onwards. As Barbara Harriss notes:

From July 1982 ... rural pre-school children registered from the age of 2 at balwadis or nurseries and all of the 3.8 million registered school attenders under the age of 10 have been entitled to one free meal daily throughout the year. 5.6 million participated in the scheme at its inception. Then in September 1982 it was extended to children in urban areas and in the cities of Madras, Madurai and Coimbatore adding an increment of 6.5 lakhs of participants. Two months later a monthly supply of tooth powder was distributed via the infrastructure built up ... In January 1983, old age pensioners were included, netting in a further 1.9 lakhs. A year later ex-servicemen's widows became eligible for a free meal. (Harriss 1984: p. 4)

The noon meal programme is run professionally. Over 90 per cent of the schools have proper kitchen infrastructure which is periodically upgraded and modernised. The mid-day meal centres are also equipped with weighing scales, mats for children to sleep on, educational charts and toys. The programme is not managed by school teachers but by a team consisting of a noon meal organiser, a cook and a helper (Rajivan 2006). They are paid adequate salaries with pension benefits. Panchayat-level vigilance committees regularly monitor the functioning and leakages. Local communities too contribute by, among other things, developing kitchen gardens for the mid-day meal centres. The success of the programme has been attributed to pressure from both above and below. A political will and well-functioning bureaucracy from above ensure the required budgetary support while the pressure from below makes officials accountable (Rajivan 2006; Narayan 2018).

Over the years the programme has become integrated with the larger goal of addressing malnutrition and promoting child development in the state. In addition to mid-day meals, the ICDS has also contributed to the state's success in improving the nutritional status of children. The aim of the ICDS is to provide integrated health, nutrition and pre-school education services to children under the age of six through local anganwadis (childcare centres) (Drèze and Sen 2013). The programme has become mandatory after the Supreme Court's intervention making it available to all children under six as a matter of legal entitlement. Given the history of its success in mid-day meals, Tamil Nadu has also done well in implementing the ICDS. A report by Focus On Children Under Six (FOCUS) (Drèze 2006)[17] also points out that the awareness level of various welfare programmes is very high in Tamil Nadu when compared to other states in India. This takes us to the processes that empowered people to make claims to healthcare access in the state.

POLITICALLY AND SOCIALLY DRIVEN DEMAND

In earlier sections, we pointed out how improvements in educational attainments and age at marriage may have indirectly contributed to awareness-induced claim-making on healthcare resources. In addition, we identify three distinct pathways that forged better collective demand, especially from marginal social groups. To begin with, apart from forging a 'politically integrated region',[18] political mobilisation also generated awareness among people of their rights and entitlements. Undermining of caste hierarchies has made institutions more responsive to collective action (Srinivasan 2010). As a result, social popular interventions could be extended all the way to the poorest and the most marginalised social groups. When this does not happen, Srinivasan points out, it is common to see people resorting to 'public action' for violation of their entitlements. If proper care is not given by a PHC doctor, patients write to the district medical officer, local newspaper or confront the doctor themselves—a culture of protest and public action that ensures better accountability.

Second, Narayan (2018) also points to the role of Dravidian party functionaries as intermediaries in linking marginalised social groups to the state apparatus. He argues that while collective action from below may have emerged as pressure groups to ensure better public services later, it was the party functionaries who initially represented the grievances of marginalised groups through petitions, protests and so on. Third, social diversification of health professionals is an important pathway through which access gets socially broad based. Literature suggests that social diversification and adequate representation of marginal groups in public administration in a stratified society offers a 'feeling of affinity' among communities.[19] Following Granovetter (1973), there has been a recognition that 'weak ties', that is, social ties that are not intimate and personal but widespread, are crucial to the diffusion of information in a society. His contention is that when information is passed through a network where ties are strong among a smaller group, it is likely to diffuse less among those outside these strong ties. Weak ties, on the other hand, by virtue of the fact that they are more widespread and link relatively disparate groups, are likely to be more useful for dissemination of information and access. In the context of the United States, Cornwell and Cornwell (2008) for example, demonstrate how concentration of access to 'experts' and 'expert knowledge' within high-status groups (in terms of class and race) and the exclusivity of such networks have led to the widening of disparities between whites and minorities. Disparities in access to expertise may therefore be a key pathway through which social and economic hierarchies are reproduced. Given the importance of social networks, particularly caste and kinship networks in accessing information in India (Munshi 2014), networks between members of a marginalised community and a service provider in a caste stratified system are likely to be critical to improved access. Having people from their community as a provider of public services can motivate those from marginal sections to access such services. Political mobilisation in Tamil Nadu is likely to have enabled the expansion of weak ties on the one hand and reduced the disparities in access to expert knowledge on the other. By forging a pan-Tamil-Dravidian identity (Singh 2015), the movement paved the way for the formation of 'weak' ties across multiple marginalised social groups. Affirmative action enabled the emergence of health experts from different marginal groups and hence broad base vertical ties with such experts. Horizontal bridging networks linked to such broad-based vertical ties can forge improved demand and access to public healthcare.

POPULIST INTERVENTIONS AMIDST REFORMS

We have argued that the state's better outcomes in health and nutrition have been made possible by ensuring relatively more equitable access to public health services and ensuring better utilisation. While the coverage may be short of World Health Organization (WHO) standards, it is still better than that in most states in India. We related this to the state's century-long track record of effective public health policies contrary to elite capture of the health system in most other parts of the country. Another significant achievement of the Dravidian experiment is its success in ensuring efficiency in health outcomes. Apart from an incentive structure, entry of lower castes in the bureaucracy brought in valuable insights into processes on the ground that ensured better design and implementation of key health policies. They further contributed to improved access by virtue of their 'weak ties' with marginal groups. Mobilisation around the Tamil identity and social justice has produced horizontal solidarities and generated awareness among people of their entitlements, which in turn made institutions accountable and ensured effective delivery of certain public services. Economic popular interventions like incentive schemes for specific healthcare access also contributed to this process.

Subsequent developments in tertiary delivery in the state are also suggestive of the ability of the state's populist slant to negotiate with market-based reforms. The growing demand and greater opening up of tertiary care to the private sector in the post-reform period meant a dramatic expansion of corporatised healthcare providers in the state. As Hodges (2013) argues, Apollo, India's first private limited hospital, offered a business template for other private players to corporatise health services in the state. In fact, this led to the emergence of the state as a major hub for healthcare services in the country. Of the 30 districts in the state, 18 districts have at least one big private hospital.[20] This also led to a growing perception of quality differences emerging between public and private care providers within this segment. Squeezed fiscally and unable to expand tertiary care capacity in the public sector, the state launched a state-funded health insurance scheme for the poor that enabled them to access private healthcare since 2006. The domain of economic popular interventions has thus expanded with the growing cost of tertiary care and the inability of the public sector to universalise this care. Subsequently, the scheme was also extended to public hospitals too so that patients could choose between the two streams of providers. The insurance premium is covered by the state government. Kailash and Rasaratnam (2015) in fact suggest that Tamil Nadu and Kerala have modified the health insurance scheme to give an advantage to public hospitals unlike in other states. Though the insurance-based model has not led to market failures as it has happened elsewhere thanks to the prevalence of a robust public health infrastructure, evidence of slippages in delivery of certain public health services has been observed (Balagopal and Vijayabaskar 2019). What kind of state and public action can address such slippages, however, remains to be seen.

APPENDIX 4A

Under-five Mortality Rate (Per 1,000 live births, 2015)

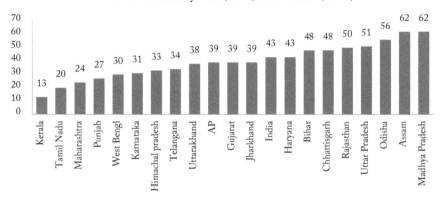

Figure 4A.1 Subnational Variation in Under-five Mortality Rate

Source: NFHS-4 (2014–15).

Maternal Mortality Ratio (Per 100,000 live births, 2016–17)

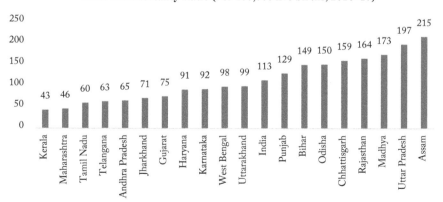

Figure 4A.2 Subnational Variation in Maternal Mortality Ratio

Source: Special Bulletin on Maternal Mortality in India 2016–17, Sample Registration System, Office of the Registrar General, Government of India.

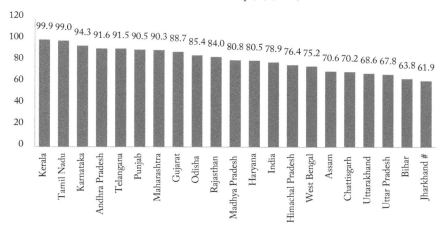

Figure 4A.3 Subnational Variation in Institutional Delivery
Source: NFHS-4 (2014–15).

NOTES

1   Tamil Nadu has underperformed in most of these indicators in the last decade. Until 2005–06, the state was one of the better performing states but the reverse is seen in 2015–16. The percentage of child immunisation was 81 in 2005–06 and but came down to 69 in 2015–16. While the level of indicators is still better in the state as compared to most states, the rate of change has come down during the last decade.

2   Interview with a senior bureaucrat in the health ministry on April 11 2019.

3   Circular 9/2014, dated June 24, 2014, National Health Mission, State Health Society, DMS complex, Chennai -6.

4   The Government of India constituted a committee under A.L Mudaliyar in 1962 which recommended the establishment of one medical college for a population of five million.

5   The *TNHDR* 2017 (Government of Tamil Nadu 2017) offers a figure of 29 medical colleges while the report also estimates the presence of 166 private nursing colleges along with 27 nursing institutions in the state.

6   Eighty-five per cent of public health expenditure in India is by state governments. While the share of state governments' expenditure in overall

public health expenditure is decreasing, especially after the introduction of the NRHM, it still constitutes the major part.

7   Following the all-India sanitary conference in 1912, Captain Hutton, sanitary engineer, complained that the advance of sanitation in the Madras Presidency was necessarily slow owing to '… the reluctance of responsible authorities to provide sufficient funds and the backward condition of the people in understanding sanitary methods …' (Harrison 1994: p. 200).

8   The Act specifies the legal and administrative structures for the public health system in the state. It provides a framework of well-defined responsibilities of different government agencies within the structure, with corresponding budget allocations.

9   The UP cabinet tried giving capital subsidies for private players who would invest in setting up medical colleges but could not build the momentum. (*Indian Express* 2013).

10 The estimation was done based on the provisional merit list released by the Directorate of Medical Education for the academic year 2015–16. The breakup of the total seats (31,525) is—BC: 12,944, MBC/DNC: 6,754, Backward Class Muslims: 1,694, SC: 7,257 and SC–Arunthathiyar: 1,079, while the figure for the remaining open category is 1,493. The list is still available on https://realitycheck.files.wordpress.com/2015/06/mbbs2015-16.pdf (accessed 24 December 2019).

11 See Tamil Nadu Governor's speech (2006): https://tnrd.gov.in/Announcement_pdf/governor_addr_May2006.pdf (accessed 12 March 2019).

12 Private colleges are mandated to offer 50 per cent seats to the Government of Tamil Nadu for which the reservation policies of the state become applicable.

13 See for details, http://www.tnsocialwelfare.org/pages/view/marriage-assistance-schemes (accessed 15 March 2019).

14 A Planning Commission (2011) expert group on universal health coverage, too, acknowledged the success of Tamil Nadu in providing essential drugs, and proposed to the Government of India that 'an increase in the public procurement of medicines from around 0.1% to 0.5% of GDP would ensure universal access to essential drugs, greatly reduce the burden on private out-of-pocket expenditures and increase the financial protection for households' (Planning Commission 2011: p. 10).

15 The setting up of the TNMSC, a state-owned company, is being seen as key to ensuring essential drugs at affordable prices (for further details see Basu 2010).

16 The scheme was introduced in 1956 by K. Kamaraj, the then chief minister, known for his pro-poor and pro-lower-caste policies, to ensure that education reaches the poor and the marginalised.

17 The report was brought out by the Citizens' Initiative for the Rights of Children Under Six (2006), based on a survey of 200 anganwadis in 2004 in six states—Chhattisgarh, Himachal Pradesh, Maharashtra, Rajasthan, Tamil Nadu and Uttar Pradesh.

18 Paul Brass (1979) argues that subnational identification became strong in Tamil Nadu, quoted in Singh (2015: p. 122).

19 Mark Granovetter (1973) offers insights on how social networks among small groups facilitate the flow of information on mobility opportunities between community organisations.

20 Hooda argues that India has seen an escalation of private enterprises in the healthcare market since the 2000s. Most such enterprises are placed in urban and the most-developed regions in the country. About 60 per cent of districts in Tamil Nadu as against 29 per cent at the all-India level have at least a private allopathic enterprise consisting of medical and dental hospitals, diagnostic centres/labs and blood banks. See Hooda (2015).

5

BROADENING GROWTH AND DEMOCRATISING CAPITAL

If social justice, as the Dravidianists imagined, was rooted in a process of inclusive modernisation, what does it mean for the process of capital accumulation? There are two interpretations of the unfolding of the process of accumulation in the state. According to one, both Dravidian parties have focused on welfare politics, leaving the elites to dominate the realm of capital accumulation (Harriss and Wyatt 2019). Harriss (2003) in fact observes that the prominent business leaders have continued to remain at the top for decades. Harish Damodaran (2008), though not exactly contesting this position, argues that there has been a 'democratization of capital' in southern India including Tamil Nadu, due to certain historical factors. Drawing upon works by historians like Mahadevan (1992, 2017), Damodaran argues that the absence of a dominant trading community (Vaishya) in the south allowed for entrepreneurs from lower castes to emerge, bringing about a process of 'democratisation of capital'. He thus attributes this 'democratisation' to a combination of opportunities opened up by colonial commerce and the ability of specific lower castes rooted in particular geographies to take advantage of these opportunities. In other words, this process has happened independent of any deliberate policy interventions. On a similar note, while Swaminathan (1994) suggests a relative absence of entrepreneurship in the state, Sinha (2005) argues that there has been inadequate state support for industrialisation. Partly contesting these propositions, in this chapter we make a case for the role of state intervention backed by a political imagination in facilitating and 'democratising' capital accumulation in Tamil Nadu.

According to ideologues of the Dravidian movement, there were two factors that hindered democratising capital accumulation in the region. First, they held that the caste system rendered actors from some castes 'born capitalists' and those from others 'born labourers' (Vidiyal 2017: pp. 737–38). Addressing railway workers in 1952, Periyar called upon the workers to understand that it was being born into a specific caste that made them a part of the working class while members of the upper castes become capitalists by virtue of their birth. Their struggle should therefore be to destroy the institution that generates and sustains this class divide. Second, the dominance of Marwari ('north Indian') capital in the country and in the region was seen to prevent modernisation of the economy and entry of 'Tamils' into business (Annadurai 2017 [1949]). Such dominance meant not only that the surplus was being siphoned off but also led to the neglect of the region by the union government in a context where the Indian state was leading industrialisation through licensing and setting up public-sector enterprises (Annadurai 2017 [1949]). Simultaneously, they held that the social domination of caste elites and their collusion with dominant business communities helped them to monopolise the sphere of capital accumulation. We argue in this chapter that notwithstanding other factors at work as pointed out by scholars like Damodaran (2008) and Mahadevan (1992, 2017), political mobilisation and state-level policies have ensured better prospects for capital accumulation as well as ensured a relatively better share of lower castes in this domain.

We trace three pathways through which this process unfolded. First, we argue that the diffusion of a productivist ethos and a belief that industrialisation is critical to undermine social hierarchies translated into a broad-based political consensus leading to consistent demands in this regard. This translation is also partly tied to the transformation of social relations that may have otherwise hindered entry. Second, as infrastructure was critical to modernisation, such demands translated into investments in physical and social infrastructure which allowed for more diffused entry into the domain of capital accumulation. Finally, we point out that specific policies in the domain of industrialisation and servitisation have also enabled this process. We therefore contest the claim that 'politicians concentrated on the social sectors, leaving entrepreneurs pretty much to themselves'. The state pursued active industrial and infrastructure policies since the 1950s responding to the consistent pressure of mobilisation built around a narrative of regional neglect, which was reworked in the post-1990s period of economic reforms as well. While the narrative of regional neglect translated into a demand for greater resources and autonomy from the union government, the narrative of domination by 'north Indian' capital led to the consolidation of an aspirational 'Tamil' identity that could be mobilised to demand redistribution of material resources towards the Tamil region. Such a demand thus enabled development through subnational solidarities (Singh 2015) and also helped constitute a spatial distributional politics based on a politics of recognition. Questioning the vertical imbalance in resource mobilisation and sharing between the union and regional governments, the state has consistently claimed greater devolution of resources and rights. The Rajamannar Committee, constituted by the DMK government in 1969 for example, was the first committee by a state government mandated to look at centre–state fiscal relations and recommend more transfers to states as well as more taxation powers for regional governments (Panneerselvan 2018). We thus suggest that a programmatic intervention driven by a 'social popular' imagination has enabled a relatively more inclusive process of capital accumulation.

We distinguish four temporal phases over which these pathways traversed. The first phase overlaps with the colonial period marked by the emergence of a productivist ethos and a popular demand for modern industries to improve the regional economy along with state support for early industrialisation. This popular demand was an outcome of a mobilisation that managed to establish equivalence between demands for social justice, dominance of a collusion of caste and business elites in the cultural and material domain, and perceived absence of adequate industrial development. The second phase corresponds to the post-1947 period until 1967 when the DMK came to power. This was a phase when the Congress government was in power and when equivalence of these demands was strengthened and articulated consistently by both the DMK seeking formal political power and the DK. The last two phases correspond to the period when the Dravidian parties have alternated in power. While the first of these phases pertains to the pre-reform period when state-led industrialisation continued to dominate, the last phase coincides with the post-reform period that saw an increase in the role of regional governments in attracting private investments. As these phases also overlap with regime and policy shifts at the national level, policy interventions are also shaped by such shifts.

Apart from using secondary data to map patterns of economic growth and enterprise ownership, we rely on government orders (GOs) and other policy documents pertaining to industrialisation in Tamil Nadu as well as on field-based research. The analysis is organised in three parts. First, we map the outcomes in terms of economic growth and the contribution of different sectors to growth. In the second part, we map the broadening of industrialisation and the social base of entrepreneurship in Tamil Nadu. Finally, we map the processes shaping such outcomes.

GROWTH AND STRUCTURAL TRANSFORMATION

In this section, we look at the trends in the composition of growth to establish that the state has not only witnessed better structural transformation than most states, but also has created conditions for sustaining the process. We rely on data on the state domestic product (SDP) and its components (agriculture, industry and services from the Central Statistics Office [CSO], compiled by Economic and Political Weekly Research Foundation [EPWRF]). We use the net state domestic product (NSDP) because it is available for a longer period of time (for the method and computed results, see Appendix 5A). Table 5.1 provides the log-linear growth for the last 55 years starting from the 1960s. While the SDP has grown at 4.7 per cent per annum during this phase, there are variations across sub-periods. Beginning with 2.1 per cent per annum in the 1960s, there is a slight increase in the 1970s (3.4 per cent per annum) and further in the 1980s (4.9 per cent). It is, however, only in the 1990s that the state registered an average growth rate of 6.2 per cent, and entered a phase of much higher growth (a rate of 8.4 per cent) during 2000–14.[1] While the trajectory mirrors all-India patterns, the growth rate in the post-1990s is higher than that at the all-India level (see Figure 5.1). If we compare with Gujarat and Maharashtra, until the 1980s, the state grew at a much lower rate than the other two, particularly Maharashtra. It is only in the 1990s that the state picked up its growth, and stood at 8.4 per cent during 2000–14—the same rate as that of Maharashtra, but less than that of Gujarat.

Table 5.1 Economic Growth (NSDP)

	Tamil Nadu	Maharashtra	Gujarat	All-India
1960–1970	2.1	2.9	2.7	3.3
1970–1980	3.4	5.6	4.6	3.2
1980–1990	4.9	5.4	4.7	5.2
1990–2000	6.2	6.7	7.7	5.8
2000–2014	8.4	8.4	9.3	6.8
1960–2014	4.7	5.6	5.5	4.8

Source: Data converted to 2004–05 base year using the method described in Appendix 5A.

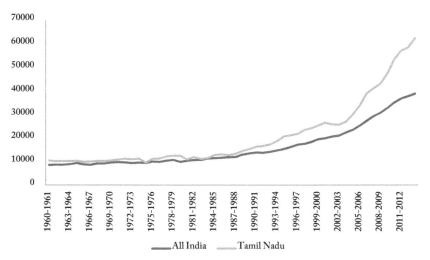

Figure 5.1 Trend in Per Capita Income (in INR at 2004–05)

Source: Data converted to 2004–05 base year using the method described in Appendix 5A.

This higher growth rate is also reflected in the widening difference in per capita income between the all-India average and that of Tamil Nadu (see Figure 5.1). The gap in per capita income between Tamil Nadu and India has increased from 14 per cent in the 1960s to 55 per cent in 2010 (Chapter 1). In the sub-periods, the relative position of Tamil Nadu vis-à-vis the all-India number was stagnant during the 1970s and marginally declined in the 1980s. It improved only in the 1990s—from 15 per cent in the 1970s to 27 per cent in the 1990s. In the 2000s, the state decisively entered a higher growth path, with the difference in per capita income growing larger. In terms of position, while

Table 5.2 Growth by Sectors in Tamil Nadu

	Agriculture	Industry	Services	NSDP	Per Capita Income
1960–1970	-0.8	6.0	3.6	2.1	0.0
1970–1980	1.0	5.7	3.9	3.4	1.7
1980–1990	3.5	4.0	6.4	4.9	3.4
1990–2000	2.9	5.1	8.7	6.2	5.1
2000–2014	3.1	8.2	9.6	8.4	7.7
1960–2014	1.9	5.0	6.1	4.7	3.4

Source: Data converted to 2004–05 base year using the method described in Appendix 5A.

the state stood at fourth place among 12 large states in the 1960s, it has steadily improved and moved up to the second position in 2014 (Chakravarthy and Dehejia 2016; Figure 5.1).

What is significant, however, is the sectoral composition of this growth (Table 5.2)

SECTORAL GROWTH AND SHIFTS

If we disaggregate by sector, agriculture, at 1.9 per cent, has been the lowest growing sector among the three sectors for the entire period. Its share has come down to just 7.2 per cent in 2014–15. Agriculture was obviously the dominant sector during the 1960s with an average share of 45.2 per cent in the SDP. While growth was relatively stagnant until the 1970s, it picked up in the 1980s, growing at 3.5 per cent thanks to the spread of Green Revolution technologies. Its growth fell to 2.9 per cent in the 1990s but improved to 3.1 per cent in 2000–14. The sector's relative contribution to aggregate growth has been declining faster than at the all-India level. The share of agriculture in Tamil Nadu has fallen from about 52 per cent in 1960–61 to just 7.2 per cent in 2014–15 while the corresponding figures at the all-India level are 48 per cent and 14 per cent, respectively. Despite this sharper fall in share, the agricultural economy performs well in terms of productivity. The state has the highest productivity for maize, groundnut and other oil seeds in the country.[2] Productivity in overall food grains too is 22 per cent more than the all-India average. In fact, while food grain production increased 2.21 times in five decades since 1965–66, the population doubled from 3.3 crore to 7.2 crore during 1961–2011, implying better per capita food availability over time at the state-level.

While the industrial sector has grown at 5.0 per cent per annum during the entire period, the growth rate was the highest (8.2 per cent per annum) in the period—2000–14. Though the higher growth in this period is in line with all-India trends, the upward trend is again stronger. Despite the share of manufacturing having marginally fallen in recent years,[3] the state still retains the status of the most industrialised state in the country. As discussed in Chapter 1, the state has specialised in more labour-intensive sectors like textiles, garments, leather goods and automobile manufacturing, compared to Gujarat and Maharashtra.[4] Sectors such as automobiles (18 per cent), textiles (11 per cent), food products (9 per cent) and basic metals (7 per cent) constitute about half of the output in the factory sector in Tamil Nadu. As a result, the state has the highest share of manufacturing to total employment in the country.

Apart from labour intensity, a distinguishing feature is the spatial spread of the process of industrialisation. We use the Herfindahl–Hirschman Index (HHI) to measure the spatial concentration of industrialisation in districts, based on the Economic Census (2013–14). The index number for the state is 796 as against 867 in Maharashtra and 1,076 in Gujarat. It suggests that enterprises are relatively better distributed across sub-regions in the state, indicating a better spatial spread. While it is true that the western (Tiruppur and Coimbatore) and northern (Chennai and Kancheepuram) regions are the most industrialised regions in the state, manufacturing is still spatially diverse. Each region hosts specific industrial clusters. For instance, Sivakasi in southern Tamil Nadu specialises in safety matches, firecrackers and printing, Karur, Erode and Salem in power looms and home textiles, Tiruppur in knitted garments, Ambur, Vaniyambadi and Ranipet in leather goods, Coimbatore in textiles and engineering and Chennai in auto and auto-component and electronics production (Damodaran 2016).[5] While the state inherited a better manufacturing base (15 per cent of the SDP as against 11 per cent at the all-India level) in the 1960s, Tamil Nadu has transformed into a service-led economy in the last decade with the latter being a more dynamic sector than in most states.

At a rate of 6.1 per cent, the services sector has registered higher growth than other sectors, and grew faster (9.5 per cent per annum) post-2000, even more than the industrial sector. The sector accounted for about 67 per cent of the state's income in 2014–15 while the all-India average was 58 per cent. In the 1960s, the service sector's share was the same as the national average (around 30 per cent of the SDP). Importantly, services is a catch-all category and its dominant share need not reflect economic dynamism as often labour productivity is low in several segments of the services sector. The Tamil Nadu story is, however, different. Within the service sector too, the state has better diversification as is evident in the performance of modern subsectors. Apart from software services where the state is a major player along with Karnataka and Telangana, the state is also home to vibrant tourism, medical and educational services. To summarise, it has a dynamic manufacturing and services sector, with manufacturing being a lot more spatially diffused. It is also important to note that high-end services like information technology (IT), education and health also rely upon human capabilities for their competitive edge, apart from access to infrastructure. While we address this aspect later, we next point out that this dynamism and spatial diffusion of the growth process have been accompanied by relative social inclusion in the ownership of enterprises.

BROAD-BASING ENTREPRENEURSHIP

Indian business has been dominated by a few caste communities (Damodaran 2008; Bagchi 2012). Though market reforms may be expected to undermine social barriers to entry, studies indicate that this has not happened, with Dalits continuing to be poorly represented within the business community (Prakash 2012; Harriss-White et al. 2013; Iyer, Khanna and Varshney 2013). The studies attribute such persistent barriers to exclusivity of social networks and access to capital, among other factors. Though the share of Dalits among entrepreneurs continues be low, Tamil Nadu has seen a relatively higher degree of entry of lower castes in business.

The latest Economic Census (2013–14) provides information regarding ownership patterns among different caste groups, the size of enterprises and

Table 5.3 Distribution of Enterprises by Ownership Pattern
(Economic Census 2013–14)

	Category of 100 and above Workers			Category of 20 to 99		
	Tamil Nadu	Gujarat	Maharashtra	Tamil Nadu	Gujarat	Maharashtra
Public Sector	243	208	807	2,362	2,165	4,988
Private	1,735	947	1,804	26,080	7,880	14,559
Private Joint Stock		1,144	1,658	1,884	3,954	8,382
Others	538	376	409	4,273	2,237	2,372
All	3,219	2,675	4,678	34,599	16,236	30,301
Population per Enterprise	22,413	22,594	24,022	2,085	3,723	3,709
Mean Size of Enterprise	373.0	341.0	321.4	38.0	38.0	36.5
Per Capita Income (2014–15 at 2004–05)	66,635	68,575	72,200			
Population (In Millions)	72.1	60.4	112.3			

Source: Computed from Economic Census 2013–14.

the source of finance, among other parameters. Census data indicate that the state has more enterprises per given population compared to other states (Table 5.3).

The table also indicates that the state has a larger share of small enterprises (in the 20–99 workers category) than the other two industrialised states, though fewer in the larger enterprises (medium and large) category. If we, however, standardise this in relation to the population, the state has a large enterprise (with above 100-workers category) per 22,413 persons while it is 24,022 in Maharashtra and 22,594 in Gujarat, which actually suggests that even overall, the state has more entrepreneurial ventures, and not just in the small-scale sector. The mean size of enterprises for Tamil Nadu is 373 workers per firm, while the corresponding figures are 321 and 341 for Maharashtra and Gujarat, respectively. We next look at the caste composition of ownership (Table 5.4).

Table 5.4 Distribution of Enterprises by Caste Status of Ownership (Per Cent)

Caste Groups	Tamil Nadu	Gujarat	Maharashtra
	All size		
SC/ST	6,45,455 (14.1)	6,11,289 (17.3)	7,30.440 (13.1)
OBCs	31,26,013 (68.2)	14,43,918 (40.2)	13,24,793 (23.8)
Elites	8,11,683 (17.7)	15,34,952 (42.6)	35,14,846 (63.1)
All	45,83,151 (100)	35,90,159 (100)	55,70,079 (100)
	Size of 20–99 workers		
SC/ST	2,532 (9.7)	1,249 (15.9)	1,022 (7.0)
OBCs	18,777 (72.0)	917 (11.6)	1,442 (9.9)
Elites	4,771 (18.3)	5,714 (72.5)	12,095 (83.1)
All	26,080 (100.0)	7,880 (100.0)	14,559 (100.0)
	Size of 100 and above workers		
SC/ST	100 (5.8)	115 (12.1)	109 (6.0)
OBCs	1,169 (67.4)	102 (10.8)	143 (7.90)
Elites	466 (26.9)	730 (77.1)	1,552 (86.0)
All	1,735 (100.0)	947 (100.0)	1,804 (100.0)

Source: Computed from Economic Census 2013–14.

Caste details are available for those firms which are privately owned.[6] We have excluded details on enterprises with 'less than 20 workers' in the table as such enterprises are likely to be petty producers who produce to survive rather than accumulate. The data for overall enterprises, however, includes the caste details of such enterprises as well. Looking at the break-up of enterprises by caste groups, other backward classes (OBCs) have a much higher share in ownership compared to other states (Table 5.4). Of the total enterprises (privately owned) in the state, OBCs have 68 per cent and Dalits have 14 per cent while the elites have about 18 per cent. If we disaggregate by size and compare with the other two states, they still do better. In the category of 100 workers and above, OBCs control about 67 per cent of enterprises in Tamil Nadu, 11 per cent in Gujarat and 8 per cent in Maharashtra. Dalits have about 6 per cent of the total enterprises in this size category in both Tamil Nadu and Maharashtra while it is 12 per cent in Gujarat. These findings must be read in the context of the caste distribution of the population in these states. While OBCs in Tamil Nadu account for about 74 per cent of the state's population, they account for about 52 per cent in Maharashtra and about 40 per cent in Gujarat, as per National Sample Survey (NSSO) 2011–12. While the share of the OBC population in the state is higher than that in Gujarat or Maharashtra, it is clear that their share in entrepreneurship is much higher than in the other two states. Similarly, the share of the Dalit population in the state is 21 per cent which is quite similar to Maharashtra and Gujarat, yet the state does better as compared to Maharashtra though not as well as Gujarat. Though the Dalits' share in enterprises is less than their share of the population, the Dalit Indian Chamber of Commerce and Industry (DICCI) records that the state is home to one of the highest concentrations of Dalit enterprises in India (Naig 2015). As per the Economic Census 2013–14, one out of every four Dalit enterprises in the '20–99 workers' category is located in Tamil Nadu. Hence, the overall trend shows a process of socially inclusive capital accumulation.

This democratisation is, however, uneven across regions, especially the two industrially dominant regions in the state, the north and the west. The northern region corresponds to the greater Chennai region while the western region comprises of Coimbatore, Erode and Tiruppur districts. In the northern region, caste elites (non-OBC and non-SC) owned about 38 per cent of the total small-scale enterprises and 37 per cent of the above-100-workers category which is about seven times higher than their population share whereas they owned only 22 per cent (Economic Census 2013–14) in the western region. Capital accumulation in the northern region is therefore less socially democratised compared to other parts of the state.

The OBCs' entry into the domain of capital may also not be even across castes, but we do not have caste specific break-up. Studies on entrepreneurship globally indicate that the phenomenon has a strong regional bias (Acs, Audretsch and Lehmann 2013). Given that castes in Tamil Nadu are concentrated in specific regions, this regional bias implies that the process of entry into entrepreneurship among the lower castes is likely to be uneven. Micro-level studies by Chari (2004), Mahadevan (1978), Hardgrave (1969) and Kawlra (2018) indicate a relationship between specific castes and entrepreneurship. Such differences may emanate not merely from differential distribution of capabilities required for entrepreneurship but may also be tied to the specific historical geographies that caste groups are embedded in. Neelakantan (1996) narrates the process of democratisation of entrepreneurship within a region, based on his observations of Karur, a hub for textiles, home furnishings and body-building for transport vehicles. In an anecdotal narrative of the transition that has taken place in Karur, Neelakantan points out that in the 1950s, most of the wealthy were from the landed gentry. However, by 1995, he argues that out of the 200 odd millionaires, there were very few who were from landed households and most would qualify for the 'rags to riches' tag. Even in the case of big business, a Nadar business group owns Hindustan Computers Limited (HCL), one of the leading technology firms in the country, with the group diversifying its interests into healthcare and education as well.

What needs to be, however, understood is that though larger business enterprises may continue to be predominantly under the control of upper castes, the ownership of small and medium enterprises that the state is known for has been open to lower castes. In other words, capital accumulation in the state has been made possible by a large number of small and medium enterprises owned significantly by backward castes. We now turn to the explanations and processes that made this possible. In terms of processes driving capital accumulation, both hard and soft infrastructures are found to play an important role, apart from direct policies meant to boost industrialisation (Morrison and Schwartz 1996; Audretsch and Lehmann 2013; Audretsch, Heger and Veith 2015). In the next section, we map the building up of physical infrastructure critical to capital accumulation in the state.

INFRASTRUCTURES OF GROWTH

The National Council of Applied Economic Research (NCAER) has been publishing an investment potential index for states (State Investment Potential Index) in recent years that is a composite index of six broad parameters of infrastructure (physical and social) and governance. According to the latest one published for 2018, Tamil Nadu has the best index after Delhi (National Council of Applied Economic Research [NCAER 2018]).

The role of human capital in driving both economic growth and entrepreneurship is well established (Marvel, Davis and Sproul 2016). Tamil Nadu, as we elaborated in Chapter 3, has come to be recognised for its ability to generate one of the largest pools of technically skilled labour in the country. In fact, the NCAER index ranks the state at the top in this regard. Creation of higher education infrastructure and ensuring higher and more broad-based enrolment, particularly in technical education, have contributed to this. Importantly, this is also critical to ensure that the resources for entrepreneurship formation are socially more widespread than in other states. Affirmative action policies have not only democratised the labour market but are also likely to have ensured new entrants from diverse caste groups into the space of entrepreneurship. While we discuss this in detail later, we next map the transformations in physical infrastructure.

The state had achieved 100 per cent rural electrification by the 1970s itself and earlier than Gujarat and Maharashtra. As per the NCAER index, it has the narrowest gap between supply and demand for power, and also ranks third in the information technology (IT) readiness index. The state has the third largest (after Maharashtra and Gujarat) installed capacity of power with 24,433 MW in 2016. Even by the early 1960s, it had built above average capacity in electricity generation. This was a phase when the Dravidian narrative of 'south waning, north flourishing' was dominant.[7] Importantly, such building up of infrastructure was also accompanied by relatively low cost access for marginal and small producers.

The perspective planning document prepared by the first state planning commission in 1972 too highlights the importance of electricity and how its lack may constrain industrial growth.[8] The state has since then diversified its energy resources over time, particularly through the renewable energy route. Established as a nodal agency in 1985, the Tamil Nadu Energy Development Agency (TEDA) sought to improve renewable energy generation in the state. At present, renewable energy accounts for more than 40 per cent of the total energy produced in Tamil Nadu,[9] with the state emerging as one of the leading producers and markets for renewable energy in the world (*Down to Earth* 2019). In fact, as Cullen (2019) points out, it was active collaboration between policy and private actors at the state level that made this possible, with the government devising a range of innovative incentives to attract investments in this sector. Cullen also contends that it was the extent of networked grid infrastructure laid out by the state electricity board that helped installation of wind energy plants on a large scale.

Apart from production, the state has also responded to demands from small producers for price subsidies. Since the 1970s, it has not only expanded coverage of electrification, but has also favoured certain economic sections like farmers and weavers in response to agitations and protests by them. Tamil Nadu was one of the first to provide farmers with free electricity. As the majority of cultivators depend on well and tube-well irrigation, power has been a significant input into their cultivation since the 1970s. As a result, both Dravidian parties have subsidised electricity and waived payment of dues from farmers following large-scale farmer agitations in the state in the 1980s.[10] Since then, subsidised electricity to farmers has been institutionalised in the state which enabled accumulation within agriculture through exploitation of groundwater and diversification of agrarian surplus into non-farm investments, although the same has also led to an ecological crisis (Rukmani 1993; Varshney 1995; Damodaran 2008; Heyer 2016). Public investments in irrigation too facilitated the formation of agro-industrial capital (Harriss-White 1996). Another group of producers that enjoy free power is weavers. In 2006, the DMK introduced a scheme of 100 units bimonthly to handloom weavers having their own work shed and 500 units bimonthly to power-loom weavers (Rao 2017). The government also introduced a scheme of free power for Scheduled Caste/Scheduled Tribes (SCs/STs) who use open irrigation wells in the state. Hence, rather than see this subsidisation as a tool of state patronage for votes (Ramakrishnan 2018), its role in capital accumulation in rural Tamil Nadu, particularly in the 1980s and 1990s, needs to be recognised.

The state also has a well-established road network with a road density that is 2.5 times that at the all-India level. Tamil Nadu is particularly known for the spread and development of 'minor' roads, namely, roads other than highways connecting every major district road in the state—and bus services that ensure the flow of people and goods across the state. As Nagaraj (2006) points out, rural–urban linkages in the state have been strengthened particularly from the 1970s. The decades of the 1960s, 1970s and 1980s witnessed a significant increase in the spread and development of the road network—of 'minor' roads and major district roads, in particular (see Table 5.5)—along with improvements in public transportation.

In addition to improvements to road networks, the state also paid attention to increasing the mobility of goods and people through strengthening bus networks. After assuming power in 1967, the DMK-led government appointed a high-level committee to analyse the efficiency of the Tamil Nadu State Transport Department. Based on the committee's recommendation, the Tamil Nadu Fleet Operating Stage Carriage (Acquisition) Act was passed in 1971 to nationalise private bus transport units having 50 or more permits.[11] In the process, the government established 15 passenger transport corporations during the period 1972–90, which were finally merged into the Tamil Nadu State Transport Corporation (TNSTC). In order to finance the corporations, the state established the Tamil Nadu State Development Finance Corporation in 1972. Thanks to the nationalisation of bus transport in the early 1970s, the state could build one of the best public transport networks in the country, linking most rural areas to nearby towns (Vignesh Karthik and Karunanithi 2018). Again, as in the case of education and healthcare, the state's efficiency of resource utilisation has been better than that of other states with studies indicating that its transport corporations have the highest productive efficiency in the country (Singh 2000). Such policies integrated the countryside with the towns and created diversification options outside of agriculture for livelihoods. The fact that non-farm business accounts for one of the largest sources of income for rural households in the state is indicative of the facilitating role of such infrastructural support (Chapter 6). The government has also managed to ensure one of the lowest freight rates and passenger fares in the country. The state has the lowest fares in the country with the fare per kilometre being 42 paisa for an ordinary mofussil bus.[12] Over time, innovations such as the mini bus have been introduced to improve links between remote rural areas and urban areas. Having established the role of systemic interventions in the domain of infrastructure, we map the evolution of a 'productivist' ethos in colonial Madras that translated into political demands, policy decisions and outcomes in succeeding phases of the state's development.

Table 5.5 Road Infrastructure in Tamil Nadu

	Major roads					Minor roads			Minor Roads as % of all roads
	National highways	State highways	Major district roads	Municipal, P.W.D and others	Total	Other district roads	Panchayat union roads	Total	
1960–61	1,754	1,754	13,742	5,827	23,077	1,194	19,748	20,942	47.6
1965–66	1,754	1,780	13,591	6,423	23,548	6,859	35,160	42,019	64.1
1970–71	1,804	1,780	13,776	7,235	24,595	9,537	40,032	49,569	66.8
1975–76	1,865	1,745	13,866	7,956	25,432	15,833	53,468	69,301	73.2
1980–81	1,865	1,814	14,028	7,956	25,663	18,118	71,527	89,645	77.7
1985–86	1,884	1,864	14,004	9,169	26,921	21,927	99,112	1,21,039	81.8
1988–89	1,884	1,885	14,008	15,022	32,799	29,254	1,02,515	1,31,769	80.1
1989–90	1,884	1,885	14,008	15,022	32,799	30,420	1,02,515	1,32,935	80.2
1990–91	1,884	1,896	13,923	15,156	32,859	31,733	1,02,515	1,34,248	80.3
1991–92	2,002	1,915	13,930	15,156	33,003	33,110	1,02,515	1,35,625	80.4
2001–02	3,850	7,163	48,325	N/A	N/A	37,122	N/A	N/A	N/A
2013–14	4,974	11,594	11,289	41,701	69,558	34,160	1,43,071	1,77,231	71.8

Source: Tamil Nadu: An Economic Appraisal 1992–93 (Government of Tamil Nadu 1993) and Applied Research, Government of Tamil Nadu, Chennai, https://www.tn.gov.in/dear/Transport.pdf (accessed 11 January 2019).

THE EMERGENCE OF A PRODUCTIVIST ETHOS

The idea of inclusive modernisation envisioned by the Dravidian movement was borne out of specific political and economic processes that unfolded in the Madras Presidency as a result of colonial interventions. To begin with, the land tenure system introduced in the region by the colonial government established a set of incentives for the process of modernisation, particularly in the domain of agriculture. Bannerji and Iyer (2005) demonstrate that the *ryotwari* tenurial system generates incentives for both improvements in productivity and infrastructure because individual cultivators could appropriate greater returns from such improvements. Tamil Nadu was historically largely under the *ryotwari* system, and since it did not have an all-pervasive regional trading caste, there were incentives for generation of surplus within agriculture and the possibility for agrarian castes to diversify through trade and other non-farm investments. Further, as productive development was visible, Gupta (2012) argues that in *ryotwari* regions, social movements that emerged during the colonial period were engaged more with the productive domain and sought to link social emancipation with incentivising modern production. This was visible in the Madras Presidency as well.

By the end of the first decade of the 20th century, the non-Brahmin movement began to articulate a vision of inclusive modernisation that saw a role for state-of-the-art industries, and supported measures for technical education and sophisticated industries (see Chapter 3). As Kalaiyarasan (2017b) points out, though both Bengal and Tamil Nadu had a sound industrial base at the end of the colonial period, the two states witnessed a different trajectory subsequently, with the former failing to make much of its first mover advantage. Tamil Nadu, on the other hand, despite not having as many modern industries as the Bombay and Bengal Presidencies regions or 'Cawnpore' until the first decade of the 20th century (Swaminathan 1992: 57)[13] managed to expand this base much better. As discussed in chapter 2, many leaders of the Justice Party and subsequently the SRM echoed this ethos in their demand for modernisation and industrialisation.

Theagaraya Chetty, a founding member of the Justice Party is also credited with having had a key role in setting up both the Victoria Technical Training Institute in the late-19th century and the Chengalvarayar Technical Training

School in 1905.[14] Geetha and Rajadurai (2008) also point out how he contrasted the emphasis on technical education in Japan with the thrust given in British India to literary skills. Soon after the Justice Party came to power, the State Aid to Industries Act was passed in 1923, the first of its kind in the country (Tyabji 1988), which sought to ensure state support for the setting up of industries. Though it didn't work well, debates around it illustrate the general approach to industrialisation in the region. When the Congress members of the legislative council were demanding support for handloom weaving, the government said that public funds should not be spent on activities that do not generate much revenue or income for workers. The resistance to promotion of traditional weaving without the use of mechanised technologies was based on the fact that its low productivity in relation to modern textile production would mean that not only will workers earn less, but importantly this would prevent the expansion of modernisation.

This emphasis on productive labour was also shaped by the activities of sections of missionaries who trained lower-caste youth in certain trades, and in instances, also set up manufacturing enterprises. The role of Basel Mission in the Malabar region of the Presidency is noteworthy in this regard (Raghaviah 2014). In fact, this Mission pioneered the hosiery industry in the Presidency, which in turn contributed to the subsequent rise of Tiruppur as a major global hub of cotton hosiery production (Vijayabaskar 2001). Being a colonial city, Madras also witnessed the emergence of a few modern industries. Chennai's growth during this phase owes in good part to what Krishna Bharadwaj (1982) has termed as the port-enclave mode of development. However, in comparison to Bombay or the Bengal Presidency, the Madras Presidency did not develop enough industries (Swaminathan 1992). Though not all colonial officials were in favour of promoting industries in the colony, there were some like Chatterton who argued otherwise and pioneered a set of initiatives in this regard (Swaminathan 1991a).[15] His work with chrome leather tanning, for instance, played a critical role in the growth of the leather and leather-goods cluster in the state (Swaminathan 1991b).

The promotion of industries was also partly tied to the promotion of artisanal castes, and this is particularly visible in the case of the leather goods sector. L.C Gurusami, a Dalit leader from the leather working community and associated with the Dravidian movement, not only championed the cause of modern education for Dalits and opened hostels for lower-caste students, but was also instrumental in starting a cooperative society for leather goods production in Madras city.[16] This sustained emphasis on a productivist ethos was thus also tied to a strong belief that modernisation is critical to the upliftment of the lower castes.

Even as such broad based aspirations for industrial development were emerging, colonial Madras also witnessed the emergence of a few modern enterprises, largely European to begin with, and subsequently by natives, primarily caste elites (Damodaran 2008). Damodaran documents how sections of caste elites entered into modern industries, particularly in the automobile sector in the Chennai region. Meanwhile in western Tamil Nadu, a different set of processes of industrialisation were unfolding (Mahadevan 1992). Referred to as Manchesterisation, western Tamil Nadu saw the expansion of cotton cultivation, particularly after the introduction of Cambodia cotton in the region. In the backdrop of a 'Vaishya vacuum' (Mahadevan 2017), a few of the cultivators among the Kamma Naidus first and followed by the Kongu Vellala Gounders, managed to enter into cotton trade and subsequently into the setting up of gins and presses as well as composite mills. There were also a set of entrepreneurs from the weaving castes like Devanga Chettis and Kaikolars whom Mahadevan and Vijayabaskar (2014) refer to as handloom capitalists. The region became a major textile hub in south India by the time of Independence in 1947.[17] The provision of electricity with the launch of hydroelectric projects in Pykara first and then in Mettur in the 1930s also contributed to the expansion of industries and the use of electric power in existing operations in the region. Power looms and hosiery machines began to be adopted by entrepreneurs. Use of electric pumps for drawing water also spawned entrepreneurial diversification into agricultural machinery and later into textile machinery. Technical training institutions too were set up by businesses. It was this symbiotic linkage between agriculture and industry that made the accumulation processes in Coimbatore and later Tiruppur distinct from capital accumulation elsewhere.

By the 1940s, a trenchant critique of the Gandhian imagination of a swadeshi economy on the one hand and the emphasis on modernisation and industrialisation on the other transformed into a common-sense that subsequent political regimes in postcolonial Madras could ill afford to ignore. Importantly, the argument that the southern region was industrially backward compared to the 'North' translated into a popular demand to counter such neglect. Over the next two decades, successive Congress governments in the state sought to respond to this 'common-sense' built by Dravidian mobilisation.

PHASE II — 1947–67: DRAVIDIAN DEMANDS AND PLANNED INDUSTRIALISATION

The phase of planned industrialisation meant that the state was to play a lead role in not only creating production infrastructure but also in directing private capital into specific sectors and specific regions. Though policies for industrial development were in the concurrent list of the Constitutional division of responsibilities between the union and state governments, recourse to licensing meant that the union government had a greater role in both resource allocation and location. If the Justice Party emphasised technical education and modern industries, the post-1947 regime led by the Congress continued this legacy in many ways. This was a period when it had to confront the growing popularity of the DMK, formed in 1949 with the explicit aim of capturing political power. Periyar, who wanted to confine his conduct of politics to the terrain of civil society fell out with leaders of the DMK. But he threw his weight behind the Congress government after Kamaraj, a lower-caste leader, assumed chief ministership in 1954 as he saw him as a true 'Tamilian' (Venkatachalapathy 2018). While Periyar was working through the Congress government to spread his ideas, he also conducted agitations whenever the government acted against the principles of social justice upheld by the Dravidian movement. As a result of this 'double-barrelled gun' formation, Venkatachalapathy argues that the ideas expounded by the Dravidian movement became more popular in Tamil society during this period.

In the sphere of industrialisation, this is quite visible in the recurrent demands for setting up new industries and criticisms of the government for failure to act on this front in the Assembly. A. Govindasami (Manian and Sampath 2017), for instance, narrates his observations about Chandigarh and Ludhiana in the course of one of his speeches in the Assembly. He says that during an official visit to these towns, he saw that there were as many as 30 factories specialising in varied activities like weaving, matches and oil engines in a town which had a population of only 30,000 (Vol. 2, p. 13). He also claims that there are no beggars there and according to a businessman in Ludhiana, even if there are, they are likely to have come from south India! Pointing out how shameful it is for him to listen to this, he goes on to ask the government about the plans it has to ensure that there are no beggars. On another occasion, he asks whether the government agrees that a weaver's child should not necessarily take up weaving and if yes, whether the government has plans to support the weaver households in this regard (Manian and Sampath 2017: Vol. 2, p. 431). He also enquires whether and when modern industries can be set up or modern technologies introduced in agriculture. For example, he asks whether a modern milk factory like the Aarey milk factory in Bombay can be built in the state (Manian and Sampath 2017: Vol. 2, p.3), about the nature of state support for an aluminium factory (p. 14), type of industries that can be set up because of the Neyveli lignite corporation power plant (p. 79), need for large-scale iron smelting units (pp. 400–01) and so on. Such demands are generally embedded in a sense of neglect of the region by the union government in terms of disbursal of funds, industrial licenses to entrepreneurs (Manian and Sampath 2017: Vol. 2, pp. 402–03), or the setting up of public sector enterprises. On another occasion, C.N. Annadurai, founding member of the DMK, speaking in the Rajya Sabha in 1962, invoked the 'Southern Question' in Italy to seek economic advancement of the Tamil region:

> For the information of the house I may say, that the very same problem arose in Italy. Southern Italy was industrially very backward compared to Northern Italy and then the Italian Government took very intelligent, very bold and very radical steps formulating a special scheme for Southern Italy. They offered tax concessions for new industries to be started in Southern Italy. They gave loans and other aids for this purpose in order to improve this part of Italy (Ramachandran 1975: pp. 103–04).

The persistent difference in the allotment of industrial licenses and the domination of a few Indian business houses belonging to powerful pan-Indian mercantile communities at the national level continued to fuel the sense of industrial neglect and a simultaneous forging of a subnational identity. Even earlier, there was a call by the movement to take over the property owned by religious organisations like temple mutts to use for investments in productive activities or modern education. Responding to such pressures, the Congress governments through the 1950s and until the mid-1960s, brought in public sector enterprises (PSEs) and secured licenses for a few private entrepreneurs in Tamil Nadu. While caste elites benefited disproportionally from such initiatives, particularly in securing industrial licences, such policy measures did lay the foundations for broadening industrialisation as such ventures led to the development of ancillary industrial clusters around these PSEs such as the ones near Bharat Heavy Electricals Limited (BHEL) in Trichy and the Avadi defence factory in Chennai. This response from the Congress governments, it needs to be remembered, was unlike in several other Congress-ruled states where the political pressure was a lot weaker. Apart from such initiatives, the government also set up the Tamil Nadu Industrial Development Corporation (TIDCO) and the Tamil Nadu Small Industries Corporation Limited (TANSI) in 1965 for the promotion of enterprises in the state. The DMK sustained such interventions after it came to power in 1967.

PHASE III — 1967–90: INSTITUTIONALISED POPULISM AND STATE-LED INDUSTRIALISATION

The DMK not only continued this legacy, but also broadened its scope. During the first phase of its being in power—1967–76—the government set up two corporations, the State Industries Promotion Corporation of Tamil Nadu (SIPCOT) and the Tamil Nadu Small Industries Development Corporation (SIDCO) to promote both large and small enterprises. Incorporated as a public limited entity in 1971, SIDCO's objectives were to ensure efficient and equitable distribution of raw material to small firms, supply expensive machinery on a hire–purchase basis, to create work sheds and also provide technical support. The Tamil Nadu Small Industries Development Corporation not only took over the management of existing industrial estates, but has established more than 50 estates since its inception. The role of TIDCO too was expanded.

It pioneered the joint sector model, partnering with the private sector to establish industries (Ravindranath 2015). The first major project of TIDCO was a joint venture, Southern Petrochemicals Industries Corporation Limited (SPIC), to manufacture fertilisers in Tuticorin which could also feed into the commercialisation of agriculture. Established in 1971, SIPCOT developed industrial complexes by providing infrastructure facilities for medium and larger investors to build their factories.

While ancillary industrial estates were promoted around large enterprises, the government also mooted a proposal in 1976 to set up a special ancillary and instruments cluster in Hosur, located close to Bangalore, to tap into demand from PSEs in Bangalore such as Bharat Electronics Limited (BEL), Indian Telephone Industries Limited (ITI) and Hindustan Aeronautics Limited (HAL) (Government of Tamil Nadu 1976: p. 314). Importantly, Hosur's location in a backward district was highlighted. The subsequent setting up of a joint venture Titan with the Tatas in Hosur and emergence of an industrial hub in the region is an instance of successful, state-induced, industrial cluster development. By the mid-1970s, government policy documents also report TANSI units producing jigs, tools and fixtures for BHEL, Scooters India and the heavy vehicles factory, Avadi (Government of Tamil Nadu 1976: p. 325). Units (TANSI engineering works) in Karur and Namakkal were engaged in designing and fabricating carts for transporting sugarcane. The state government also set up support facilities, like testing laboratories, for small and medium firms. The Central Electrical Testing Laboratory, set up in Thiruvallur district in 1973, is one such example. A regional testing laboratory was also set up in Madurai in 1972 to cater to industries from the southern districts.

There were also specific sectoral interventions. The Tamil Nadu Textile Corporation was started in 1969 as a fully owned state government enterprise to take over and run sick textile mills (Government of Tamil Nadu 1976: p. 335). While initially it sought to support the spinning mills in the cooperative sector by centrally purchasing yarn and other equipment, it was subsequently instrumental in setting up 10 power-loom complexes in different parts of the state. It is worth mentioning in this context that this also paved the way for a booming small-scale power-loom sector in the state, with looms often started by ex-workers of textile mills. Importantly, given the availability of power and offer of subsidies, power-loom production is highly decentralised in the state, and spread across several villages, unlike the power-loom clusters in Maharashtra or Gujarat. The Tamil Nadu Dairy Development Corporation, formed in 1972 to support the milk producers in the state with regard to procurement, processing and marketing, culminated in the formation of the Tamil Nadu Co-operative Milk Producers' Federation (TCMPF) in 1981 along the lines of AMUL, and is now a successful model of a state-level dairy cooperative in the country. But as we documented in the first part of this chapter, the non-agricultural economy witnessed a more radical transformation and dynamism in the post-reform period, particularly since the 2000s.

PHASE IV — POST-REFORM INTERVENTIONS AND THE NEW PROFESSIONAL ELITE

Economic reforms initiated in the 1990s were also accompanied by political reforms that sought to devolve more functions to state governments (Kennedy 2014). Accompanied by a decline in central transfers, states were made responsible for mobilising resources through private investments unlike in the past when investments were directed through licensing by the union government. While providing a degree of autonomy, this shift implied competition between states to attract investment, and implementation of institutional reforms directed towards drawing private capital (Kennedy 2004). Following this shift, the state initiated a slew of reforms to embed growth within private capital in the absence of adequate resources.

Given the need to augment resources for infrastructure, the state created the Tamil Nadu Urban Development Fund (TNUDF), a special purpose vehicle, in a public–private partnership (PPP) mode to generate long-term debt for urban infrastructure development.[18] Though it ran into trouble after a decade due to rigidities in the lending model, the fund is supposed to have been successful in providing finance for infrastructure development to several urban local bodies (ULBs), particularly for roads and sanitation.[19] The Tamil Nadu Road Development Company was another joint venture launched by TIDCO to promote road infrastructure in 1998. According to its website, it has come to be a benchmark in this sector and has served as a model for other state governments.[20]

The state also set up the country's 'first operational SEZ [special economic zone]', Mahindra World City, in a public–private mode as a collaboration between TIDCO and the Mahindra and Mahindra group (Vijayabaskar 2014). Both TIDCO and SIPCOT, in tune with the larger shifts in policy orientation, became facilitators for industrial development through support for infrastructure creation and easing of procedures for setting up of industries. The move by SIPCOT to acquire land since the mid-1990s facilitated the creation of a land bank that proved useful when SEZ promotion began a few years later. The state was also one of the first to formulate a SEZ policy in 2003, and is home to one of the largest number of SEZs in the country. The Nanguneri SEZ in southern Tamil Nadu was one of the first two SEZs at the national level launched through the export–import (EXIM) policy of 2000. This SEZ was also seen as a way to address caste conflicts in the region as the judicial commission enquiring into caste violence suggested that the industrial backwardness of the region should be addressed to mitigate such violence.[21] Importantly, unlike several states where SEZ promotion was more a speculative activity, the state did witness creation of productive capacities through this route.[22] The development of a hardware hub in the Sriperumbudur region, the arrival of a number of auto majors and the expansion of established software firms into tier-II towns like Coimbatore are all considered facets of this success story. Such broad-based investments in infrastructure need not, however, necessarily broad-base entrepreneurship. The latter was made possible during this phase primarily through the state's support for human capital development combined with such expansion of physical infrastructure.

We conducted a series of interviews with entrepreneurs in the engineering sector (including auto-component making) in the Chennai region and also in the Coimbatore region during the period June 2017–December 2019 intermittently. We also interviewed Dalit entrepreneurs through the DICCI and other contacts in the second half of 2019. A couple of features stand out. Most of them are from second-generation-educated households with their parents having a steady job either in the government (particularly so for Dalits) or in the private sector. After having acquired a technical qualification, they have taken the entrepreneurial route. Often networks forged in colleges and schools have had a role. Some of the backward caste entrepreneurs also had some access to land.

The entry of entrepreneurs from non-traditional business families is even more evident in the case of the software services economy (Varrel and Vijayabaskar 2019). Coimbatore has emerged as a modest hub for software services with the government and private actors setting up IT parks for development centres. Outside these parks, the city is also home to several small start-up firms in this domain that include sophisticated ones such as in robotics and the internet of things (IoT). Two incubation centres in leading engineering colleges in the city too have contributed to this development. More interesting, however, are the enabling networks forged by entrepreneurs with little link to traditional business families. They had all attended school in the city and some of them studied in colleges in the city or in Chennai. They have then gone on to work for IT majors including MNCs like IBM. After having worked for a few years, they have come back to Coimbatore to set up firms. They tend to partner with friends from school, college or workplaces who are likely to be based in places outside Coimbatore, with some of them continuing to work in other firms. The business model is often based on inter-city networks. While the actual software development takes place in Coimbatore, the marketing end of the business is taken care of through their partners based in Chennai, Bangalore or even in the United States. Through this, they are able to leverage the advantages of networks created in metropolitan regions. Their partners are engaged in marketing, sourcing orders from new clients or trying to access venture capital funding. Damodaran's discussion of democratisation of capital in the region, however, does not consider this possibility. This phenomenon also nuances the contention that caste elites and their caste networks dominate the software business community elsewhere as suggested by Taeube (2004).[23] Outside the domain of software services, the city is also home to a vibrant medical services sector established largely by medical professionals hailing from the region. A leading orthopaedic hospital in Coimbatore city, for example, is run by a doctor from a backward caste with no prior business networks. While democratising higher education has opened up spaces for entrepreneurship among non-elites in new economic sectors, there are shifts taking place in older sectors as well. In western Tamil Nadu, Tiruppur has emerged as the biggest centre of garment exports in the country. Industrial estates by SIDCO, both in the pre-reform period and subsequently in the 1990s, have contributed to its development along with support for common effluent treatment plants. Given the fragmentation of the production process, entrepreneurs from lower economic and social backgrounds could easily enter the industry (Chari 2004). The state government also set up an industrial estate exclusively for Dalit entrepreneurs in the region though it did not do well (Vijayabaskar and Kalaiyarasan 2014). However, over time, with the demands of the global market and the need to network with global clients, not only have highly educated second-generation entrepreneurs emerged from owner families, a new set of entrepreneurs with better educational qualifications have managed to take advantage of market opportunities.[24] The networks they are embedded in are less about kinship than about ties formed in modern social spaces like the classroom.

Apart from the entry of the Kongu Vellala Gounders into manufacturing, the entry of Nadars, a backward caste, into this space is unique. Though tapping of palmyra trees was their primary traditional occupation, they have become successful professionals and businessmen, even forming one of the largest IT enterprises in the country.[25] Their mobility has been both through education leading to a professional elite who went into business, and also through entry into trade. While Christianity and early investments in education allowed them to enter into modern professions such as IT and medicine, others could transit from toddy tappers to merchants by trading in palm gur, dried fish, salt, and assorted agro produce (Damodaran 2008: p. 181). Early diffusion of aspirations for modern education and interventions by both the colonial and postcolonial subnational governments thus enabled their mobility.

Better road and energy infrastructure has allowed firms to also move further away from towns to take advantage of lower land costs as well as access to labour. As Ghani, Goswami and Kerr (2012) argue, organised manufacturing in India has moved to rural and semi-urban areas since the 1990s. The broad-basing of social and physical infrastructure has contributed to furthering this process in the state. An industrial estate set up by the state for knitwear production on the outskirts of Madurai has now helped move production of segments of knitwear away from Tiruppur to an industrially backward region.

Developments in the Coimbatore region too are important in this regard. From being a hub for agricultural and textile machinery, it has diversified into auto components, kitchen equipment and electrical home appliances among others. The Coimbatore District Small Scale Industries Association (CODISSIA), started in 1969 for lobbying with the state for infrastructure and other support, has now emerged as one of the largest business associations for small-scale entrepreneurs in the country. Once again, the emergence of a pool of technically qualified entrepreneurs has contributed to such dynamism in the region, with many of them emerging from non-elite backgrounds.

DEMOCRATISING OPPORTUNITIES AND INCLUSIVISING GROWTH

Hariss and Wyatt (2019), based on Washbrook's formulation, argue that the role of the state in Tamil Nadu is 'neither … developmental nor … social democratic … while having some elements of both …' They further argue that it did not contribute much to industrialisation as such roles were pretty much left to the entrepreneurs themselves, while it confined itself to the social sectors. Such a reading, we have tried to establish does not explain either the sectoral diversification that the state has witnessed or the shifts in the social basis of entrepreneurship. While factors that Damodaran alludes to in explaining the process of democratisation of capital in the state did play a role, we have sought to establish how a particular imagination of social justice made possible a set of interventions that simultaneously expanded capital accumulation and broad-based entrepreneurship. While the questioning of caste-based division into 'born capitalists' and 'born workers' allowed for capacities to aspire among lower castes, broad-basing education and physical infrastructure allowed for translation of aspirations into actual capabilities for entry into spaces of accumulation. This diffusion of entrepreneurship has been embedded within the growth process itself.

It is true that upper castes like the Brahmins and Nattukottai Chettiars continue to dominate big business. We, however, point to a process of democratisation of capital in the lower rungs, with new entrants from among the backward castes and a section of Dalits, especially through access to professional education. As a result of such pluralisation, it is difficult for one or a few business groups to exercise control over policy-making in the state. Pareto (1968) distinguishes the modern governing elite from its traditional counterpart, as one that acquires its stability through recruiting members from across different socio-economic groups and also offers scope for the movement of persons from non-elite to elite positions and vice versa. The coming to power of the Dravidian parties in 1967 opened up such possibilities for many lower-caste groups to be a part of the ruling elite. This was made possible by a political imagination that upheld demand for, or actual mobility of specific lower castes to be essential to undermining of caste hierarchies (Karthick 2020). This imagination in conjunction with a belief in economic transformation in undermining caste hierarchies has fostered a relatively more inclusive growth process in the state. This inclusive character has been sustained by circulating elites emerging across several caste groups. It therefore suggests that once a path is created by a set of interventions, it generates a trajectory of growth and development fairly independent of specific and more immediate policy measures.

Such interventions have led to structural shifts in the economy that ensured the movement of people out of traditional livelihoods much more than in most states in the country. What are the implications of this process for lower-caste labour in rural and urban Tamil Nadu? How has the political regime responded to the demands of these classes? The next two chapters engage with these questions.

APPENDIX 5A

SDP data is available from 1960 to 2014 in five different series, that is, with five different base years: 1970–71, 1980–81, 1993–94, 1999–2000 and 2004–05. We have therefore made the series comparable by using 2004–05 prices as the base by *splicing*. Since we do not have data for all the years (1960 to 2014) with the same base year, using the splicing technique provided by Kumar and Chandra (2003), data with different base years are converted to the same base year. We have spliced individual components—agriculture, industry and services—and then added them up to arrive at the SDP for each year. We use here two growth rates; annual growth rate and log-linear growth for longer periods. The annual growth is estimated using the following method; using the sub-components of SDP, the growth rate between two years, t and (t + 1)

$$g_{t+1} = g^A_{t+1} \times s^A_t + g^I_{t+1} \times s^I_t + g^S_{t+1} \times s^S_t$$

where the contribution of each sector to overall growth is a combination of its own growth rate (g) and its share in the NSDP. We then add them up for aggregate annual growth rates.

For estimating the growth rate for longer periods, we use the log-linear model. For example, growth between the time period 1980–81 and 1989–90 is defined as

$$\ln (SDP_i) = \alpha + gt$$

Where i = 1980–81 ... 1989–90, α is the intercept and t = 1 ... 9, is the time variable.

NOTES

1   While growth has significantly picked up since the 2000s, when we tried endogenously testing for a structural break using the Zivot–Andrews method, the analysis suggested a break at 2002 at 10 per cent significance with a chosen lag length of 2. It means while the growth has seen acceleration in the 2000s, it has been gradual over time.

2   Policy Note: Demand no. 5—2017–18. Department of Agriculture, Government of Tamil Nadu.

3   Swaminathan (1994) argues that though the state has managed to remain among the top 3 industrialised states in the country, it has not only lost ground to Maharashtra and Gujarat but has also not taken advantage of new economic opportunities.

4   As Nagaraj and Pandey (2013) show, export-oriented petroleum refining alone accounts for about a quarter of the gross value added in registered manufacturing in Gujarat.

5   Damodaran in fact attributes the absence of unrest among agrarian communities like the Jats in Haryana, Marathas in Maharashtra, Kapus in Andhra Pradesh and Patels in Gujarat, to this model of decentralised industrialisation in the state.

6   We do not, however, have caste details for private joint stock companies and corporations which are excluded from the caste survey.

7   A debate in the state assembly in the early 1960s illustrates this. Mr A. Govindasami, a major voice in the DMK who also served as the Minister for Agriculture when the DMK assumed power in 1967, was speaking in the assembly during his term as an MLA in 1957–62. He points out that though the Congress repeatedly claims that the south has done better than the north in terms of electricity, there are still parts of the state where supply of electricity is poor (Manian and Sampath 2017: 280–81).

8   Perspective Plan prepared by Malcolm Adiseshiah (1972)

9   See http://teda.in/ (accessed 17 March 2020).

10   The farmers, particularly those who use pump sets in western Tamil Nadu, were agitating for waiving off the 'belated payment surcharge' (BPSC)—a payment levied on the amount of electricity dues (Rao 2017)

11   Order dated November 8, 1971 (G.O. No:86)

12   Policy Note: Demand No. 48 2014–15. , https://cms.tn.gov.in/sites/default/files/documents/transport_e_pn_2014_15.pdf (accessed 15 April 2019).

13   Swaminathan cites a note prepared by Alfred Chatterton, School of Arts, Madras to make these observations.

14   See http://siragu.com (accessed 8 May 2020).

15   Alfred Chatterton, an engineer by profession, was appointed by the colonial government as Superintendent of the School of Arts in Madras in 1897. He was responsible for laying the foundation for technical education, experimenting in industrial clusters and modernising caste-based industries in the Madras Presidency. His initiatives among others are (a) the development of the aluminium industry, (b) the inspection and reorganisation of existing industrial schools and the establishment of new ones and (c) the development of indigenous industries and the establishment of a manual training class in the college of engineering workshop or elsewhere. (Swaminathan 1991a: p. 4).

16 See http://chamaar-today.blogspot.com/2019/04/lc-gurusamy-1.html (accessed 23 April 2020). Bharathidasan (2015) also makes a similar argument based on his ongoing study of L. C. Guruswamy.

17 Coimbatore accounted for 82 per cent of the investment in south India, and 26 of the 30 units that came to be promoted between 1940 and 1957.

18 See http://tnuifsl.com/tnudf.asp (accessed 15 March 2020).

19 See http://tnuifsl.com/tnudf.asp (accessed 15 March 2020).

20 See http://tnrdc.com/about/ (accessed 15 March 2020).

21 Report of the High Level Committee formed under Justice S. Mohan (Rtd.) for Prevention of Caste Clashes in Southern Districts of Tamil Nadu (January 31, 1998: pp. 20–21).

22 This is, however, not to deny the speculative dimension of large-scale land acquisitions for SEZs in the state (Vijayabaskar 2014).

23 Taube (2004) suggests the dominance of caste elites within entrepreneurial networks of the dynamic software sector in the country. He also traces the global mobility of caste elites through the software industry and how caste networks sustain such mobility.

24 This information is drawn from a series of interviews conducted in the Tiruppur region during March 2009 and again during February–April 2018.

25 In August 1976, Shiv Nadar created Hindustan Computers Limited (HCL). The firm has become one of the country's leading IT conglomerate.

6

TRANSFORMING RURAL RELATIONS

Many scholars have suggested that identity-based mobilisation in the state has ignored class- based issues such as land reform or empowering of labour (Mencher 1975; Thangaraj 1995; Subramanian 1999). In this and the next chapter, we argue for a more nuanced understanding of how the subnational state has negotiated the question of labour welfare even as it sustained capital accumulation. In this chapter, we focus primarily on how mobilisation and policy interventions have improved the terms of work, incomes and status of rural labour including small holders and tenant farmers. As we argued in Chapter 2, ensuring inclusive structural transformation was critical to the Dravidian vision of social justice. Translated into developmental challenges, this implies two sets of processes. First, interventions ought to ensure shifts of people out of agriculture and other traditional occupations into secure livelihoods in the non-agricultural sector to undermine caste hierarchies. Second, while this involves shifts over time, interventions should also secure place-based livelihoods and income security at a given point in time.

We map three policy interventions that have made this possible. First, though land reforms were not pushed through strongly by legislation at one stroke, land transfers from upper-caste landlords to lower-caste tenant farmers did take place through molecular interventions and pressure from collective mobilisation. Second, investments in physical and social infrastructures have enabled diversification of rural livelihoods away from agriculture. Such diversification, accompanied by investments in education, in turn has led to better bargaining power for labouring households within agriculture. Third, an important argument that both this chapter and the next make is that substantial interventions in the labour market have been indirect through economic popular and social popular measures outside the domain of the workplace. Rural welfare interventions primarily through the public distribution system (PDS) and caste mobilisation sought to undermine hierarchical labour relations between the landed and the landless. Availability of food through the PDS weakened the basis of labour control and opened up economic possibilities for labouring households outside the domain of agriculture and the rural milieu. Such mediations outside the workplace have not only transformed rural social relations, but have also helped poorer households diversify into the non-farm sector on relatively better terms.

The chapter is organised in three parts corresponding to the three domains of interventions. In the first part, we map the changes in land relations and the factors that brought about such change. We next address the extent of non-farm diversification and the drivers of the process. Finally, we trace welfare interventions of the state and their impact on labour, particularly, the process of weakening of the social hierarchy in rural Tamil Nadu. The section takes up two such schemes, the PDS and the Mahatma Gandhi National Rural Employment Guarantee Act (MNREGA) to demonstrate how these schemes weakened hierarchical labour relations between the landed and the landless. We begin with the changes in land relations in the state.

WEAKENING RURAL HIERARCHIES: *CASTE AND LAND*

Micro-level studies hint at the decline of landlordism in the state (Harriss and Jeyaranjan 2016). Macro-level data on landholding size in rural Tamil Nadu indicates that the share of land held as large landholdings is much lower than the all-India average (see Table 6.1 and Table 6A.1). We map the trend in landholdings since the 1970s based on the agriculture census. The agriculture census collects data from comprehensive land records on villages, and hence offers reliable information on operational holdings in India from the first census conducted in 1970–71 to the latest—2015–16.

Data from the above tables shows that marginal and small landowners, who constituted about 78 per cent of all landowners, controlled 37.6 per cent of the total land in 1970–71. By 2015–16, while their share in the number of total

Table 6.1 Distribution of Rural Households by Size Class (Landholdings) for Tamil Nadu

	Marginal (up to 1)	Small (1 to 2)	Semi-medium (2 to 5)	Medium (5 to 10)	Large (10 and above)	All	Average Size Holding
			Size of Landholding (in Hectare)				
1970–71	58.8	20.9	13.1	6.1	1.1	100	1.5
1980–81	69.7	16.8	9.2	3.7	0.6	100	1.1
1985–86	71.3	16.3	8.4	3.4	0.5	100	1.0
1990–91	73.1	15.9	7.7	2.9	0.4	100	0.9
1995–96	74.3	15.4	7.5	2.5	0.3	100	0.9
2000–01	74.4	15.6	7.3	2.5	0.3	100	0.9
2005–06	76.0	15.1	6.6	2.1	0.2	100	0.8
2010–11	77.2	14.6	6.2	1.9	0.2	100	0.8
2015–16	78.4	14.1	5.7	1.6	0.2	100	0.8
			Area under Control of Different Sizes				
1970–71	17.1	20.5	24.8	24.6	13.0	100	1.5
1980–81	24.7	22.2	23.6	20.2	9.3	100	1.1
1985–86	25.9	22.7	22.8	19.3	9.2	100	1.0
1990–91	28.3	24.0	22.6	17.4	7.7	100	0.9
1995–96	30.3	23.6	22.2	15.5	8.4	100	0.9
2000–01	31.0	24.6	22.2	15.7	6.5	100	0.9
2005–06	33.5	25.2	21.5	14.0	5.7	100	0.8
2010–11	35.3	25.3	20.9	13.1	5.4	100	0.8
2015–16	36.3	26.0	20.3	12.0	5.3	100	0.8

Source: All-India Rural Financial Inclusion Survey, 2016–17 (NAFIS), NABARD.

landholdings had increased to 92 per cent, their control of the total land had increased to 62.3 per cent. These figures refer to operational holdings. There may be variations between operational holdings and ownership patterns but in the absence of tenancy, one may assume that the differences are not large. Their share in the total number of holdings and the amount of land held is also higher than the all-India average suggesting that the state has a relatively better share of land operated as small and marginal land holdings. Similarly, the average size of holdings in the state has come down from 1.5 hectares in 1970–71 to 0.8 hectares in 2015–16 as against 2.3 to 1.1 hectares at the all-India level during the same period. Scholars cite division of holdings due to inheritance as a major factor behind decline in landholding size over time in India (Mahendra Dev 2018). Given the much sharper decline in fertility in the state, this factor is likely to have played less of a role. In fact, across the state, the share of Dalit households who reported as cultivators has gone up from 6.5 per cent in 1993–94 to 13 per cent in 2017–18 while it has declined for non-Dalits from 25 per cent to 17 per cent (see Table 6A.2 in Appendix 6A). Harriss, Jeyaranjan and Nagaraj (2012) observe that in 2010, land was predominantly owned by Pallars (a Dalit caste) and Thevars (a backward caste) in the case village they studied in southern Tamil Nadu.

Based largely on Jeyaranjan's work (2020), we argue in this section that legislative measures combined with pressure brought on landlords through collective mobilisation by the Dravidian and Left parties, and the coming to power of the DMK did result in transfer of land to the lower castes. After assuming power in 1967, the DMK government enacted the Tamil Nadu Agricultural Lands (Record of Tenancy Rights) Act, 1969. Through this formal institutional process (de jure mechanism), the state managed to transfer some land to tenant cultivators. However, more transfer of land to its tenants took place through non-institutional processes that Jeyaranjan refers to as de facto mechanisms. If de jure processes involved a slew of formal legislation, de facto transfers worked through political mobilisation.

Jeyaranjan argues that Brahmin and Vellala elites who historically inherited land in the fertile deltaic region of the Cauvery basin often migrated to cities after selling their lands to backward caste and Dalit tenant households on terms that were favourable to the tenants. According to him, the dislodging of caste elites from the rural areas was not an organic process driven merely by the attraction of accumulation and economic mobility prospects in urban areas. Mobilisation played a key role in this regard.[1] Jeyaranjan starts with the dominant consensus in existing literature on land reforms in the state. Citing a range of literature from the early 1970s up to the first decade of the 21st century, he points out that they all concur that despite the passing of several pieces of legislation in favour of tenants and agricultural labourers since the 1940s, the proximity of the landowning classes to those in state power enabled them to flout such formal legal measures. Jeyaranjan questions this hypothesis by starting from the present. If indeed this was true, how does one explain the collapse of landlordism in the state? Further, he points to the disappearance of tenancy in several parts of the state as well as the substantially improved terms of tenancy in the Thanjavur delta that is historically known for wealthy landlords exercising control over the labour of tenants and agricultural labourers through extreme non-economic forms of coercion. He then goes on to demonstrate that this shift in power from the landlord to the tenant was an outcome of molecular changes at the micro-level which in turn were enabled by legislation and collective action. He demonstrates this through a study of land transfer records from 1967 to 2014 and changes in tenancy in a village in the western part of the Cauvery delta that is historically known for its high levels of tenancy and control over land by caste elites.

While the role of the Communist Party in mobilising tenants and agricultural labourers in the region is well known (Gough 1981), Jeyaranjan highlights the less known but equally significant role played by the Dravidar Vivasaya Thozhilalar Sangam (DVTS) (Dravidian Agricultural Workers' Union) formed by the Dravidar Kazhagam in 1952.[2] Citing a memoir by an activist Kasthurirangan, which documents the struggle in the region, he points out that the union had a membership of '15,000 dalit agricultural workers and another 5,000 backward caste workers as members in [the] Nagappatinam[3] area alone' (2020: p. 258). In another region, he cites an even stronger presence with more than 50,000 members. Mobilisation by the union was originally against the hegemony of Brahmin landlords. The union often collaborated with the Communist Party union but also had conflictual relations with them. Due to political contingencies, members of the DVTS joined the Communist Party union and even assumed leadership of the union. In a recent work, Thiruneelakandan (2017) recovers another micro-history of the SRM taking up the cause of Dalit agricultural workers against upper caste landlords in the Thanjavur delta during the 1930s. Such collective action translated into a set of empowering interventions in the domain of land relations.

Although the Congress party had passed acts like the Thanjavur Tenants and Pannaiyals Protection Act, 1952, the Tamil Nadu Cultivating Tenants Protection Act, 1955 and the Tamil Nadu Cultivating Tenants (Payment of Fair Rent) Act, 1956, these acts were ineffective in the absence of a registry of tenants. Tenants could not provide documentary evidence in courts that they were actually working as tenants on a particular landlord's land. The DMK passed the Tamil Nadu Agricultural Lands (Record of Tenancy Rights) Act, 1969, that sought to address the issue. Revenue officials were instructed to prepare a register of tenants in each village. Tenants were given a document certifying their claim to tenancy rights. Importantly, the tenants were not required to provide documentary proof of their status to get such a certificate. Oral evidence and statements by neighbouring households were deemed sufficient evidence to demand their tenancy rights. This proved to be a major victory for the movement with nearly 7,00,000 acres of land being registered under about 5,00,000 tenant farmers. While the Congress government passed the land reform act restricting a family of five members from owning more than 30 acres, the DMK government reduced it further to 15 acres. Rental shares too were reduced, allowed to be paid in instalments and also waived on occasion. While the latter is an economic popular intervention that provides only short-term relief, the earlier interventions have clearly sought to undermine the basis on which the power held by landlords was being reproduced. Another important legislation passed by the DMK government in this regard was the Conferment of Ownership of Homestead Act, 1971 which gave ownership to all those living in homesteads belonging to someone else or on land belonging to the government. This move further enhanced the freedom of the tenant or the agricultural labourer.

Jeyaranjan also highlights some of the failed legislative efforts in this regard. One bill that gave the right to purchase the landlord's land by payment of 12 times the fair rent by the tenant failed to receive Presidential assent. Resistance by religious mutts which controlled vast tracts of land is seen to have played a part in this. Subsequent developments led to consolidation of backward-caste tenant power in the delta, their de facto rights becoming stronger than what legislation allows. As a result, according to a senior party functionary of the Communist Party of India-Marxist (CPI-M), tenancy is a dead issue in the delta region at present (Jeyaranjan 2020: p. 268). Jeyaranjan goes onto further map the transfer of land from the upper castes to the backward castes and to a lesser extent, to Dalits, over the last 40 odd years.

This narrative overlaps partly with processes mapped by Neelakantan (1996). Discussing the rural and urban transformation of the Karur region (in central Tamil Nadu), Neelakantan provides anecdotal evidence of the increasing costs that landlords had to incur to retain their lands and resist claims by tenants. While he attributes this to increased transaction costs, he does not engage with the possibility that transaction costs have actually increased because of the power of tenants and their ability to resist them and the local bureaucracy and judiciary. He shows how on occasion tenants, including Dalit tenants, managed to acquire ownership through shifts in rural power relations made possible by political mobilisation. Such accounts demonstrate how caste and land relationships have been reconfigured in rural Tamil Nadu and the strong ties that bound lower-caste landless labourers and tenant farmers to land and landowners stand dissolved. Another significant move that undermined elite power in the Tamil countryside is the abolition of traditional village heads.

DEMOCRATISING BUREAUCRACY

To abolish caste in rural areas, Periyar had suggested that traditional administrative jobs such as that of the accountant or revenue collector, held by caste elites, should be handed over to Dalits (Thirumavelan 2018: p. 8). The abolition of hereditary village heads (*karnam*) by the DMK in 1975 in line with such reasoning changed social dynamics in the rural hinterlands (Narayan 2018). Until then, village administration was in the hands of the village heads (*karnam*) who usually came from upper castes and were appointed by inheritance. The village heads used to be a part of the colonial bureaucracy introduced in Indian villages for revenue and other administrative purposes. The abolition of such hereditary appointments opened up space for participation of lower castes in village administration. Recruitment through the public service commission meant that control over land administration was no longer with the landed elites. Harriss, Jeyaranjan and Nagaraj (2010) in their case study of a village in northern Tamil Nadu observe that the village had only one president between 1957 and 1977 who was a landlord in that village. It was only in the 1980s, however, that things started changing on the ground. At the time of their study, the village panchayat had four Vanniyar members (classified as a 'most backward caste') and two Dalits while the president is a Dalit widow. The appointment of village administrative officers through the Tamil Nadu Public Service Commission (TNPSC) unsettled the inherited social power of the dominant castes and opened another pathway to democratise rural caste relations. Such efforts to reconfigure rural land relations were also accompanied by shifts in rural labour relations that contributed much more to the mobility of Dalit households.

LABOUR DIVERSIFICATION

Recent micro-level studies suggest that rural Tamil Nadu has become 'post-agrarian' with a reduced role for agriculture in contributing to household income (Harriss, Jeyaranjan and Nagaraj 2010, 2012). In this section, we establish using unit-level data of various NSS rounds that this is indeed a state-level phenomenon, with rural labour considerably diversifying out of agriculture. Though the rural non-farm sector has become a significant source of livelihood for rural households across India (see Table 6A.3 in Appendix 6A), the levels, patterns and drivers of the non-farm sector are distinct in the state. For the purpose of this chapter, we define the non-farm sector to include all income-generating activities that are not agricultural but located in rural areas.[4]

The share of the rural workforce in agriculture which was 70 per cent in 1993–94 has come down to about 42 per cent in 2017–18. The decline is much faster than in Gujarat or Maharashtra (see Table 6.2). Rural Tamil Nadu has a higher share of population dependent on income accruing in the non-farm sector compared to other high income states in the country. Non-farm sectors have in fact emerged as the biggest source of livelihood. According to the recent National Bank for Agriculture and Rural Development (NABARD) All-India Rural Financial Inclusion Survey (NAFIS) conducted in 2016–17 (see Figure 6.1), only 13 per cent of the rural households in the state can be classified as 'agricultural' even under a very generous definition of what constitutes an agricultural household.

Clearly this is much lower than the all-India average of 48 per cent or that of Maharashtra or Gujarat, and along with Kerala, is the lowest among the major states. Income of farm households from wages and salary and from non-farm business in Tamil Nadu is the second highest among all the states. Household income from cultivation has also declined. Among farm households in the

Table 6.2 Rural Non-farm Employment

| | 1993–94 | | | |
	Agriculture	Non-farm (including MFG)	MFG	All
Tamil Nadu	70.1	29.9	12.9	100.0
Gujarat	78.5	21.5	9.2	100.0
Maharashtra	82.4	17.6	5.0	100.0
All-India	78.1	21.9	7.0	100.0
	2017–18			
	Agriculture	Non-farm	MFG	All
Tamil Nadu	42.5	57.5	14.3	100.0
Gujarat	66.6	33.4	9.1	100.0
Maharashtra	74.5	25.5	5.4	100.0
All-India	59.4	40.6	7.8	100.0

Source: Estimated from various rounds of NSS–EUS unit-level data sets.

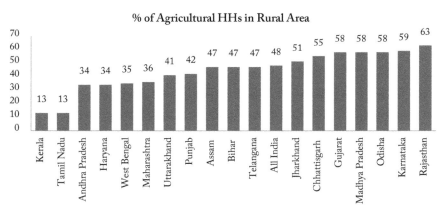

Figure 6.1 Share of Agricultural Households in Total Rural Households

Note: An 'agricultural household' is defined as a household that has received some value of produce more than INR 5,000 from agricultural activities (for example, cultivation of field crops, horticultural crops, fodder crops, plantation, animal husbandry, poultry, fishery, piggery, bee-keeping, vermiculture, sericulture and so on) and having at least one member self-employed in agriculture either in the principal status or in a subsidiary status during the last 365 days. The condition of land possession was dispensed with.

Source: NABARD All-India Rural Financial Inclusion Survey, 2016–17 (NAFIS), NABARD, 2018.

state, only about 43 per cent of the household income is from agriculture, as against 60 per cent for the rest of India (see Table 6A.3 in Appendix 6A). In fact, if we take cultivation alone, it accounts for just 27.5 per cent of agricultural households in the state as against 48 per cent for all India. Diversification into livestock accounts for a significant share of farm incomes. The percentage of cultivators in rural Tamil Nadu has also come down from 29 per cent of the rural workforce in 1981 to just 13 per cent in 2011, which is again one of the lowest shares in India (Vijayabaskar 2017). Further, about 40 per cent of the rural households live in areas classified as semi-urban[5]—having a population less than 50,000—in Tamil Nadu as against 16 per cent at the all-India level. The rural is no longer synonymous with agrarian life in Tamil Nadu, with the working population moving out of agriculture at a faster pace than in other Indian states.

If the declining share of agricultural labour in the total workforce indicates the opening up of opportunities in the non-farm sector, increased bargaining power due to new non-farm opportunities is likely to have weakened the control that the landed could exercise over agricultural labour. This is also borne out by the increase in agricultural wages. The state has seen an increase in real agricultural wages (Harriss and Jeyaranjan 2016) in spite of a relative stagnation of the agricultural economy. The recent wage data (2017) from the Labour Bureau suggests that agricultural wage rates in the state are the second highest after Kerala (See Figure 6.2).

Wage rates are also relatively higher in the non-farm sector. The average nominal daily wage in the non-farm sector, as Figure 6.3 indicates, is once again the second highest in the country after Kerala.

If we compare over time, the state has seen a faster rate of growth of real wages compared to either Gujarat or Maharashtra (see Table 6.3). Real wage has increased from INR 72 in 1993–94 (at 2011–12 prices) to INR 179 in 2011–12, an increase of 148 per cent while it increased only by 72 per cent in Gujarat and 109 per cent in Maharashtra. We also see the wage picking up from the second half of last decade. Between 2004–05 and 2011–12, the real wages witnessed a rise from INR 114 to INR 179, an increase of 57 per cent. The remarkable increase in wage rates, particularly in rural areas, is generally attributed to the spillover effect of MNREGA on the one hand, and the shortage of labour, partly due to higher participation in education, on the

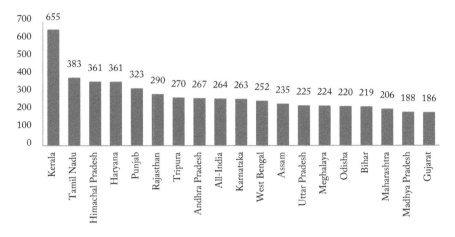

Figure 6.2 Inter-state Differences in Rural Agricultural Wages (2017)
Source: Labour Bureau (2018), Ministry of Labour & Employment.

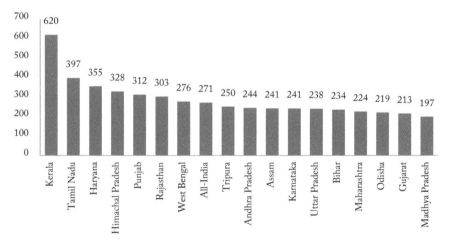

Figure 6.3 Inter-state Differences in Rural Non-agricultural Wages (2017)
Source: Labour Bureau (2018), Ministry of Labour & Employment.

other (Mehrotra et al. 2014). The demand for workers in the non-farm sector, particularly in states like Tamil Nadu, too, is likely to have played a role.

This diversification out of agriculture has also importantly been accompanied by relatively lower wage inequality between rural and urban areas (see Table 6.3). The ratio of rural to urban wage—a measure of disparity—is

Table 6.3 Trends in Wage Disparities (in Per Cent)

	1993–94	1999–2000	2004–05	2009–10	2011–12
	Rural–Urban Ratio Comparison				
Tamil Nadu	50.4	52.9	46	52	55.3
Gujarat	48.1	42.5	43.4	40.9	49.7
Maharashtra	30.5	35.1	34.8	27.8	38.5
All-India	41.1	41.4	41.4	39.6	45.4
	Rural Wages				
	1993–94	1999–2000	2004–05	2009–10	2011–12
Tamil Nadu	72	108	114	151	179
Gujarat	85	103	112	119	146
Maharashtra	80	102	120	135	168
All-India	75	98	119	112	171

Source: Estimated from various rounds of NSS–EUS unit-level data sets.

not only higher as compared to other states but also improving over time indicating that the rural labour markets are getting better integrated with urban labour markets. This diversification has also been relatively inclusive in terms of caste. The share of Dalit households in agriculture is 37 per cent in Tamil Nadu as against 68 per cent in Gujarat, 57 per cent in Maharashtra and 47 per cent at the all-India level. Their dependence on agricultural labour has also come down. The percentage of Dalits working as agricultural labourers declined from 71 per cent in 1993–94 to 24 per cent in 2017–18. The corresponding figures for non-Dalits in the state are 32 per cent and 14 per cent, respectively. What we see therefore is a trend of Dalits moving away from being agricultural labourers and accessing increased job opportunities outside agriculture. A section of them have also become cultivators as we pointed out in the previous section.

Data also suggests that within the non-farm sector, Dalits in the state have been able to access a relatively higher share of 'regular salaried' jobs, an indicator of better quality jobs (Table 6A.2). Twenty-four per cent of Dalit households held regular salaried jobs in rural Tamil Nadu as against 20 per cent among non-Dalits. The corresponding figure for Dalits in the rest of India is about 12 per cent (see Table 6A.2. This is indeed significant though we are aware that 'regular, salaried' jobs may not always imply better quality jobs. We therefore also traced the educational background of salaried workers. 'Graduates accounted for 32 per cent (see Table 6.4) of such salaried Dalit worker households which is similar to that of non-Dalits suggesting that education has indeed enabled mobility of Dalits into relatively better quality jobs.[6] The remaining Dalits are engaged in casual jobs in the rural non-farm sector. Dalits employed under this category have gone up from 12 per cent in 1993–94 to 20 per cent in 2017–18 while the corresponding figures for non-Dalits are 13 per cent and 19 per cent, respectively. Thus, a section of Dalits is reducing the economic distance between them and the non-Dalits in rural Tamil Nadu, at least those occupying economically and socially lower rungs of the rural hierarchy. This, as recent episodes of caste violence suggest, poses anxieties among sections of other caste groups.[7] In sum, Dalits are a lot less dependent on the landed non-Dalits for livelihoods with a section of them entering into relatively remunerative jobs in the non-farm economy. While the educational mobility of Dalits is a trend that is visible across India,[8] it is much sharper in Tamil Nadu.

To understand the extent to which labour relations have been democratised in rural Tamil Nadu, it is worth recalling the extent to which labour relations were caste-hierarchical in the past. Besides being agricultural labourers for daily wages, Dalits historically worked as *panaiyal* or *padial* (attached labour) for landlords—a tradition of semi-servitude in this region that can be witnessed in both the colonial and postcolonial period. The system of *padial* tied labour to land and the landlord's family. *Padial* did not have mobility and she or he could not work on others' land. She/he was paid in kind usually

Table 6.4 Educational Status of Rural Workers (in Per Cent)

	Salaried Workers		All Workers	
	SCs	Non-SCs	SCs	Non-SCs
Illiterate	11.8	7.5	27.6	24.7
Primary and Middle	31.5	33	46.8	47.5
Secondary and Higher Secondary	24.6	27.7	15.2	17.5
Graduate and Above	32.2	31.8	10.4	10.3

Source: Estimated from NSS–Periodic Labour Force Surveys (PLFS) unit-level data sets.

through food grains. As Gilbert Slater, who pioneered village studies in India, defines it:

> ... 'padial' is a sort of serf, who has fallen into hereditary dependence on a landowner by debt ... Such a loan never is repaid, but descends from one generation to another; and the padials themselves are transferred with the creditor's land when he sells it or dies (Cited in Harriss, Jeyaranjan and Nagaraj 2010: p. 55).

Padial is different from daily agricultural labour. While agricultural labour was also paid in kind through food grains, she or he was not tied to land or the landlord's family permanently. The system of *padial* continued as late as the 1980s. Guhan and Mencher (1983a, 1983b) observe the presence of 36 *padial*s working largely in households of persons belonging to the dominant caste of the village they studied. Harriss, Jeyaranjan and Nagaraj (2010) who visited those villages in 2008 observe that while the system of *padial* had vanished, there are still some who are engaged in such jobs though with better remuneration. Given this history of such limited mobility and strong bonds of dependence on the landowning castes, economic diversification in rural Tamil Nadu has helped weaken these dependent relations and improved livelihoods for Dalits.

The question therefore is what made this diversification possible? Standard explanations for non-farm employment are broadly two-fold (Davis et al. 2009). One source of expansion is rooted in agricultural dynamism which allows for surplus to be transferred to investments in the non-agricultural sector, particularly in agro-processing, trade in inputs and output, repair and maintenance of assets and infrastructure related to agricultural production and trade. The other mode of diversification is distress-induced. While agro-processing has contributed to non-farm dynamism, the state has witnessed more penetration of other modern manufacturing activities.

RURAL MANUFACTURING AND INFRASTRUCTURE

At 14 per cent, the share of manufacturing in the total rural workforce is one of the highest in the country (see Table 6.2). Rural Tamil Nadu has a sizeable number of units. There are 5,036 units with 20 or more workers, higher than the 3,356 factories in Gujarat and 3,075 in Maharashtra. The share of rural manufacturing units in total manufacturing in the state is about 41 per cent in Tamil Nadu as against 31 per cent in Gujarat and 34 per cent in Maharashtra (Economic Census 2013–14). It is, therefore, plausible to argue that manufacturing is an important source of productive employment in rural areas in the state (Sarkar and Karan 2005). The reduced gap between average rural and urban wage rates may also be because of such penetration. Though construction is the biggest employer of rural labour after agriculture, the relatively higher wages in construction in the state (Government of Tamil Nadu 2017) suggest that wage rates are influenced by demand across such sectors.

In addition to this process, two more variables shape the rise of the non-farm sector in the state: rural transport and electricity infrastructure. As we discussed in the previous chapter, a significant increase in the spread and development of the road network, particularly 'minor' roads has enabled intra- and inter-state mobilities of people, goods and services. The percentage of minor roads to total roads increased from 47 in 1960–61 to 80 per cent in 1990–92 (Rukmani 1994). Thanks to policy interventions to build broad based road transport infrastructure and lower costs of access, the state has managed to link the rural and urban, and expanded the scope for non-farm livelihood options among rural households.

Similarly, we pointed out in the previous chapter that the state was a pioneer in rural electrification.[9] The long term-trend towards higher non-farm diversification is therefore rooted in the provisioning of rural infrastructure such as electrification and transport that allowed not only for accumulation within agriculture but also for non-agricultural activities to take off in rural areas. In addition, free power for poor households was introduced in Tamil Nadu in the 1970s. Initially, each hut (up to 200 square feet) was to be provided with a single light bulb not exceeding 40 watts under various schemes including the Jawahar Velai Vaiippu Thittam (Jawahar Employment Opportunity) and TAHDCO Kamarajar Adi Dravidar housing, which was increased to 100 watts after 2006.[10] Apart from diversification contributing to the tightening of rural labour markets and facilitating greater integration with the urban labour market, there were other policy moves that undermined traditional relations of power. Welfare interventions like the PDS not only offered freedom from hunger, but also substantially weakened relations of dependence and hierarchy. Access to food was a significant factor that tied labour to land and the landlord's family. The PDS contributed in good measure to break such ties of economic coercion.

WELFARE AND LABOUR

The state's better ability to design and implement welfare interventions like the PDS and other central schemes like MNREGA is well recognised (Vivek 2014; Drèze and Sen 2011; Vijayabaskar and Balagopal 2019). Some of these schemes are path dependent and have become irreversible given their link with electoral political appeals. The rural population has also acquired an ability to negotiate with the state over the years to ensure that such welfare schemes are implemented better. Put simply, what began as economic popular appeals have evolved to become legitimate claims of people and if the state fails to deliver such services, people resort to collective action. Srinivasan (2010) maps the process of how collective action has worked towards making public institutions more accountable and implement welfare schemes better. Here, we discuss two schemes—the PDS and MNREGA, which have direct implications for changing labour relations in rural Tamil Nadu.

MAKING OF THE PUBLIC DISTRIBUTION SYSTEM

The PDS has become an important institution in shaping and influencing the way the economy works in rural Tamil Nadu. This section explores briefly the functioning of the PDS in Tamil Nadu, its effect on rural social relations and reasons for its relative success in the state. We suggest that the PDS and its evolution in the state is intimately tied to the history of the Dravidian movement and its vision of social justice.

The DMK came into power with a promise to supply three measures of rice per rupee which was part of its election manifesto (Venkatsubramanian 2006).[11] The new DMK government declared food policy to be a central concern. The first step taken in this regard was the establishment of Tamil Nadu Civil Supplies Corporation (TNCSC) in 1972. Until then, food supply policies were designed by the union government. The state government was dependent on the central pool for food grains and had to seek the permission of the union government to procure them from other states. Guided by its commitment to state autonomy, the DMK established the TNCSC to govern supply and distribution of food grains without interference from the union government. Mirroring the union government's procurement and distribution architecture like the Food Corporation of India (FCI) at the state level, the TNCSC began to procure paddy directly from farmers, process and distribute it to various parts of the state through its transport contractors. The government established fair price shops across the state and enacted guidelines to ensure that no PDS beneficiary has to travel more than 2 kilometres to access a fair price shop. Using cooperatives as the primary instrument for extending these shops to all villages across Tamil Nadu, by 1982 there were 17,536 fair price shops in the state.

Political commitment to the PDS continued to be firm in the state even when the union government attempted to dilute it following the macro-economic reforms of the 1990s. In 1997, the union government initiated the Targeted Public Distribution System (TPDS) by introducing below poverty line (BPL) and above poverty line (APL) categories and setting differential prices for the two. The DMK government that was in power rejected the proposal and reaffirmed its commitment to a universal PDS (Venkatsubramanian 2006). The state's commitment to the programme is visible in the amount of subsidies that go into it. In its initial stage, the open market price, central price and the state procurement price within the PDS were the same for rice (Venkatasubramanian 2006). It was perhaps meant to ensure the availability of food grain more than subsidising it. The state, however, started to gradually subsidise it to the extent that the price at PDS stood at 22 per cent of the open market price (see Table 6A.4 in Appendix 6A). When the centre imposed the TPDS, the state continued the universal PDS, at times bearing the associated fiscal cost too.

CONTENT OF THE PUBLIC DISTRIBUTION SYSTEM

Along with the increased coverage, the basket of commodities provided within the PDS has also widened. Initially, the TNCSC provided rice, wheat, sugar and kerosene. Under a special PDS, it further included *tur* dal, *urad* dal, palmolein oil, fortified wheat flour, *rava* and *maida* at subsidised prices. In addition, the TNCSC also started supplying cement at concessional rates, free LPG stoves and LPG connections to poor families. Importantly, the price of essential commodities under the PDS in Tamil Nadu is much lower than the price fixed by the Government of India. The issue price of rice under the PDS as fixed by the Government of Tamil Nadu was INR 1 per kilogram during 2006–11, after which it was made completely free. This is against the Government of India's issue price of INR 3 per kilogram under the Antyodaya Anna Yojana allotment, INR 5.65 per kilogram under BPL allotment and INR 8 per kilogram under APL allotment (Venkatasubrmanian 2006).

As it is universal, the PDS has become a source of income support and social protection in the state (Drèze and Khera 2013). Drèze and Khera's study (2013) study estimates that the state offers the highest implicit subsidy through the PDS. The same study also provides estimates of the potential effect of the PDS in reducing poverty. Income transfer through the PDS accounts for about 11 per cent of the total poverty reduction in rural India whereas for Tamil Nadu, the effect of the PDS in reducing poverty is as high as 44 per cent, which is again the highest among all states in India. Commitment to the PDS is reflected in its efficiency and coverage as well.

PDS: EFFICIENCY AND COVERAGE

Khera (2011b) ranks the performance of the PDS across states based on eight parameters such as degree of inclusiveness, quality of PDS grain and physical access. At 4.4 per cent, Tamil Nadu has one of the lowest diversion rates (the proportion of grain that does not reach beneficiary households) compared to the all-India average of 44 per cent. The state has an efficient tracking mechanism in place to prevent diversion (Vydhianathan and Radhakrishnan

2010). Further, card holders can also check the stocks by sending short message services (SMSs). In addition to such technical interventions, awareness and mobilisation of users of PDS also contributes to its effective and transparent functioning (Vivek 2014). As a result, both coverage of and consumption through the PDS are better compared to other major states in the country. Importantly, as Tables 6A.5 and 6A.6 in Appendix 6A indicate, this is true for households at the bottom of the economic and social hierarchy. The coverage of the PDS measured as a percentage of households availing ration cards, percentage of people availing BPL cards and access among lower castes and lower income groups are all better in Tamil Nadu than in other major states.

The success of the programme becomes more evident if we look at the actual reliance of rural households on the PDS for food consumption. The National Sample Survey Office (NSSO) consumption survey (68th round—2011–12) offers insights on the consumption of various goods (see Table 6A.6 in Appendix 6A). The monthly per capita average consumption of rice in rural Tamil Nadu is about 9 kilograms, of which, the PDS alone accounts for about 5 kilograms (56 per cent). In other words, on average more than half of the household consumption of rice comes from the PDS in the state while the corresponding figure at the all-India level is just 29 per cent (see Table 6A.6 in Appendix 6A).[12] If we disaggregate by deciles, for the bottom decile—the poorest of the poor, about 73 per cent of the consumption of rice comes from the PDS in Tamil Nadu while such category gets only 42 per cent in the rest of India. The PDS in fact accounts for more than 50 per cent of household rice consumption for 70 per cent (until the 7th decile) of households in Tamil Nadu. While the programme is universal, the poor and lower castes gain more from such universal provisioning.

Apart from its role in social protection and poverty reduction, an important outcome of the scheme is that it has enabled Dalits to be freed from food-related servitude. As pointed out earlier, food grains constitute the single most dominant factor in controlling labour. The PDS, on an average, accounts for 59 per cent of the total rice consumption of Dalit households in Tamil Nadu (see Table 6A.7 in Appendix 6A). The poorest households among Dalits (the bottom decile) actually get 74 per cent of their rice from the PDS. The PDS therefore, apart from ensuring a degree of food security, has also undermined relations of coercion. This once again shows how interventions in the domain of the economic popular have implications for the social popular domain. This undermining is likely to have been accompanied by better bargaining power apart from a rise in the reservation price of labour. The PDS in addition to ensuring freedom from hunger has also worked in conjunction with MNREGA to enhance the bargaining power of labour in the state. The next section maps this process.

THE MAHATMA GANDHI NATIONAL RURAL EMPLOYMENT GUARANTEE ACT (MNREGA)

This section explores three aspects with respect to MNREGA, a national legislation passed in 2005: its relative performance in the state, factors that made the programme successful and finally, its implications for rural power relations. The Mahatma Gandhi National Rural Employment Guarantee Act is a rural job guarantee programme funded largely by the central government through which rural households have the legal right to get up to 100 days of on-demand employment in public works every financial year. The programme is generally evaluated based on the three stipulated components in the Act: (a) at least 100 days of guaranteed wage employment to each household requesting work in a rural area, (b) every worker entitled to wages at the specified wage rate for each day's work based on minimum wages set by the government and (c) one third of the beneficiaries of the programme to be women. A study by Princeton University (Bonner et al. 2012) shows that Tamil Nadu has topped all states in ensuring women's participation in the programme and also does better on the other two dimensions.[13] Though higher women's participation may well have to do with the possibility that male workers access higher wage jobs in the rural economy and hence prefer to not seek MNREGA work, effective implementation has nevertheless made it possible for women in rural Tamil Nadu to enhance their incomes. The higher level of women's participation in Tamil Nadu is also endorsed by other micro-level studies (Drèze and Oldiges 2011; Carswell and de Neve 2014).[14]

The state also scores better with regard to caste-wise inclusiveness. As per NSSO data (2012), a larger share of lower castes participated for more than 60 days in Tamil Nadu. The macro-level success story in terms of caste inclusiveness is also borne out by evidence from micro-level studies such as by Carswell and de Neve (2014).

Interviews with bureaucrats reveal how efforts were made by the state government to ensure that persons from the lower castes, particularly Dalit households, could access MNREGA work.[15] Rather than using the village as the basis for identifying work sites, they worked with data on habitations within villages. As residential neighbourhoods in rural areas are segregated on the basis of caste, it is possible that some work sites cannot be accessed by Dalits. Further some sites may not be close enough for residents in some habitations to access. Working with habitations as the unit to identify work sites, bureaucrat respondents are of the opinion that they were able to ensure employment access across caste groups better.

Scholars agree that MNREGA has pushed up rural wages (Chandrasekhar and Ghosh 2011; Mehrotra 2013). Given the rapid sectoral changes in the structure of the state economy with negative employment generation in agriculture, MNREGA has also helped sustain the livelihoods of those in rural Tamil Nadu who cannot access the non-farm sector for work. As stated earlier, the rural real wage has doubled between 2004–05 and 2011–12 both in Tamil Nadu and at the all-India level. It can therefore be argued that such welfare interventions do enhance bargaining power in the rural labour market. Though the number of days of employment has been falling in agriculture, a combination of investments in education, demand from the non-farm sector, a universal PDS and MNREGA employment has pushed agricultural wages up as well. Such interventions therefore not only effect changes in rural labour markets but, as Carswell and de Neve (2014) point out, can also contribute to a progressive shift in social relations and empower historically marginalised caste groups in rural areas.

As in the case of PDS, the relative success of the programme in the state is definitely in part due to the presence of an efficient bureaucratic–administrative mechanism for its monitoring and implementation (Abraham 2016). But as a senior bureaucrat who was in charge of implementing the programme clarified, 'It is only because of the political will that we are able to implement better. Without the political leaders giving us direction, we would not be in a position to implement.'[16] Leveraging this programme to seek electoral support, as in the case of other welfare measures, has therefore contributed to populist politics in the state. Further, awareness has also led to increased public demand for employment. Often, the administrative mechanism has been forced to meet the heightened public expectation due to collective action by people at the ground level.[17] Vivek (2014) argues that the reductions in caste inequalities due to social movements the state has witnessed for a century have expanded the 'substantive freedom of lower caste groups', changed the unequal social norms and influenced institutions to deliver better. In other words, while lower-caste mobilisation has led to better implementation of programmes like MNREGA and the PDS, better implementation in turn contributes to expanding the substantive freedom of the poor and lower castes in rural areas. If the PDS worked to free labour from food-related dependence on landlords, MNREGA has certainly worked in setting a reserve wage and freeing them from dependency on landowners and petty capitalists in rural Tamil Nadu.

CONCLUSION

Rural Tamil Nadu is arguably the least agrarian in the country with the exception of Kerala. While this transformation is in line with the Dravidian vision of moving the subaltern out of caste bound traditional occupations, limits to structural transformation also imply that those who are unable to make the transition have to be provided with a degree of social protection. The analysis clearly shows that the state has not only seen greater economic transformation in rural areas, but such transformation has also been accompanied by improvements in the well-being of people and undermining of traditional labour and land relations. Contrary to popular perception, rural land has indeed been transferred to backward castes and to a lesser extent to Dalits. The non-farm sector has acquired a predominant role in providing opportunities in rural Tamil Nadu. It has undermined rural wage relations, offered a degree of mobility for the lower castes and supplemented farm incomes for the lower classes of farmers. Such diversification only affirms the 'post-agrarian' character of the state. State intervention through infrastructure, education and welfare has only accelerated such transformations. If rural–urban connectivity through roads and transport opened up new opportunities and widened access to the world, the network of primary health centres (PHCs), mid-day meals for school children and education for all contributed to building the capabilities of individuals. Economic popular welfare interventions such as the PDS and MNREGA have not only worked to cushion the rural poor from economic shocks but have crucially freed lower castes from social bondage and weakened hierarchical labour relations between the landed and the landless. If promotion of the rural non-farm sector opened up opportunities for the mobility of lower castes, state welfare interventions equipped them to participate in the market and negotiate with the state. Mobilisation that sought to undermine status based inequality and populist policy interventions in response have therefore not only improved socio-economic conditions of lower castes in rural Tamil Nadu, but have also improved the terms on which they could participate in the labour market.

APPENDIX 6A

Table 6A.1 Distribution of Rural Households by Size Class (Landholdings)—All-India

	Marginal (up to 1)	Small (1–2)	Semi-medium (2–5)	Medium (5–10)	Large (10 and Above)	All	Average Size Holding
Size of Landholding (in Hectare)							
1970–71	50.6	19.1	15.2	11.3	3.9	100.0	2.3
1980–81	56.4	18.1	14.0	9.1	2.4	100.0	1.8
1985–86	57.8	18.4	13.6	8.1	2.0	100.0	1.7
1990–91	59.4	18.8	13.1	7.1	1.6	100.0	1.6
1995–96	61.6	18.7	12.3	6.1	1.2	100.0	1.4
2000–01	62.9	18.9	11.7	5.5	1.0	100.0	1.3
2005–06	64.8	18.5	10.9	4.9	0.8	100.0	1.2
2010–11	67.1	17.9	10.0	4.2	0.7	100.0	1.2
2015–16	68.5	17.7	9.5	3.8	0.6	100.0	1.1
Area under Control of Different Sizes							
1970–71	9.0	11.9	18.5	29.8	30.9	100.0	2.3
1980–81	12.0	14.1	21.2	29.6	23.0	100.0	1.8
1985–86	13.4	15.6	22.3	28.6	20.1	100.0	1.7
1990–91	15.0	17.4	23.2	27.0	17.3	100.0	1.6
1995–96	17.2	18.8	23.8	25.3	14.8	100.0	1.4
2000–01	18.7	20.2	24.0	24.0	13.2	100.0	1.3
2005–06	20.2	20.9	23.9	23.1	11.8	100.0	1.2
2010–11	22.5	22.1	23.6	21.2	10.6	100.0	1.2
2015–16	24.2	23.2	23.7	20.0	9.0	100.0	1.1

Source: Computed from the First Agricultural Census 1970–71 to the 10th Agricultural Census 2015–16 compiled by the EPWRF.

Table 6A.2 Rural Occupational Classification of Households

	Tamil Nadu					
	SC			Non-SC		
	1993–94	2011–12	2017–18	1993–94	2011–12	2017–18
Cultivator	6.5	6.7	13.3	25.3	18.4	16.8
Self-employed	4.3	6.5	9.4	16.3	14.5	15.7
Regular Salaried		14.3	23.9		15.6	20.1
Agri-labour	0.7	49.7	24.1	31.9	29.7	13.9
Non-farm Labour	12.3	15.4	19.6	12.6	15.6	18.9
Others	6.2	7.5	9.8	14.0	6.3	14.6
All	100.0	100.0	100.0	100.0	100.0	100.0

	All-India					
	SC			Non-SC		
	1993–94	2011–12	2017–18	1993–94	2011–12	2017–18
Cultivator	20.1	19.55	26.8	43.4	37.7	39.8
Self-employed	10.7	14.2	12.3	14.4	17.1	16.3
Regular Salaried		8.54	11.5		10.5	13.6
Agri-labour	49.3	31.4	19.6	23.3	17.2	9.3
Non-farm Labour	10.1	21.28	20.3	6.8	11.1	10.3
Others	9.8	5.08	9.5	12.1	6.4	10.8
All	100.0	100.01	100.0	100.0	100.0	100.0

Source: Estimated from various rounds of NSS–EUS unit-level data sets.

Table 6A.3 Average Monthly Income (INR) from Different Sources and Consumption Expenditure (INR) per Agricultural Household for July 2012–June 2013

	Average monthly income					
States	Income from wages/ salary	Net receipt from cultivation	Net receipt from farming of animals	Net receipt from non-farm business	Total income	Average monthly consumption expenditure
Tamil Nadu	2,902	1,917	1,100	1,061	6,980	5,803
Kerala	5,254	3,531	575	2,529	11,888	11,008
Andhra Pradesh	2,482	2,022	1,075	400	5,979	5,927
Telangana	1,450	4,227	374	260	6,311	5,061
Karnataka	2,677	4,930	600	625	8,832	5,889
Maharashtra	2,156	3,856	539	834	7,386	5,762
Gujarat	2,683	2,933	1,930	380	7,926	7,672
All-India	2,071	3,081	763	512	6,426	6,223

Source: The Situation Assessment Survey of Agricultural Households, NSSO (2013).

TRANSFORMING RURAL RELATIONS

Table 6A.4 PDS Subsidies

	Open Market Price	Central Issue Price		State PDS Price	Ratio of PDS Price to Open Market Price
		BPL	APL		
1978	1.6	1.5		1.6	100
1979	1.65	1.5		1.6	97
1980	2	1.65		1.6	80
1981	2.9	1.75		1.75	60.3
1982	2.71	1.88		1.75	64.6
1983	3.71	1.88		1.75	47.2
1984	3.12	1.88		1.75	56.1
1985	3.38	2.17		1.75	51.8
1986	3.52	2.31		1.75	49.7
1987	3.75	2.39		1.75	46.7
1988	4.17	2.44		1.75	42
1989	5.54	2.89		2	36.1
1990	4.37	2.89		2	45.8
1991	4.9	3.77		2	40.8
1992	5.67	4.37		2	35.3
1993	6.81	5.37		2.5	36.7
1994	6.85	5.37		3.5	51.1
1995	8.35	5.37		2	24
1996	9.15	5.37		2	21.9
1997	8.53	3.5	7	2	23.4
1998	9.09	3.5	7	2	22
1999	10.1	3.5	9.05	2	19.8
2000	10.55	5.9	11.8	3.5	33.2
2001	10.36	5.65	8.3	3.5	33.8
2002	10.69	5.65	8.3	3.5	32.7
2003	11.79	5.65	8.3	3.5	29.7

Source: Venkatasubramanian (2006).

Note: The distinction between 'below poverty line' (BPL) and 'above poverty line' (APL) was introduced only from 1997.

169

Table 6A.5 Coverage of PDS (in Per Cent)

	Poor		Non-poor		Total	
	Tamil Nadu	All-India	Tamil Nadu	All-India	Tamil Nadu	All-India
Rural	90.9	80.6	88.4	81.9	89.2	81.4
Urban	82.2	71.8	76.6	65.8	77.6	67.0

	Caste-wise Coverage of PDS				
	Tamil Nadu				
	ST	SC	OBC	Others	Total
Rural	93.7	91.3	89.0	71.6	89.2
Urban	68.4	79.2	79.4	81.6	79.4
	India				
Rural	75.6	83.0	81.3	82.0	81.0
Urban	53.0	70.1	68.8	69.3	68.8

Source: Estimated from NSS–Consumption Expenditure Survey (CES) 68thunit-level data set.

Table 6A.6 Average Per Capita Quantity Consumed in 30 Days (Kg)—Rural

MPCE_ MRP_ Decile	Tamil Nadu			All-India		
	PDS Rice	Total Rice	Share of PDS (%)	PDS Rice	Total Rice	Share of PDS (%)
0–10	5.74	7.92	72.5	2.76	6.59	42.0
10–20	5.23	8.23	63.5	2.07	6.44	1
20–30	5.58	8.82	63.2	1.97	6.43	30.6
30–40	5.12	9.04	56.6	1.83	6.32	29.0
40–50	5.12	8.90	57.5	1.63	6.14	26.5
50–60	5.21	9.37	55.6	1.83	6.26	29.2
60–70	5.49	9.65	56.9	1.58	6.03	26.2
70–80	4.55	9.42	48.3	1.60	6.12	26.1
80–90	4.42	9.66	45.8	1.38	5.79	23.8
90–100	3.48	8.87	39.2	1.21	5.80	20.8
Total	4.99	8.99	55.6	1.79	6.19	28.9

Source: Estimated from NSS–CES 68th unit-level data set.

Table 6A.7 Average Per Capita Quantity Consumed in 30 Days (Kg) for Caste Groups

MPCE_ MRP_ Decile	SC			Non-SC		
	PDS Rice	Total Rice	Share of PDS (%)	PDS Rice	Total Rice	Share of PDS (%)
0–10	5.92	7.96	74.3	5.29	8.03	65.8
10–20	5.42	8.41	64.4	5.31	8.33	63.7
20–30	5.18	9.03	57.3	4.90	8.53	57.4
30–40	5.15	8.90	57.9	4.69	8.55	54.9
40–50	5.76	9.17	62.8	4.79	8.83	54.2
50–60	5.89	10.10	58.3	4.23	8.84	47.8
60–70	4.64	8.97	51.7	3.70	8.46	43.7
70–80	3.94	8.46	46.6	3.43	8.30	41.3
80–90	2.71	7.12	38.1	2.79	8.02	34.8
90–100	1.31	3.96	33.1	1.43	6.17	23.2
Total	4.91	8.37	58.7	4.01	8.21	48.8

Source: Estimated from NSS–CES 68th unit-level data set.

NOTES

1   Tenant farmers in the region were largely from the following castes—Thevars, Vanniars, Pallars, Paraiyars and Nadars, who were lower backward castes and Dalits.

2   Thirumavelan (2018) too discusses this mobilisation in the delta region.

3   The lower delta region.

4   Some understand the non-farm sector as all those income-generating activities that are not agricultural but located in rural areas (Lanjouw and Lanjouw 2001), while others also include remittances and rural infrastructures such as roads, schools and hospitals under the non-farm label as they are integral to the rural economy (Davis and Bezemer 2004).

5   The NAFIS adopted the definition of 'semi-urban' based on the RBI classification: Tier-III to Tier-VI centres with a population of less than 50,000.

6   Even if one considers all workers among Dalits, graduates constitute about 10 per cent which is the same as for non-Dalits (See Table 6.4).

7   Several recent micro studies show how this new mobility for Dalits has generated anxiety among the intermediate castes as they no longer wield

control over them in the way that they used to in the past (Pandian 2013). Further, state interventions through a slew of welfare measures, as well as urbanisation, have improved the position of Dalits vis-à-vis sections of intermediate caste groups (Anandhi and Vijayabaskar 2013).

8 The recent study by Asher, Novosad and Rafkin (2020) shows, based on historical time series data, that the upward educational mobility of Scheduled Castes (SCs) is higher than that of other social groups in India.

9 See https://recindia.nic.in/download/TAMILNADU.pdf (accessed 6 August 2019).

10 Government of Tamil Nadu, Amendment to the Schedule to the Tamil Nadu Revision of Tariff Rates on Supply of Electrical Energy Act, 1978, Notification, http://cms.tn.gov.in/sites/default/files/gos/energy3-e.pdf (accessed 3 August 2019).

11 Faced with a serious food and financial crisis, the government could manage to provide only one measure of rice per rupee.

12 A similar trend prevails even if we compare wheat consumption, although its consumption is relatively very limited in the state. The per capita average consumption of wheat in rural Tamil Nadu is just about one kilogram, and the PDS alone supplies about 80 per cent of it. On the other hand, expectedly, the per capita consumption of wheat is about 5 kilograms at the all-India level but the PDS contributes only 26 per cent of it.

13 The study compares the performance of states in India in implementing the programme using certain basic indicators such as the number of days worked, level of wages and women's participation.

14 The study by Carswell and de Neve (2014) was carried out in two villages in the Tiruppur district of Tamil Nadu.

15 Interviews were conducted for the study by Vijayabaskar and Balagopal (2019).

16 Personal interview with a senior bureaucrat closely associated with the implementation of MNREGA in Tamil Nadu, June 20, 2016.

17 Srinivasan (2010) provides a detailed account of how the programme worked at the ground level in Tamil Nadu, and what changes it brought about in the socioeconomic institutional set up at the village level.

7

POPULAR INTERVENTIONS AND URBAN LABOUR

In the last chapter we argued how traditional rural labour relations were destabilised and new opportunities opened up for lower castes due to a set of measures informed by Dravidian common-sense. Identity-based mobilisation was not merely about a politics of recognition but also a politics of redistribution that ensured a degree of material improvement in rural Tamil Nadu. In this chapter, we turn to ask: How did such mobilisation shape the material conditions of urban and non-agrarian labour in the state? Given the different institutional embedding of formal and informal labour, we make a distinction between interventions and outcomes in the two labour market segments. Establishing that the condition of labour in both formal and informal segments is relatively better than in other states characterised by industrial dynamism, we map a set of processes that made this possible. The study of Tamil Nadu's interventions in the domain of urban labour, we argue, suggests a solution to an interesting puzzle. A state which embraces economic reforms including the key tenets of labour market flexibility also does relatively better with regard to wages, working conditions and social protection for labour in both organised and unorganised sectors. Tamil Nadu's commitment to liberalisation has been accompanied by a relatively higher degree of social protection of informal workers.

Apart from secondary data and literature, the chapter also relies on detailed interviews with trade union officials, labour bureaucrats, activists and professionals employed in the software sector. We observe that the state has a relatively better share of decent jobs in the labour market, better wages and conditions of work. Importantly, while the state has not been able to counter the process of contractualisation of labour that we witness all over the country, it has nevertheless managed to contain it. The share of wages in organised manufacturing too is higher vis-à-vis other states in India. We explain such relatively better conditions for labour in terms of collective mobilisation and better embedding of the state's political regime in the interests of the lower castes and labouring classes. While Left unions and the DMK-affiliated Labour Progressive Front (LPF) played an important role in mobilisation, political regimes tend to respond to such demands better than in other industrially dynamic states. Next, based on survey data and a case study of the software services sector, we establish that affirmative action policies have made the organised labour market socially more inclusive despite persistent caste differences. We also use a micro-level intervention to show how the idea that caste-based differences in access are not because of intrinsic differences in capabilities but due to social deprivation is widely diffused in Tamil civil society. We suggest therefore that Dravidian common-sense has de-naturalised the idea of merit to an extent.

Moving to the domain of informal work, we show how welfare interventions have shaped labour well-being. Such measures have enabled the state to sustain accumulation even as it provides a degree of protection to vulnerable workers. Interventions outside the domain of work are also likely to contribute to a relatively higher reservation wage. Wage rates for urban casual labourers are not only the second highest in the country but are closer to those of regular workers. Apart from such universalist interventions outside the workplace, we emphasise the constitution of welfare boards for different segments of unorganised workers and the political processes leading to this constitution.

We begin with a comparative account of different labour market outcomes in the state and link it to the structural shifts of the state's economy in terms of employment. The second section offers insights on how jobs are distributed across castes and the role of affirmative action. In the third section, we demonstrate how labour institutions mediate labour welfare in the organised sector. The fourth section presents strategies adopted by the state to address labour market vulnerabilities generated by rapid economic transformation particularly among workers in the urban informal economy.

LABOUR MARKET: STRUCTURE AND QUALITY

STRUCTURAL CHANGE IN EMPLOYMENT

As stated in Chapter 1, the state has the most structurally diversified workforce in India. Though the diverging structures of output and employment that are evident at the national level hold true for the state as well, the growth path is distinct. Hasan, Lamba and Sen Gupta (2015) argue that Tamil Nadu is one of the few states which has achieved structural change and poverty reduction simultaneously in India. A key indicator of this structural shift, as we pointed out in the previous chapter, is the much lower share of agriculture in total employment in the state as against the all-India average. Apart from having the highest share of its workforce in manufacturing (see Table 7A.1 in Appendix 7A), the state also has a larger share of its workforce in the service sector (37 per cent) than Gujarat or Maharashtra. Combined with the high levels of urbanisation, Tamil Nadu thus has a relatively larger share of its workforce employed in the urban economy.

This structural shift in employment has been accompanied by relatively lower additions to the workforce in the last three decades thanks to the decline in fertility rate in the state[1] (see Table 7A.2 in Appendix 7A). Between 1993–94 and 2017–18, the agricultural sector has seen a withdrawal of 6.2 million from its workforce, registering one of the highest reductions in the country. This withdrawal of the workforce from agriculture started in the 1990s in Tamil Nadu whereas this began to happen only from the mid-2000s in most other states. Though this diversification has still not kept pace with diversification in incomes, the state has seen a faster diversification of its workforce in the three decades compared to all-India trends. Importantly this is true even in the case of the female labour force. Women's participation in paid employment, as Arthur Lewis (1954: p. 404) remarks, '… is one of the most notable features of economic development'. Notwithstanding the possibility of such paid employment leading to a 'double burden' for women, entry into new spaces of participation and access to independent incomes may contribute to undermining of gender hierarchies as well (Kabeer 2012).

In India, we are actually witness to a reversal of this process, with the female labour force participation rate (FLFPR) declining.[2] Despite following the national trends, not only is the overall labour force participation rate (LFPR) much higher for women in the state (Government of Tamil Nadu 2017), women workers are also engaged in a higher share of jobs in the non-farm economy. Women's participation in service and manufacturing is 64 per cent as against 44 per cent in Gujarat, 35 per cent in Maharashtra and the all-India average of 43 per cent. This sectoral shift of women away from agriculture in Tamil Nadu is significant given the larger national trend towards feminisation within agriculture (Government of India 2018b). We next turn our attention to the quality of jobs generated in the urban economy.

THE QUALITY OF URBAN EMPLOYMENT

Belying the anticipation of economic modernisation, a substantial section of the workforce in India continues to be self-employed (NCEUS 2009). Self-employment is often survival driven and tends to be higher in lower-income states.[3] The process of diversification in Tamil Nadu has been accompanied by increases in wage-led employment, both regular and casual, and much less in self-employment. The share of self-employed persons in total non-farm jobs is only 26 per cent in 2017–18, as against 38.4 per cent in Gujarat and 32.8 per cent in Maharashtra, while the all-India average is 35.6 per cent.[4] The share of casual jobs is, however, much higher in Tamil Nadu than in Gujarat or Maharashtra (see Table 7A.3 in Appendix 7A). The share of regular jobs with a stable contract and wage structure is about 46 per cent in Tamil Nadu and not too different from Gujarat or Maharashtra (see Table 7A.3 in Appendix 7A). Populist interventions in the domain of urban labour have to therefore respond to two structural constraints. First, despite having the best parameters of structural transformation, labour absorption in the non-farm sector continues to lag behind income shifts taking place across sectors. Second, regular employment with security of employment continues to account for only a small share of urban employment. While this is partly tied to macro policy shifts that tend to view labour as a cost to be minimised, the inability of the modern sector to absorb the workforce exiting agriculture on 'decent' terms should also be recognised. In the absence of adequate regular waged employment, workers are therefore more likely to be engaged in casual wage work than be self-employed. This wage-led employment, however, has implications for social policy in the state.

Based on the sectoral definition put forward by the National Commission for Enterprises in the Unorganised Sector (NCEUS) (NCEUS 2009), we compute the extent of employment generated by formal enterprises from the NSSO–EUS unit-level data.[5] Forty-seven per cent of enterprises (for industry and the services sector) in Tamil Nadu were still in the organised sector in 2017–18, higher than that in Gujarat, Maharashtra and the all-India average (see Table 7A.4 in Appendix 7A). If we go by the employment definition of informality, a greater share of the workforce within manufacturing is in the unorganised sector compared to Gujarat or Maharashtra. However, when we look at the share of informal workers in both industry and services, the state has a lower share compared to Gujarat or Maharashtra (see Table 7A.4). Nevertheless, only around 23 per cent of the workforce is formally employed indicating the dominance of informality in the labour market and consequent vulnerability. Notwithstanding such high levels of informal employment, the state still has a relatively better wage share in organised manufacturing.

TRENDS IN WAGES AND WAGE SHARES

The wage share in national income has been falling across the world due to increases in capital intensity as well as a policy regime that privileges labour market flexibility (OECD and ILO 2015). Going by the wage share in organised manufacturing in the state, Tamil Nadu is no exception (see Figures 7.1 and 7.2). In relative terms, however, the state has a higher share of wages in gross value added (GVA) in the factory sector (Government of India 2014) than most states in India.

The average wage share in GVA for the period 2008–15 is 22 per cent in the state which is about twice that of Gujarat (10 per cent) and Maharashtra (12 per cent). The share of total emoluments in GVA too is the highest.[6] This higher share accruing to labour in the state can be attributed to two possible factors. First, wage levels are higher because of lower levels of contractualisation and the better bargaining strength of labour. Or, it may have to do more with the

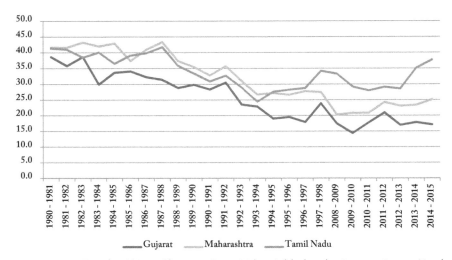

Figure 7.1 Trend in Wage Share in Gross Value Added in the Factory Sector (Total Emoluments)

Source: Estimated from *ASI* data series, EPWRF.

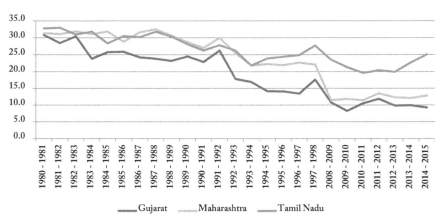

Figure 7.2 Trend in Wage Share in Gross Value Added in the Factory Sector (Per Cent Wage and PF Alone)

Source: Estimated from *ASI* data series, EPWRF.

sectoral composition of manufacturing in the state, with a higher share of labour-intensive sectors. While it is true that the state has a number of labour-intensive sectors like textiles, garments and leather goods, the wage share is higher even in these sectors than in Gujarat or Maharashtra suggesting relatively better bargaining strength in the formal sector. Second, a larger share of workers in the factory sector are directly employed against the prevailing trend of contractualisation in the country. The percentage of directly employed workers in the state is 80 as compared to 62 per cent in Gujarat, 58 per cent in Maharashtra and the all-India average of 66 per cent (Kalaiyarasan 2020).

Outside the world of formal manufacturing, we find that the urban casual wage in Tamil Nadu (INR 205 in 2011–12) is one of the highest in the country and much higher compared to Gujarat or Maharashtra (see Table 7A.5 in Appendix 7A). The state has also seen a faster rate of growth of urban real wages compared to the other two states. The combined (casual + regular) urban real wage has gone up from INR 144 in 1993–94 (at 2011–12 prices) to INR 323 in 2011–12, an increase of 125 per cent while it increased by only 57.7 per cent in Gujarat and 104 per cent in Maharashtra (see Table 7A.6). Apart from better returns to labour in the organised sector as well as in the urban casual wage segment, we also find that wage inequality between the unorganised and organised segments is relatively lower than other industrially dynamic states. The ratio of the urban casual to urban regular wage rate is 55 per cent for Tamil Nadu which is higher than the 45 per cent in Gujarat, 31.5 per cent in Maharashtra and 38 per cent at the all-India level. This once again suggests a role for regional labour market institutions and policy interventions. Before we examine this dimension, we highlight the caste dimensions of the organised labour market given that affirmative action has been a key plank of social justice in the state.

CASTE AND LABOUR

IDENTITY AND LABOUR IN URBAN TAMIL NADU

While caste differences in rural Tamil Nadu have been undermined over time as we demonstrated in the previous chapter, caste inequalities continue to exist in urban Tamil Nadu. If it was the rural caste elites who migrated initially responding to opportunities opened up during colonialism and Nehruvian policies, it was a new segment of elites who exited the rural areas during the economic reforms that began in the early 1990s. Together, they have cornered a disproportionate share of opportunities in the formal urban labour market. Affirmative action policies in public sector employment may have addressed this to an extent, but the privatisation of services and expansion of private sector employment since the 1990s is likely to have undermined the effectiveness of this measure. Nevertheless, affirmative action policies in the domain of higher education may have helped broad base employment in the private sector.

Going by occupational categories of the NSSO, about 68 per cent of caste elites are in salaried jobs as against 50 per cent among the SCs and 48 per cent among OBCs (see Table 7A.7 in Appendix 7A). There are also variations within salaried jobs if we disaggregate by the educational level of workers and their skill-based occupations. About 72 per cent of the salaried among the elites are graduates as against 45 per cent among OBCs and 30 per cent among Dalits. If we take all of them as workers, 37 per cent of workers among the elites are graduates while it is only 19 per cent among OBCs and 13 per cent among SCs (see Table 7A.8 in Appendix 7A). Thus, while entry into salaried employment has been broad-based, earlier entry into urban spaces and probable use of social networks[7] to 'hoard opportunities' (Tilly 1998) or access to premium private educational institutions continue to provide elites with an advantage over lower castes in accessing quality employment.

Observations on skill-based occupations too affirm such caste divisions in urban Tamil Nadu. Occupational groupings are constructed from occupation categories of employment given in NSSO data. The National Classification of Occupations (NCO)-2004 provides information on skill levels and number of years of education which are helpful to categorise the occupations held by workers. We have grouped occupations into three categories: professional, skilled and unskilled. We find that caste does play a role in skill formation and entry into high productivity jobs. In 2017–18, around 63 per cent of the salaried among elites were found to have been employed as professionals while this share was only 36 per cent among OBCs and 24 per cent for SCs. If we take all workers, 58 per cent of elites are professionals while it is 31 per cent among OBCs and 17 per cent among SCs (see Table 7A.9 in Appendix 7A).

However, despite such inter-caste differences in access to the state's premium labour market, OBCs and SCs in Tamil Nadu are relatively better off across all these parameters—nature of jobs, educational level of workers and skill-based occupations—compared to the all-India level. The percentage of graduates among the salaried class of SCs in Tamil Nadu is 30 as against 23.7 per cent at the all-India level. Even if we take all workers, 13 per cent of SCs are graduates in Tamil Nadu as compared to 4 per cent in the rest of India. When we disaggregate by skill levels, about 24 per cent of SCs are professionals in the salaried category as against 22 per cent in the rest of India. This suggests that while economic modernisation has led to a degree of mobility among lower castes within the urban labour market, it has not been able to unsettle caste hierarchies as much as in rural Tamil Nadu despite increased access to higher education among the lower castes in the state.

To illustrate that lower castes have indeed been able to access higher segments of the urban labour market, we provide a case study of employment in the software sector to demonstrate how affirmative action policies have rendered the labour market relatively more inclusive through incorporation of employees from lower-social-status households in Tamil Nadu.

CASTE INCLUSIVENESS IN THE SOFTWARE SECTOR

Though software and IT-enabled services (ITeS) have been key sources of quality employment generation in post-reform India, social exclusion plagues the IT labour market. Given the requirements of knowledge of English and tertiary education, it has been pointed out that the growth of this sector may aggravate labour market inequities given the wide disparities in access to tertiary and English language education across castes and regions. Though there is no large-scale data on caste-based distribution of the workforce in the IT sector, micro-level studies by and large affirm the predominance of upper castes in the workforce (Rothboeck, Vijayabaskar and Gayathri 2001; Upadhya 2007) across the country. In fact, Upadhyay brilliantly argues how the sector deploys a narrative of 'merit' to generate such exclusivity. In this section, we discuss the impacts of reservation in higher education in the case of Tamil Nadu. The state not only has a longer history of reservation in higher education, but importantly, has been at the forefront of the IT sector's growth in India along with Karnataka, Andhra Pradesh and the NCR. With regard to the growth of the software sector, the state accounts for nearly 14 per cent of the total exports from the country in addition to a major share of business process outsourcing (BPO) exports (Dubbudu 2017).

While the dominance of upper castes in terms of magnitude persists, it is our contention that the long history of reservation for OBCs and Dalits in higher education has made a difference. The expansion of the IT sector has led to a growing demand for technically qualified engineers to undertake programming and coding tasks. Tamil Nadu, as we indicate in Chapter 3, accounts for the highest share of engineering seats in the country.[8] Sixty-nine per cent of seats in government colleges and aided colleges are reserved for OBCs, the most backward castes (MBCs) and SCs/STs. In private colleges, 50 per cent of seats come under the government quota and reservation is applicable to only that share of the total number of seats. Also, 32 per cent of those enrolled in tertiary education are in technical or professional courses in Tamil Nadu as compared to 15 per cent at the all-India level. It is also fairly distributed across castes.

Apart from campus recruitment, bigger firms also recruit personnel through referrals and weekly interviews. As a result, it is difficult to get detailed data on the profile of employees though it is unlikely that only elite caste students will be recruited given the large share of students from lower castes entering into these colleges. We therefore rely on information provided by insiders with long-term experience in the industry. Since 2008, we have conducted interviews with 12 middle- and senior-level professionals in the software sector in the state who have studied in Tamil Nadu. Out of the 12 informants, all except one are middle-level managers in software firms located in Chennai. The exception is a manager working in a multinational corporation (MNC) in Coimbatore.[9] Informants acknowledge that there has been a change in the social profile of entrants into the software sector since the early 2000s. Early entrants into the software sector from Tamil Nadu have been primarily from the upper castes. A testimony to that is their overwhelming presence in top managerial positions which continues to this day. One informant working in a leading Indian IT firm in Chennai said that at least 80 to 90 per cent of such positions were occupied by caste elites. As we go down the hierarchy to the middle levels of management, the profile does change. Among the 30 project managers he knows, he can recall at least 12 who are caste elites. Of the remaining, he knows for sure that six of them are not. In his own project team, a largish team consisting of 24 members, 10 are from Tamil Nadu. Of these, three are elites, and the rest he felt, going by their names, should belong to the non-elite castes. Identifying Dalits' share is almost impossible, he feels. According to another key informant, caste elites may not account for more than 20 per cent of the workforce at the lower and intermediate levels in her firm.

Other informants, including a human resources (HR) consultant, concur on the entry of personnel from smaller towns of Tamil Nadu and from less affluent backgrounds. Often, they belong to the first generation in their families to have accessed tertiary education. Though informants point out a similar social broad-basing in the case of recruits from undivided Andhra Pradesh, evidence for such opening out is lacking in the case of recruits from north India. According to one key informant, a good share of colleagues from the north are vegetarian, indicative of their high-caste status. Apart from Chennai, Coimbatore is emerging as a destination for software service investments among tier-II cities in the country. A project manager in a leading MNC there says that out of his project team of around 120, most are Tamil speakers of whom none are from an elite background to the extent that he is aware of. He further remarks that many are first generation graduates who often talk about how but for Periyar and the Dravidian movement, they wouldn't have got this opportunity. In fact, the emergence of Coimbatore as a hub for software is actually owing to the availability of labour from such backgrounds as metropolitan elites may not prefer to work in smaller cities.

As we stated earlier in chapter 3, there has been a steady reduction in the difference between cut-off marks for entry into technical and medical education for different caste groups. However, the software sector continues to erect high barriers to entry through its emphasis on consistent performance from the 10th standard onwards. A minimum of 70 per cent is required in the 10th, 12th and undergraduate examinations. Such requirements pose considerable barriers for students from lower-caste backgrounds as according to the educationist Anandakrishnan, it is not easy for students from non-elite backgrounds to do well consistently given the vulnerabilities they confront. He further points out that what the IT employers do not comprehend is the trainability of graduates from less privileged backgrounds who have much less access to soft skills that are demanded by the industry. Students from rural and lower socioeconomic backgrounds tend to access the near-free education provided through the public education system. This system offers instruction to a large extent in Tamil, with English being taught only as a second language. Even when English is the medium of instruction, the social milieu does not allow for acquiring skills to communicate in English. The software sector, catering to global markets, places a premium on soft skills like communication and interaction skills, primarily in English.

This demand for soft skills obviously creates a tremendous entry barrier for students from less affluent households. K. B. Chandrasekhar, a leading entrepreneur in the Silicon Valley and an alumnus of Anna University, Chennai, however, points to the possibility of imparting soft skills to students from such backgrounds through an interesting exercise he was a part of at Anna University.[10] An external HR trainer was hired for six weeks to train 50 students from colleges located in the most backward areas of Tamil Nadu, who were in the third year of their engineering course in the University. They were trained to speak about themselves for a minimum of 30 seconds and 87 per cent of them cleared the test at the end of the training. The students who received the training have been asked to carry forward this system by contributing to the training of future students. Thanks to the Dravidian movement, he says that Tamil Nadu has come to be one of the most socially progressive states offering a higher degree of mobility to the lower castes. The shift to knowledge-based growth has enabled children from these castes to aspire higher. This is one reason, he argues, why tier-2 cities are attracting software investments. Such training in soft skills for socially less privileged students is also now being offered by the state government though the impacts of these measures in terms of access to employment are not clear.[11] The government has also introduced soft skills courses in all state universities as a part of regular degree courses in addition to initiating steps to set up separate finishing schools in the state.[12] This shows how the idea of merit is called into question within Tamil civil society. Public policies such as affirmative action have therefore addressed pre-entry barriers in the labour market to an extent. Supply-side interventions, like reservations for the marginalised castes, have made a difference, albeit insufficient, in rendering the labour market more inclusive. Other interventions in the labour market in response to labour mobilisations too have led to a relatively better distribution of gains in the organised labour market.

LABOUR INSTITUTIONS AND ORGANISED LABOUR

As per the Indian Constitution, labour regulation comes under the concurrent list, allowing state governments to legislate on certain matters. Macro deregulation measures since the early 1990s emphasise the need for labour market flexibility as a key attribute for building competitive production structures and attracting private investments. As a result, several regulations that have sought to protect labour in the past have been called into question. Among the most contentious is the Industrial Disputes Act (IDA), 1947, that deals with closure, lay off and retrenchment of workers in industries employing 100 or more workers. The other is the use of contract labour under the Contract Labour (Regulation and Abolition) Act, 1970. Over the last three decades, there has been a shift against workers both in the interpretation of these acts in courts and on the ground across India (Gopalakrishnan 2015). But, it does appear that the state has ensured relatively better protection for labour. Shyam Sundar (2010) shows that contractualisation has been relatively low in the state. Trade union activists point out that it is their mobilisation and claim-making, which in turn pressured the government to act in favour of labour, that have made this possible.[13] We illustrate this with two pieces of evidence.

One important intervention undertaken by the state is in amending the IDA in 1982 by inserting Section 10B (Sundar 2010).[14] The amendment empowers the state to offer interim relief in industrial disputes, particularly for workers, until the grievances are settled. Employers have to accept the terms and conditions including payments to workers based on the order issued from the Labour Court or Industrial Tribunal. It also offers discretionary powers to the government to intervene in dictating terms and conditions of work to both employers and workers. Interviews with those associated with the trade union movement in the state reveal that this allowed workers to often use this provision to force the state to act in their favour. One instance cited by them is the lockout in 2007 by Madras Rubber Factory Limited in response to labour unrest. Responding to the workers' demands, the government passed a resolution in the state assembly declaring that it would nationalise the factory if the management did not reopen it.[15] Though such instances are not many, the labour department does play a relatively more effective role in conciliation and negotiation.

Another instance pertains to reliance on apprentices. At present, several firms appoint apprentices in large numbers who are replaced with a fresh set once the period of apprenticeship is over. While the Apprentices Act is meant to facilitate skill formation, firms often use this law to recruit a set of workers on short-term contracts and at lower costs. In response to the pressure from trade unions, the state has recently amended the provisions to restrict the extent of employment of apprentices in factories.[16] While this may not reflect the actual levels of apprentices in specific firms as unionisation is not evenly distributed across firms, it nevertheless provides them with legal scaffolding to negotiate with the management.

Such interventions pose the question: What makes them possible, especially when the Left parties are politically marginal in the state? We suggest that this negotiation between workers and the state becomes possible due to a specific history of political and labour mobilisation in Tamil Nadu. It can be understood partly by the distinction that Sennett (2012) makes between two modes of building solidarity across the poor—the social Left and the political Left. The former is a bottom–up approach that helps build an ethos of community and cooperation whereas the latter emphasises engagement for capture or sharing of political power. Social Left mobilisation is likely to be concerned with making claims in the domain of reproduction such as education, health and housing while the latter is concerned with broader political change. To begin with, unionisation is more widespread in Tamil Nadu compared to other industrially dynamic states. While the Left parties are politically marginalised, their trade unions do have a presence in the state. Overall union density is also relatively higher, with more membership and spread across sectors. According to the NSS 2011–12, about 27 per cent of workers in the manufacturing sector reported having unions in their factories. This is higher than the 19 per cent in Gujarat, 22 per cent in Maharashtra and the 19 per cent national average. If we take the organised sector alone, the share goes up to 75 per cent (Sundar 2010).

An activist working with the Maruti Workers Union in Haryana[17] also observes that workers are more politicised, with connections to political parties, and as a result are able to bargain better with capital through such networks unlike in other states, particularly ones ruled by the Congress or the Bharatiya Janata Party (BJP). Labour mobilisation is therefore embedded within larger political mobilisations in the state. Another trade union activist with exposure to national-level trends points out that the probability of a member of the legislative assembly (MLA) or member of parliament (MP) intervening in labour disputes is high in Tamil Nadu. Besides electoral compulsions, MLAs and MPs are forced to take more pro-labour positions as there is always scope for dialogue with both the Dravidian parties. Trade unions reportedly use leaders from the DMK to voice their grievance if the AIADMK is in power and vice versa. As a result, the spaces of negotiation for labour tend to be larger. The activist working with the Maruti Workers Union points out that it is almost impossible to get a politician to speak in their favour in Haryana and contrasts it with the situation in Tamil Nadu. There are union leaders in major parties in the state who occupy or have occupied prominent positions within these parties.[18]

Further, while having multiple unions is seen to fragment and dissipate bargaining power, Tamil Nadu's experience suggests otherwise. Data on government-verified union membership suggests that the LPF, affiliated to the DMK, accounts for about one-third (34 per cent) of the total union members followed by the Centre of Indian Trade Unions (CITU): 14 per cent, Indian National Trade Union Congress (INTUC): 12 per cent and All India Trade Union Congress (AITUC): 9.5 per cent, while other regional unions account for about 17 per cent. Often workers have membership in more than one union (see Table 7A.11 in Appendix 7A). The link to political parties has made their bargaining more effective. While there maybe competition between unions within specific factories, this works to the workers' advantage. For example, when the DMK is in power, working through their union tends to yield results. Apart from political competition and embedding within party political mobilisation, there is also a difference with regard to the social embeddedness of trade unionism in the state.

Politicisation through identity-based mobilisation has also worked to create broad-based labour solidarities. Trade unions often come together in the state in support of non-labour struggles. Their support for youth protesting against the ban on *jallikattu* is one such example (Ravikumar 2017). Importantly, as the experience of the formation of the first trade union for software employees shows, identity-based mobilisation has also led to the emergence of collective bargaining institutions. The Forum for IT Employees (FITE) became the first registered trade union for workers in the IT sector in the country following its recognition by the court.[19] Originally formed to mobilise software employees to protest against the massacre of Tamils in Sri Lanka in 2009, they have since then moved on to address issues such as sexual harassment and finally to issues of the broader rights of workers. When leading software firms retrenched workers in 2014, they mobilised software employees across the country and formed the first recognised union to represent them. Interestingly, this claim-making gets recognised immediately in the policy domain. In the DMK's election manifesto for the 2019 parliamentary elections, the party promised to work with the union government to form a tripartite committee to address the grievances of workers at the state and national levels.[20] Such multiple mobilisations for economic and social issues also created better awareness among the workers, an option not available for workers in many states, says a trade union activist.[21]

Another possible factor according to union activists is their strategies. They tend to be less militant and make more incremental demands. According to a prominent CITU union leader, since unions are known to be less disruptive of production, employers tend to be more open to negotiation. Another trade unionist observes that workers have developed a culture of appealing to the government and challenging capital in the court rather than confronting the management on the shop floor. Such an approach, according to him is an accumulated outcome of a long tradition where labour is not completely alienated from the political system nor seen by the system as an obstacle to industrial development. While such mobilisations and policy response within the domain of organised labour market have contributed to better conditions of work, the growing precariousness of employment cannot be denied. As we argued earlier, rights-based intervention with certain redistributive content—wage share, nature of the work contract and conditions of work—articulated by trade unions broadly faces two constraints—structural and electoral. When unable to further its intervention in these domains, the state shifts its focus from the social popular to the economic popular—through a strategy of welfare interventions outside the workplace. We argue that welfare interventions outside the workplace have also allowed for labour to offset such labour market vulnerabilities.

One such major intervention is social protection—creation of welfare boards for informal workers within the sectors in which they work. In the next section, we map the evolution and impact of welfare boards.

WELFARE INTERVENTIONS

WELFARE BOARDS AND INFORMAL LABOUR

A welfare board is a tripartite institution that is funded by employers, states and informal workers. The state now has 17 welfare boards under the Ministry of Labour and another 17 boards working under specific departments. While the first board for construction workers was formed in 1994, the Tamil Nadu Manual Workers Welfare Board was established in 1999. Subsequently, the state has added another 15 industry-specific welfare boards in the last two decades.[22] This recognition of the need to protect unorganised sector workers predates interventions at the all-India level by more than a decade. It was only in 2009 that the Supreme Court issued an order for the establishment of similar boards for construction workers across the country (Gopalakrishnan 2015). As Agarwala (2013) elaborates, the state has been a pioneer along with Kerala in innovating the welfare board as a social security institution for informal sector workers.[23]

The idea of welfare boards has a long history in the state, says Mr Shanmugam, currently an MP and president of the LPF. He recalls how in 1974, the then Chief Minister Karunanidhi took issue with trade unionists for their treatment of informal workers. He is apparently said to have remarked that it is not fair that unions are recruiting only those who can afford to pay *santha* (member's contribution) as there are large sections of labour who cannot! Mr Shanmugham, narrates how the design and constitution of welfare boards has evolved over time, reflecting in part a shift from the domain of the social popular towards the economic popular. This in turn is linked to the changing nature of modern production and resultant global narrative on informality (Sanyal 2007). Informal labour protection was initially perceived in terms of addressing traditional demands of workers such as minimum wages and conditions of work. At present it is more about social security benefits such as healthcare, education, pension and other non-work related benefits.

While the legal basis of welfare begins with the enactment of the Tamil Nadu Manual Workers (Regulation of Employment and Conditions of Work) Act by the AIADMK in 1982, the idea goes back to the first DMK government in the 1970s, when the government constituted a committee to prepare a comprehensive report on the condition of informal workers in 1975.[24] While trade unions such as the Tamil Maanila Kattida Thozhilalar Panchayat Sangam (TMKTPS) and the Beedi workers' unions did mobilise informal workers to make demands on the state, the committee was more an initiative from the government—a fact that union activists acknowledge. The idea of a union for unorganised workers was relatively new in India.[25] As stated earlier, initial concerns were around issues like minimum wages and better conditions of work as it was believed at that point that informality is a transitory phenomenon, and workers in this segment would eventually become formalised.

Following the report prepared by the committee, the AIADMK government led by M. G. Ramachandran enacted the Tamil Nadu Handloom Workers (Conditions of Employment and Miscellaneous Provisions) Act, 1981. To expand protection to all workers, the government went on to enact the Tamil Nadu Manual Workers (Regulation of Employment and Conditions of Work) Act in 1982. The Construction Workers Act was passed in 1984 while the Construction Workers Welfare Board was formed in 1994. When it came to power in 1996, the DMK expanded the boards to cover an additional 16 unorganised sectors (see the list of boards in Table 7A.12 in Appendix 7A). It formed a second committee in May 1997 which submitted its report in 1998 after a comprehensive study of the functioning of such boards in Kerala and other parts of the country. Based on the committee's recommendations, the state created welfare boards for more sectors with the DMK government showcasing these boards as significant achievements. Not only did he take an active interest in these welfare boards,[26] Karunanidhi, who was Chief Minister at that point, personally unveiled these boards in a massive rally in Chennai in the run up to the 2001 elections, and appointed the labour minister as the head of these boards to mark their significance. A retired senior official from the Labour ministry and a member of the committee also acknowledges the political support that the DMK provided to make some important changes in the welfare boards.[27] One innovation that the DMK government introduced was to link the members registered with these welfare boards to the Chief Minister Kalaignar Insurance Scheme in 2009, a non-contributory health insurance scheme supported by the government that we mention in Chapter 4.

Two significant differences can be observed in the approaches between the two reports submitted in 1975 and 1998, respectively. First, the former focused only on non-unionised informal workers but the latter included all those who are not legally protected. Second, provisioning of welfare benefits outside the worksite was emphasised more in the latter report.[28] In other words, if the 1975 report focused on extending formal rights to informal workers, the 1998 report argued for the creation of welfare boards recognising that informality was here to stay. While the discourse on informality in the 1970s was rooted in the belief that informality is transitory, by the 1990s, particularly with the onset of reforms, informality was seen as inevitable and in fact an outcome of the development process itself (Sanyal 2007). The second report reflects this changed perspective on the informal sector.

> The five year plans have not evolved an integrated comprehensive scheme of social security for unorganized labour. The majority of the existing labour laws seek to benefit the organized sector which constitutes merely a little more than eight percent of the total 313 million workforce. A very bold policy is needed. (Government of Tamil Nadu 1998: p. 79)

As on 31 July 2019, the boards cover 43,59,728 workers registered under them. Welfare boards offer compensation for accidents at workplaces, pension, educational assistance for workers' children and marriage and maternity assistance. While the state funds most of the interventions, it also mobilises resources through cess from construction firms for the construction workers' welfare board and motor vehicle cess for the drivers' welfare board.[29] If the formation of these boards was an outcome of political intervention, better implementation can be attributed to the collective mobilisation of workers. The latter also helped to expand the benefits provided under these boards.

In response to a petition from workers' representatives, the boards now have 35 centres across the state to help workers access benefits more easily.[30] Micro-level studies confirm the relatively better functioning of these boards. Agarwala shows that all workers she interviewed received welfare benefits in Tamil Nadu while less than half of them received benefits in Maharashtra and only one worker in West Bengal (2013: p. 71). According to her, traditional unions refuse to recognise that a narrow class reading is insufficient to address the life chances and multiple axes of vulnerability of individuals in a stratified society. Citing the experience of West Bengal, Agarwala argues that the CPI-M's power over unions constrained the articulation of concerns of informal workers. When conventional collective bargaining strategies seem to be weakening, this route of political mobilisation has offered a degree of protection to informal workers, albeit insufficiently so. Importantly, Tamil Nadu has also created welfare boards for the differently abled and for transgenders indicating the importance of recognising other axes of vulnerabilities. It is the first state to constitute a welfare board for transgenders and also the first state to enable persons with disabilities to access MNREGA work (Government of Tamil Nadu 2017). Agarwala also points out that as members of welfare boards, workers are now in a position to make legitimate claims on the state through recognition and identity. It is important to note here that while many of the informal workers make claims as workers through their membership in welfare boards, they also continue to stake claims through caste identities in the realms of education and formal employment for the next generation. Access to caste-group-specific benefits therefore complements support provided to them as marginal, poor and informal workers. In addition, economic popular interventions for the urban poor have also allowed for a degree of protection from labour market vulnerabilities.

OTHER ECONOMIC POPULAR INTERVENTIONS AND THE URBAN POOR

In 1971, Chief Minister M. Karunanidhi created the Tamil Nadu Slum Clearance Board (TNSCB) as an agency separate from the Tamil Nadu Housing Board (TNHB) to deal specifically with the problem of slums. What the government sought to do was to provide in situ tenements for slum dwellers. Fishermen in Chennai city were one of the earliest beneficiaries of this effort to provide housing infrastructure. As a result of such measures, Royapuram in north Chennai, dominated by the fishing community, remained a bastion of the DMK for two decades because of its 'strategic accommodation of many fishermen and SCs in public tenements' (Subramanian 1999: 206). Such interventions in the domain of urban housing have, however, not expanded much, especially across other cities. Interventions since then have primarily been in the domain of food and education.

The recent NSSO consumption data shows that on average, the public distribution system (PDS) contributes about 43 per cent of the per capita consumption of rice in urban Tamil Nadu while it contributes just 15 per cent in the rest of urban India. For the poorest of the poor (the bottom 10th decile), about 66 per cent of the rice consumed comes from the PDS as against 30 per cent for the poorest in the rest of urban India. In fact, about 50 per cent of the rice consumed is still sourced from the PDS for one-third (30 per cent) of the urban population in Tamil Nadu (see Table 7A.10 in Appendix 7A). The PDS thus plays an important role in the lives of the urban poor even among those employed in the formal sector but on short-term contracts or at the bottom end of such markets. Such welfare interventions outside specific sectors have an important role to play in shaping the labour market outcomes of industrial growth in the state. This is particularly significant given the shift in accumulation strategies towards competing for global markets through low-cost labour among other elements. We illustrate this through a case study of labour in the Tiruppur garment cluster in western Tamil Nadu when it was affected by the global recession of 2008–09.[31]

The Tiruppur cluster is the single largest node for garment production in the country employing anywhere between 4,00,000 and 5,00,000 workers directly and several lakhs indirectly. Most workers during the 1990s and 2000s were migrants from either the immediate rural hinterlands or from poorer regions of rural Tamil Nadu employed invariably through contractors or through short-term piece-work-based contracts by exporters. The cluster has always been marked by a high entry and exit of firms as they are confronted with unsteady demand in the global market. When the global crisis hit the cluster in 2008–09, several firms cut down the number of work hours as well as days of work. Such reduction needs to be juxtaposed against the above average hours of work that workers put in under 'normal' conditions. According to a study on the impact of the recession on employment, about 40,000 to 1,00,000 workers had also completely lost their jobs by December 2008 (Jha 2009: p. 12).

Confronted with such job losses, rather than stake claims against retrenchment, workers sought to negotiate this vulnerability by falling back on rural areas for their basic entitlements through reverse migration. Workers were less severely affected because of their ability to access welfare entitlements like the PDS and MNREGA employment outside the workspaces. Interestingly, exporters had cried foul earlier when the MNREGA scheme was implemented fearing an increase in wage costs. However, when they were hit by recession, they and sections of the government too suggested that a similar urban employment guarantee scheme should be implemented so as to ensure that sectors like theirs can access labour and also prevent out-migration.[32] Welfare interventions outside the domain of work therefore allow for firms in the organised sector to rely on flexible labour markets without being encumbered by the need to provide for the social protection of labour. This once again highlights the interplay between shifts in the nature of populist interventions and macro shifts in policy regimes. When the latter does not allow for rights-based claims within the workplace, economic popular interventions outside the domain of work become attractive. Apart from helping sustain such a flexible workforce in the organised sector, welfare interventions have also contributed to bettering conditions for the urban self-employed or casual labour.

As in the case of rural areas, welfare interventions are likely to have contributed to not only higher real incomes but also to improved bargaining power by increasing the reservation wage. Heyer (2010) in her study of Dalit households in villages near Tiruppur clearly points to the critical role played by the PDS in improving their real incomes. The significance of the food component in wages becomes evident if we look at the factors going into determining minimum wages in India. The recent report on minimum wages submitted to the central labour ministry[33] suggests INR 414 as the minimum wage for Tamil Nadu irrespective of skills and occupation, of which 56.7 per cent is the food component. Another report, the *Living Wage Report*, for Tiruppur City by an international agency estimates that the 'replacement value of a free lunch to families is Rs. 24.04 per meal on average per child' as children attending a public school or government-aided school receive a free meal (p. 26).[34] This is tied to the free noon meal scheme innovated in the state and now supported through the integrated child development services (ICDS).

A less noticed but successful scheme which caters to the urban poor is Amma Unavagam,[35] a chain of low-cost canteens serving cooked food run by local self-help groups. Comparable to soup kitchens in the United States and Europe, it offers meals priced at INR 1, INR 3 and INR 5. Starting with only a few locations (15) in the Chennai Corporation and a few other major cities in 2013, it is now being run in more than 400 locations in the state. By sourcing subsidised grains, pulses and vegetables from state-owned enterprises like the Tamil Nadu Cooperative Milk Producers Federation (TCMPF) and the Tamil Nadu Civil Supplies Corporation (TNCSC) and cooperative societies, these canteens have been able to cater to casual labourers and self-employed persons like auto drivers and street vendors. This scheme is at present being replicated in other states such as Karnataka, Delhi, Rajasthan, Madhya Pradesh, Odisha and Andhra Pradesh (Doval 2017). The PDS, mid-day meals and Amma Unavagam all therefore work as implicit wage subsidies for urban labour, particularly those in the informal segments.

STRUCTURAL TRANSFORMATION AND POPULIST INTERVENTIONS

Limits to labour absorption in a transitioning economy and a policy emphasis on labour market flexibility clearly shape the nature of populist interventions in the domain of labour. Despite having been able to transform the economic structure along the lines anticipated by developmentalist accounts, the extent and terms of labour transition are clearly not along expected lines. It is under these constraints that the terrain of populist interventions needs to be understood. The limits of the extent of social protection available in the state may also be an indicator of the limits to this subnational experiment under current macro regimes. Sustained welfare-based interventions outside the domain of spaces of work not only protected labour from the shocks emanating from a flexible labour market but also helped them increase their reserve wages. This increased nominal wage could be compensated through the state's ability to supply a pool of skilled labour, and attention to physical infrastructure. The ability of the state to sustain its manufacturing base as well as its high-end services can be attributed to such investments. The latter in turn allowed for labour to enter into better bargaining arrangements with capital wherever bargaining institutions are present.

We also point out that in a society where caste-based inequalities are naturalised, anti-caste mobilisation has chipped away the basis of such inequalities and de-naturalised it. In north India, when affirmative action was introduced post-Mandal, it was seen to go against natural justice as it was against merit-based access. In Tamil Nadu on the other hand, merit was seen as a means to secure elite privilege and hence caste-based reservation has become an accepted means to ensure socioeconomic mobility and importantly, social justice. Reservation in education and jobs is seen as a rightful entitlement. This has been reinforced by the generation of a relatively more inclusive labour pool in the high-end software services sector thanks to the long history of affirmative action in the state that has managed to undermine the mainstream narrative around 'merit'.

APPENDIX 7A

Table 7A.1 Structure of Workforce

	Tamil Nadu	Gujarat	Maharashtra	All-India
		1983–84		
Agriculture	53.4	60.5	61.1	64.6
Manufacturing	17.8	14.7	10.8	10.4
Non-manufacturing	4.5	4.2	4.1	4.2
Services	24.3	20.5	24.0	20.8
All	100.0	100.0	100.0	100.0
		2017–18		
Agriculture	27.7	42.4	47.8	47.8
Manufacturing	19.5	20.0	11.7	11.7
Non-manufacturing	15.5	7.3	6.3	6.3
Services	37.3	30.2	34.2	34.2
All	100.0	100.0	100.0	100.0

Source: Authors' estimates based on NSS–EUS unit-level data.

Table 7A.2 Size of Labour Force and Workforce by Sectors (in Million)

Sectors/Years	1983–84	1993–94	1999–2000	2004–05	2009–10	2011–12	2017–18
Agriculture	13.9	15.1	14.6	14.9	14.2	11.4	8.9
Manufacturing	4.0	5.0	5.3	6.3	5.4	6.5	6.2
Non-manufacturing	0.8	1.3	1.7	2.2	3.4	4.5	4.9
Services	5.2	6.9	7.5	8.7	8.8	10.0	11.9
Total Workforce	23.8	28.3	29.0	32.0	31.8	32.4	32.0
Total Labour Force	24.6	29.0	29.7	32.7	32.5	33.2	34.6
Total Population	50.4	57.6	61.6	66.0	70.9	73.0	78.9
LFPR Male (15–59) %	92.2	89.1	87.7	78.0	85.0	84.6	84.0
LFPR Female (15–59) %	56.1	57.1	50.9	61.1	43.8	42.4	36.8
Ratio of Working Population (15–59) %	57.8	62.0	64.0	64.4	66.2	65.7	66.0

Source: Authors' estimates based on NSS–EUS unit-level data.

Table 7A.3 Types of Workforce (excluding Agriculture)

	Tamil Nadu	Gujarat	Maharashtra	All-India
		1983–84		
Self-employed	38.9	35.4	37.8	45.1
Regular	35.9	38.2	48.0	34.8
Casual	25.2	26.4	14.3	20.1
All	100.0	100.0	100.0	100.0
		2017–18		
Self-employed	25.9	38.4	32.8	35.6
Regular	46.2	49.2	54.7	39.9
Casual	27.9	12.4	12.5	24.5
All	100.0	100.0	100.0	100.0

Source: Authors' estimates based on NSS–EUS unit-level data.

Table 7A.4 Organised Enterprises and Formal Workers in Industry and Service Sectors

	2011–12 Organised				2017–18 Organised			
	Tamil Nadu	Gujarat	Maharashtra	All-India	Tamil Nadu	Gujarat	Maharashtra	All-India
Manufacturing	39.4	57.1	51.5	34.6	47.3	52.7	55.4	36.4
Non-manufacturing	55.4	46.2	45.9	40.4	54.1	50.0	35.3	32.3
Services Sector	37.0	27.9	37.4	31.7	43.9	32.1	41.9	34.1
All	41.7	41.5	41.9	34.4	47.0	41.5	44.1	34.2
	Formal				Formal			
Manufacturing	12.9	13.6	20.9	10.9	21.6	19.5	30.8	16.6
Non-manufacturing	4.3	3.4	8.3	5.3	8.4	6.9	12.3	6.3
Services	24.5	17.5	24.9	19.9	29.3	17.3	29.6	22.4
All	16.6	14.2	21.7	14.4	22.8	16.7	27.8	17.5

Source: Authors' estimates based on NSS–EUS unit-level data.

Table 7A.5 Trends in Nominal Wages

	1993–94	1999–2000	2004–05	2009–10	2011–12
			Urban Casual		
Tamil Nadu	44.9	63.6	73.9	105.9	205.4
Gujarat	25.1	61.0	68.7	103.9	141.8
Maharashtra	21.7	52.8	67.3	108.9	151.6
All-India	25.3	56.8	68.4	121.3	168.5
			Urban Regular		
Tamil Nadu	58.6	118.6	164.4	302.7	375.5
Gujarat	67.9	159.6	164.0	285.0	317.2
Maharashtra	80.1	52.6	205.3	433.1	480.7
All-India	72.8	150.0	189.7	362.0	440.5

Source: Authors' estimates based on NSS–EUS unit-level data.

Table 7A.6 Trends in Real Wages and Ratio of Casual to Regular Wages

	1993–94	1999–2000	2004–05	2009–10	2011–12
		Real Urban Wages Combined			
Tamil Nadu	144	191	230	268	323
Gujarat	186	241	246	289	293
Maharashtra	266	289	328	465	436
All-India	222	270	297	368	377
	Ratio of Urban Casual to Urban Regular Wages				
Tamil Nadu	76.6	53.6	44.9	35.0	54.7
Gujarat	37.0	38.2	41.9	36.4	44.7
Maharashtra	27.1	100.4	32.8	25.1	31.5
All-India	34.7	37.8	36.1	33.5	38.2

Source: Authors' estimates based on NSS–EUS unit-level data.

Table 7A.7 Occupational Classification in Urban Areas

Tamil Nadu

	SC			OBC			General		
	1993–94	2011–12	2017–18	1993–94	2011–12	2017–18	1993–94	2011–12	2017–18
Self-employed	20	22.1	14.2		37.2	33.7	38.9	25.6	25.3
Regular Salaried	25	45.6	50.6		41.6	48.0	39.3	66.8	67.8
Casual	55	32.3	35.2		21.2	18.3	21.7	7.6	6.8
All	100.0	100.0	100.0		100.0	100.0	100.0	100.0	100.0

All-India

	SC			OBC			General		
	1993–94	2011–12	2017–18	1993–94	2011–12	2017–18	1993–94	2011–12	2017–18
Self-employed	30.1	30.1	29.4		44.9	40.5	42.3	44.6	40.6
Regular Salaried	33.3	45.3	47.3		38.0	42.7	39.4	47.6	51.2
Casual	36.6	24.6	23.3		17.1	16.8	18.3	7.8	8.2
All	100.0	100.0	100.0		100.0	100.0	100.0	100.0	100.0

Source: Authors' estimates based on NSS–EUS unit-level data.

Table 7A.8 Educational Status of Urban Workers

| | Tamil Nadu | | | | | |
| | Salaried Workers | | | All Urban Workers | | |
	SCs	OBCs	GEN	SCs	OBCs	GEN
Illiterate	13.5	4.3	1.9	22.9	15.3	6.3
Primary and Middle	35.7	30.2	16.7	45.7	42.8	31.4
Secondary and Higher Secondary	20.7	20.9	9.6	18.7	22.6	24.9
Graduate and Above	30.1	44.5	71.8	12.7	19.2	37.4
All	100.0	100.0	100.0	100.0	100.0	100.0
	All-India					
Illiterate	12.0	8.2	5.4	37.9	32.9	25.8
Primary and Middle	36.7	32.3	26.1	44.8	45.4	45.9
Secondary and Higher Secondary	27.6	32.1	34.5	13.3	16.8	20.8
Graduate and Above	23.7	27.5	34.0	3.9	4.8	7.5
All	100.0	100.0	100.0	100.0	100.0	100.0

Source: Authors' estimates based on NSS–EUS unit-level data.

Table 7A.9 Skill Status of Urban Workers

| | Tamil Nadu | | | | | |
| | Salaried Workers | | | All Urban Workers | | |
	SCs	OBCs	GEN	SCs	OBCs	GEN
Professionals	24.4	35.6	63.1	17.4	30.5	57.8
Skilled	57.8	54.7	30.7	54.2	55.8	31.9
Unskilled	17.9	9.7	6.1	28.5	13.7	10.3
	All-India					
Professionals	22.4	31.3	40.3	18.9	27.4	40.7
Skilled	51.9	55.6	49.4	51.6	55.8	48.8
Unskilled	25.7	13.1	10.3	29.5	16.8	10.5

Source: Authors' estimates based on NSS–EUS unit-level data.

Table 7A.10 Average Per Capita Quantity Consumed in 30 Days (Kg) in Urban Tamil Nadu

MPCE_ MRP_ Decile	Tamil Nadu			All-India		
	PDS Rice	Total Rice	Share of PDS (%)	PDS Rice	Total Rice	Share of PDS (%)
0–10	4.87	7.43	65.6	1.34	4.57	29.3
10–20	4.57	7.90	57.9	1.09	4.54	24.1
20–30	4.32	8.04	53.7	0.93	4.39	21.2
30–40	3.87	8.20	47.2	0.85	4.50	18.8
40–50	3.62	7.93	45.6	0.67	4.37	15.4
50–60	3.40	8.04	42.3	0.45	4.25	10.6
60–70	2.47	7.14	34.6	0.39	4.28	9.1
70–80	2.01	6.67	30.1	0.25	4.32	5.7
80–90	1.73	6.46	26.8	0.20	3.84	5.3
90–100	0.72	4.86	14.9	0.08	3.16	2.6
Total	3.16	7.27	43.5	0.63	4.22	14.8

Source: Authors' estimates based on NSS–CES unit-level data.

Table 7A.11 Distribution of Verified Membership of Unions in Tamil Nadu

Unions	No. of Members	% of Membership
LPF	6,11,108	33.8
CITU	2,54,347	14.1
INTUC	2,17,574	12
AITUC	1,72,517	9.5
Other Regional Unions	2,99,110	16.6
Other National Unions	2,52,022	13.9
All	18,06,678	100

Source: Adapted from Shyam Sundar (2010).

Table 7A.12 Welfare Boards for Unorganised Workers

S. No.	Name of the Board	Date of Formation
1	Tamil Nadu Construction Workers Welfare Board	30.11.1994
2	Tamil Nadu Manual Workers Welfare Board	17.01.1999
3	Tamil Nadu Unorganized Drivers Welfare Board	01.09.2006
4	Tamil Nadu Tailoring Workers Welfare Board	01.09.2006
5	Tamil Nadu Hair Dressers Welfare Board	01.09.2006
6	Tamil Nadu Washermen Welfare Board	01.09.2006
7	Tamil Nadu Palm Tree Workers Welfare Board	01.09.2006
8	Tamil Nadu Handicraft Workers Welfare Board	01.09.2006
9	Tamil Nadu Handlooms and Handloom Silk Weaving Workers Welfare Board	01.09.2006
10	Tamil Nadu Footwear and Leather Goods Manufactory and Tannery Workers Welfare Board	01.09.2006
11	Tamil Nadu Artists Welfare Board	01.09.2006
12	Tamil Nadu Goldsmiths Welfare Board	01.09.2006
13	Tamil Nadu Pottery Workers Welfare Board	01.09.2006
14	Tamil Nadu Domestic Workers Welfare Board	22.01.2007
15	Tamil Nadu Power Loom Weaving Workers Welfare Board	13.07.2009
16	Tamil Nadu Street Vending and Shops and Establishments Workers Welfare Board	29.01.2010
17	Tamil Nadu Cooking Food Workers Welfare Board	24.02.2011

Source: RTI from Department of Labour and Employment, Government of Tamil Nadu.

Table 7A.13 Other Welfare Boards under Different Ministries

S. No.	Name of Board	Date of Formation	Department
1	Tamil Nadu Traders Welfare Board	25.9.1989	Commercial Tax
2	Tamil Nadu Agricultural Workers Welfare Board	22.12.2006	Revenue Department
3	Tamil Nadu Grama Koill Poosarigal Welfare Board	22.1.2007	Hindu Religious and Charitable Endowments
4	Tamil Nadu Tribal Welfare Board	20.4.2007	Adi Dravidar and Tribal Welfare
5	Tamil Nadu Denotified Communities Welfare Board	20.4.2007	BC, MBC and Minority Welfare
6	Tamil Nadu Disabled Persons Welfare Board	24.4.2007	Welfare of Differently-abled Persons
7	Tamil Nadu Folk and Artists Welfare Board	26.4.2007	Tourism, Culture and Religious Endowments Welfare
8	Tamil Nadu Scavengers Welfare Board	11.6.2007	Adi Dravidar and Tribal Welfare
9	Tamil Nadu Fisheries Welfare Board	29.6.2007	Fisheries
10	Tamil Nadu Transgenders Welfare Board	23.01.2008	Social Welfare
11	Tamil Nadu Cable TV Operators Welfare Board	28.3.2008	Information Technology
12	Tamil Nadu Narikuravar Welfare Board	27.5.2008	BC, MBC and Minorities
13	Tamil Nadu Ulemas Welfare Board	24.8.2009	Environment and Forest
14	Tamil Nadu Film Artists Welfare Board	28.10.2009	Information and Public Relations
15	Tamil Nadu Puthirai Vannar Welfare Board	19.02.2010	Adi Dravidar and Tribal Welfare
16	Tamil Nadu Khadi Spinners and Weavers Welfare Board	26.8.2010	Textiles and Khadi Handlooms
17	Tamil Nadu Coconut Farmers Welfare Board	27.8.2010	Horticulture

Source: RTI from Department of Labour and Employment, Government of Tamil Nadu.

Table 7A.14 Welfare Schemes under Unorganised Welfare Boards

S. No.	Type of Assistance	Amount (INR)
1.	Accident Relief Scheme	1,00,000
	a) Accidental Death	5,00,000
	b) Accidental Disability (based on extent of disability decided by the Tamil Nadu differently-abled welfare board)	1,00,000
2	Natural Death Assistance	2,00,000
	Funeral Expenses Assistance	5,000
3	Educational Assistance	
	(a) Girl Children studying in 10th Standard	1,000
	(b) 10th passed	1,000
	(c) Girl Children studying in 11th Standard	1,000
	(d) Girl Children studying in 12th Standard	1,000
	(e) 12th passed	1,500
	(f) Regular Degree Course	1,500
	with Hostel facility	1,750
	(g) Regular Post-graduate Course	4,000
	with Hostel facility	5,000
	(h) Professional Degree Course	4,000
	with Hostel facility	6,000
	(i) Professional PG Course	6,000
	with Hostel facility	8,000
	(j) ITI or Polytechnic	1,000
	with Hostel facility	1,200
4	Marriage Assistance	
	(a) For Men	3,000
	(b) For Women	5,000
5	Maternity Assistance	6,000
	Miscarriage or Medical Termination of Pregnancy	3,000
6	Reimbursement of cost of Spectacles	up to INR 500
7	Pension	1,000 per month

Source: RTI from Department of Labour and Employment, Government of Tamil Nadu.

NOTES

1   The state is known for the dramatic decline in its fertility rate which is now less than the replacement rate, and comparable to many developed countries.

2   The Indian case seems to be a paradox. It is witnessing an all-time low in FLFPR during one of its highest economic growth phases—2005–15. India's FLFPR is well below some of its immediate neighbours, Bangladesh (36 per cent) and Sri Lanka (35 per cent) and far below other Asian countries such as Afghanistan (49 per cent), Malaysia (51 per cent), the United Arab Emirates (51 per cent), Indonesia (52 per cent), Thailand (59 per cent) and China (61 per cent).

3   Agarwala and Herring (2020) note that besides a small section of profitable entrepreneurs, many self-employed workers are often misclassified workers operating on a contractual basis; also a substantial number of them merely survive through petty trade such as street vending, running a tea shop or rag picking.

4   Chandrasekar and Ghosh (2011) and Deshpande and Sharma (2013) argue that self-employment is often distress led in India, and cannot be seen as entrepreneurial in nature; if given opportunities in regular salaried work, the workforce will move from the former to the latter. This is particularly evident from the fact that the share of self-employed tends to be much higher in lower income states in the country.

5   Towards this, we use NSS unit-level data to arrive at resultant estimates. As per the sectoral definition, unincorporated private enterprises owned by individuals or households engaged in the sale and production of goods and services operated on a proprietary or partnership basis and which employ less than ten workers, are considered as unorganised enterprises. This definition is well-accepted as it includes both enterprise type and size criteria in its definition. However, it needs to be noted that the sectoral definition of organised and unorganised, differs from the definition of organised and unorganised in terms of workers. The NCEUS defines unorganised workers as consisting 'of those working in the informal sector or households, excluding regular workers with social security benefits provided by the employers and the workers in the formal sector without any employment and social security benefits provided by the employers'.

NCEUS *Report on Definitional and Statistical Issues Relating to Informal Economy* (NCEUS 2008: p. 11).

6   This higher share of wages in GVA has to be seen in light of the nature of work contracts.

7   Munshi (2014) points to the role of social networks in shaping access to labour markets.

8   Between 1999 and 2005, the number of private engineering colleges in Tamil Nadu doubled, so that by 2005 there were more than 240—20 per cent of the total number of engineering institutions in India—offering over 80,000 seats; a few of the colleges have become autonomous 'deemed universities'. By contrast, only nine engineering colleges, with about 4,800 seats, are government-run or state-financed (Fuller and Narasimhan 2006: 258).

9   Except for the manager based in Coimbatore, all other interviews were conducted during 2008–10.

10 Telephonic interview on August 6, 2008.

11 See https://digitallearning.eletsonline.com/2013/02/tamil-nadu-varsities-to-impart-soft-skill-training/ (accessed 8 May 2020).

12 See Government Order Ms (No. 255), Higher Education Department, 24 June 2008, http://www.tn.gov.in/gorders/hedu/hedu_e_255_2008.pdf (accessed 15 June 2012).

13 Interviews with trade union leaders and labour activists were conducted during June to September 2019.

14 See http://www.lawsofindia.org/pdf/tamil_nadu/1963/1963TN9.pdf (accessed 8 April 2020).

15 See https://tnlabour.in/automobile-industry/4502 (accessed 19 August 2019).

16 The standing order was amended but the rules are yet to be amended. Interview with Shanmugam, LPF president, 11 July 2019.

17 Interview dated 19 June 2019.

18 They include Kaalan of the Indian National Trade Union Congress (INTUC), V. P. Chintan, K. T. K. Thangamani and A. M. Gopu of the Centre of Indian Trade Unions (CITU), and Kuppusamy, Rahman and Shanmugam of the DMK-affiliated LPF. The AIADMK also had a trade union leader Chinnasamy, who went on to became an elected member in the state assembly.

19 See https://fite.org.in/ (accessed 8 April 2020).

20 See https://fite.org.in/2019/04/13/forum-for-it-employees-stands-about-2019-general-election/ (accessed 8 April 2020).

21 Personal Interview. We conducted a set of unstructured interviews with trade union activists from the LPF, CITU, AITUC and Working Peoples Trade Union Council (WPTUC) during June–September 2019 on the strategies adopted by the labour movement in their negotiations with industry representatives during the months of June and July 2019. We also conducted a set of interviews with trade union activists in Delhi a for a comparative analysis of trade union strategies.

22 Informal workers are classified into two categories; one is self-employed workers such as street vendors, domestic servants, owners of petty enterprises and so on, and the other is contract workers who work through subcontractors for informal or formal enterprises in various sectors including automobiles and textiles. Those contract workers who work in the formal sector are excluded from such policies.

23 Kerala had constituted such boards in the coir industry much before Tamil Nadu.

24 Mr Shanmugam narrated his personal involvement in the history of welfare boards in the state.

25 There were a few such as the Self Employed Women's Association (SEWA), the National Alliance of Street Vendors in India, workers' cooperatives and self-help groups such as the Delhi-based Building and Woodworkers International (Bhowmik 2008)

26 The LPF president (M. Shanmugam interviewed on July 11, 2019) suggests that this concern maybe because Karunanidhi himself was from a background of traditional informal labour.

27 Interview with a retired senior official from the Labour ministry in Tamil Nadu on 14 June 2018.

28 The *Report of Committee to Go into the Living Conditions of Workers in Beedi and Other Unorganised in Tamil Nadu* (Government of Tamil Nadu 1975a) and the *Report of the Committee Constituted to Study the Problems and Issues of Unorganised Labour in Tamil Nadu* (Government of Tamil Nadu 1998).

29 For details on welfare benefits see the Table 7A.14 in Appendix 7A.

30 Government Order (D) 486: Unorganised Workers—Construction Workers Registered with Tamil Nadu Construction Workers Welfare Board Pension

Scheme, Department of Labour and Employment, Chennai. *Monitoring Reports on Tamil Nadu Construction Workers Welfare Board* (Government of Tamil Nadu 2008b); *Monitoring Report for Welfare Boards for Unorganised Workers* (Government of Tamil Nadu 2008a).

31 The discussion in this section is based on a paper by the second author (Vijayabaskar 2011).

32 See http://www.isidelhi.org.in/hrnews/isidownload/Labour/Labour-2009. pdf (accessed 6 May 2020).

33 Report of the Expert Committee on Determining the Methodology for Fixing the National Minimum Wage submitted to the Ministry of Labour and Employment in January 2019.

34 See https://www.globallivingwage.org/wp-content/uploads/2018/05/urban-india-living-wage-benchmark-report.pdf (accessed 8 May 2020).

35 Amma Unavagam is named after the late Chief Minister J. Jayalalithaa, referred to by her partymen as Amma, which means mother (Narasimhan 2015).

8

FISSURES, LIMITS AND
POSSIBLE FUTURES

Chantal Mouffe makes a strong case for 'Left populist' mobilisation in building radical democracy. By Left populism, she refers to a populist mobilisation based on an expansive construction of a 'people' that works towards deepening equality and social justice for multiple marginalised groups. Taking cues from Laclau's works on populist reason (2005, 2006; Laclau and Mouffe 2014), she argues that radical politics requires deepening the idea of democracy so that ideas of freedom and equality are no longer confined to the domain of the liberal. They ought to be reworked so as to transform social relations towards realising substantive freedom and equality. Our narrative of the developmental trajectory of Tamil Nadu suggests that populist mobilisation around a non-essentialised Dravidian-Tamil identity and a demand for 'social justice' has indeed worked to expand freedom and reduce inequities across castes. Operating within a constitutional democratic framework, the state's experience highlights the democratic possibilities that can be opened up within such a structure. This is particularly important in postcolonial societies where mobilisations have often drawn upon essentialised and exclusionary constructions of 'people' that tend to undermine prospects for democratising social relations. The state's political experience suggests that it is indeed possible to institutionalise an inclusive populist mobilisation leading to a comparatively egalitarian developmental trajectory in the Global South.

There are thus two distinct contributions that our analysis of the state's development makes to the literature on subnational development and politics in the Global South. First, we establish that an inclusive populist mobilisation can generate sustained developmental outcomes for the marginalised social groups even when national-level interventions have an elite bias. Populist mobilisation and institutionalisation of that populist logic in the state apparatus have fostered better developmental outcomes in Tamil Nadu than in most states in the country. Such outcomes have been embedded in a growth process that has managed to structurally transform the state's economy and livelihoods. In fact, such outcomes have fed into the broad-basing of opportunities for entry into expanding modern productive sectors. Second, we have also demonstrated how an emphasis on status-based inequality has shaped this process. We thus call for greater attention to this source of inequality in the Global South.

In contrast to other political mobilisations that focused merely on class-based inequality, the Dravidian movement conceptualised injustice emanating from caste hierarchies to be more central in India. Piketty's recent work (2020) only affirms such a conception. He sees two important sources of contemporary inequality globally. One source of inequality emerges from property ownership and another from social status. He points to the sustained importance of status-based inequalities in countries like India, particularly related to caste. Caste status conditions access to education and modern sectors as well as the life chances of individuals. This is not, however, to deny the overlaps between the two sources of inequality. As we demonstrated in the case of Tamil Nadu, caste elites managed to sustain their economic dominance through their social status signifying the systemic nature of caste-based power relations. This phenomenon therefore calls attention to the pathways through which status based inequalities reproduce or transform through the process of economic modernisation in other post-colonial regions.

In this chapter, we engage with the limits to this populist developmental process. We identify slippages not only in the quality of some of the outcomes but also in ensuring adequate benefits of structural transformation or better social inclusion. These slippages are translating into popular demands that the subnational political regime is seeking to respond to, albeit with less success. Using elements of the analytical framework outlined in Chapter 2 in conjunction with a 'multi-level' approach, in this chapter, we aim to provide explanations for such slippages and the limits of the subnational political response. As we explain in Chapter 1, 'multi-level' refers to an approach that recognises that policy and political outcomes at a particular level or scale, subnational in this case, are an outcome of an interaction of variables that are more visible and embedded in higher levels with those that operate at the subnational level. In doing so, we also reflect upon the implications of such subnational politics and how these may resonate with the developmental dilemmas of the Global South. In the following section, we highlight the emerging fissures and slippages across the various domains that we have analysed in this book.

FISSURES AND SLIPPAGES

EDUCATION

As we pointed out in Chapter 3, the state has one of the highest literacy rates, particularly among marginalised social groups, and also hosts the largest share of youth in higher education. Entry into tertiary education too has been much more inclusive in terms of both caste and class. We argued that this was made possible both due to a political ethos that imagined education to be a key axis of inequality and a consequent set of policy interventions. This led to an inversion of the prevailing elite bias in education at the national level by emphasising primary education and creative affirmative action policies. There are, however, two sources of concern in this domain.

Studies point to relatively poor learning outcomes among school children in the state (Balagopal and Vijayabaskar 2018). Further, despite the fact that learning outcomes in public schools are better than in private schools, there is a growing preference for private schools not only among socioeconomic elites, but even among poorer or marginalised social groups (Balagopal and Vijayabaskar 2018). The increase in out-of-pocket expenditure on education for such households, and welfare implications are obvious. The dominant reasons that households cite for this shift are better learning environments and better training in the English language. Such shifts are generating a new axis of differentiation. The second issue relates to the uneven quality of higher education. While the state has achieved a remarkable enrolment ratio in higher education, its record in the quality of education has been uneven (Bhatnagar 2011). While some colleges do better and meet the standards set by the All India Council for Technical Education (AICTE), many fail to meet them. Poor infrastructure, inexperienced teaching staff and outdated syllabi are typical issues that these colleges have failed to address. The disparity in quality of education has a direct bearing on labour market inequities. Those who graduate from these colleges are largely absorbed in poorly paying jobs leaving those passing out of elite institutions to access premium jobs. Hence the difference in quality of education escalates wage disparities and perpetuates income inequalities. With the bulk of technical education being provided by the private sector, this also has implications for household expenditure on tertiary education and a high probability of poor returns to such investments in education.

HEALTH

We attributed the state's achievements in the domain of health outcomes to a relatively well-functioning, spatially distributed infrastructure and better rate of utilisation of services. Importantly, the state has innovated a system whereby a socially inclusive pool of health professionals feeds into the public health infrastructure. The state's achievements in preventive healthcare have also been lauded. It could retain doctors in rural areas due to its responsive reservation and incentive policies both in medical college admissions and in the appointment of medical professionals in the state medical services. Such policies not only ensured that an adequate number of medical professionals could enter the public system to meet the growing demand, but also socially broad-based entry into medical services. Hence, despite the relatively not so high average per capita health expenditure, the state could achieve better health outcomes.

The state has, however, also been a pioneer in the expansion of private medical services and one of the earliest to offer a template for corporatisation of medical services in the country. Further, the fact that a significant share of the population relies on private healthcare facilities for hospitalisation (Balagopal and Vijayabaskar 2019) suggests that once again (as in the case of education), we are possibly witnessing a segmentation of the healthcare system based on perceived or real differences in quality. There is also recent evidence of shortages of human resources in some segments of the public health system.

Importantly, the introduction of the National Eligibility Cum Entrance Test (NEET), a national-level entrance exam for admissions to medical courses may not only feed into the process of corporatisation of healthcare in the state, but can also undermine incentive structures that sustained the entry of qualified medical professionals into the public system. As the dreams of NEET aspirants who have to spend a lot of money and resources on coaching centres in metropolitan cities converge with the interests of world-class corporate hospitals like Apollo, dreams of students like Anitha would remain distant.

LABOUR OUTCOMES

Despite being embedded within a national macro-regime premised on driving growth through labour market flexibility, the state has ensured relatively better wage shares, incomes and social security for labour. While the former is an outcome of a history of labour mobilisation that drew upon both class and Dravidian-Tamil identities, expansion of the domain of social security was based on a combination of interventions in the domains of both the social and the economic popular. Importantly, a series of programmatic interventions ensured a much higher degree of structural transformation of the economy allowing for a much larger share of the population to move out of caste-marked livelihoods. A universal and an efficient public distribution system (PDS) ensured a higher degree of social protection than in most states even as it contributed to the undermining of hierarchical caste relations in rural Tamil Nadu. In conjunction with labour welfare boards for urban unorganised labour, better implementation of a national-level rural employment guarantee scheme and a slew of economic popular schemes targeted at specific social groups in the state made such social protection possible. If inclusion in education could democratise the formal labour market, welfare interventions such as the universal PDS and mid-day meal programme for school children have ensured a higher reserve wage for non-formal labour in the state. Contrary to popular perceptions, the state has also enabled transfer of land from landed elites to lower castes through a series of molecular interventions in response to political mobilisation. Enhanced public transport and road connectivity too have transformed rural–urban networks and hence people's mobility.

Slippages in this domain are along the following axes. Despite the overseeing of a better process of structural transformation, a significant number of livelihoods outside agriculture are far from 'decent'. Casual employment continues to be an important source of employment for those exiting agriculture suggesting new vulnerabilities. Gender differences too are visible. Once again, a larger share of the rural female workforce has moved out of agriculture compared to most states, but wage disparities persist. The share of manufacturing employment has continued to stagnate despite the ability of the sector to respond well to global and domestic market impulses. Further, while affirmative action policies have socially broad-based entry into the middle and lower end of the organised labour markets, caste elites continue to dominate the premium end. With declining employment in the public sector, the role of caste-based affirmative action in employment has also considerably reduced in scope. As a result, while the economic divide across caste lines has diminished in rural areas, urban Tamil Nadu that was seen as a space less marked by caste continues to reproduce caste differences despite a higher degree of social inclusion. While this may be due to differences in the quality of educational outcomes in the tertiary sector, the role of 'opportunity hoarding' by elites through caste networks cannot be dismissed. Unemployment, especially among the educated, has emerged as another worrying phenomenon. A vibrant manufacturing and high-end services economy has failed to absorb the large number of labour market entrants with higher educational attainments. As a result, economic popular schemes derogatorily referred to as 'freebies', are seen to reduce expenditure on 'productive' investments that may have helped generate more jobs for the educated youth. Such unevenness is also translating into fissures in the 'Dravidian bloc'.

SUSTAINING THE 'DRAVIDIAN BLOC': EMERGING INTER- AND INTRA-CASTE DIFFERENCES

One central characteristic of Dravidian mobilisation is its refusal to universalise specific caste interests. While it rejected the Brahminical caste hierarchy, it also refused to completely embrace the putative glorious past of 'Tamils' or civilisational claims by specific caste groups. Yet it could accommodate their diverse interests to forge a hybridised Dravidian identity rooted in a social and economic future. It also managed to draw together a range of demands for recognition and socioeconomic mobility from diverse lower castes which were often in hierarchical and antagonistic relations with one another. Fissures are therefore inevitable.

After the DMK came to power in 1967, the state managed to avoid the dominance of a single caste bloc in influencing the political or policy domain in the initial years. The DMK also managed to diffuse the dominance of landed and urban elites that the state inherited from the patronage politics of the Congress. Power was transferred to a bloc comprising a range of subaltern intermediate caste groups and a section of Dalits. The ability to sustain this heterogeneous group has been challenged in recent decades, particularly due to the uneven socioeconomic development of different castes and emergence of intra-caste disparities. Sections of backward castes resent the relative mobility among sections of Dalits. The 'slipping hegemony' of such caste groups (Pandian 2013) has led to several instances of violence against Dalits. While Dravidian common-sense provided a vocabulary to articulate their concerns, the institutionalised response has been inadequate.

Some have gained more than others across other caste axes too. While there has been a convergence of incomes in rural areas, this is not the case in urban Tamil Nadu. Many factors explain such uneven outcomes. First, are regional differences. The *TNHDR* (Government of Tamil Nadu 2017) reveals that districts that have the least levels of human development in the state are also ones marked by low levels of urbanisation and industrialisation. Many of these districts form a contiguous belt along the east starting from Cuddalore, apart from a few that are south of Madurai. Given that caste groups are often concentrated in specific regions of the state, this is also likely to translate into uneven outcomes for different lower-caste groups. Second, in the domain of human capital formation, there is a significant rural–urban divide, especially with the privatisation of education in the tertiary sector. This would imply that there are differences emerging even within specific caste groups apart from the possibility that some caste groups are more urbanised than others. Third, while land as a source of power within agriculture has declined enormously because of the structural transformation that the state has witnessed, land as a speculative asset in urban areas and in the rural areas adjoining the urban has become a source of accumulation not only in the state but across the country (Chakravorty 2013). Once again, lack of access to such speculative asset holdings, especially among non-landowning Dalits and backward castes, may be a source of unevenness. The fourth and probably the most important is the rural versus urban divide. Though rural–urban wage disparities are relatively low, given the declining share of state income from agriculture, income disparities persist. Hence caste groups who are more dependent on agriculture or agricultural labour are likely to lose out. Also, the emphasis on soft skills including spoken English as a growing pre-requisite for entry into the upper end of the labour market implies that those in rural areas or in non-metropolitan urban areas are at a disadvantage. The persistence of caste divisions in the organised segment of the urban labour market is possibly suggestive of this phenomenon. The absence of affirmative action policies in the private sector also clearly contributes to this.

Finally, as we argued in Chapter 5, though entry into the domain of capital accumulation has been broad-based, regional concentration of economic dynamism and the inability of Dalits to adequately enter into this domain constitute another axis of exclusion. A few castes, such as Nadars who have historically occupied a low caste status have become successful entrepreneurs and achieved considerable economic mobility over the last century. Members from many peasant castes too could enter into entrepreneurship on a larger scale than in other parts of the country. In fact, Damodaran (2016) contends that as a result, the state has not witnessed protests by agrarian caste groups as has happened among the Jats, Marathas and Kapus elsewhere. Failed efforts to develop industries in industrially backward regions such as Tirunelveli or Perambalur, however, signify the limits to the extent to which regional differences in this regard can be addressed through modernisation.

There is also a temporal dimension to this differential mobility. Caste groups or sections within castes who managed to access modern education earlier because of historical or geographical advantage are likely to extend this advantage through differences in household-level attainments. As Alcott and Rose (2017) point out, household-level characteristics such as income, social background and educational attainments of parents are very critical to the educational attainments of school children. They particularly highlight the role of parental education and household income levels in generating such differences. Irrespective of whether public schools are able to provide better education compared to private schools, such household differences therefore continue to perpetuate differences in schooling outcomes. Importantly such differences tend to widen over time. Unequal returns to education and adverse inclusion in the labour market reproduce differences over time. Soft skills are also attributes that first-generation students are likely to lack. Despite efforts by the Dravidian parties to constantly rework affirmative action to address the unevenness of caste mobility among OBCs and Dalits, inter-caste differences have emerged. As a result, this was also a phase when voices from specific intermediate and Dalit castes began to articulate a politics outside the fold of the Dravidian. The Dravidian-Tamil equivalence is therefore no longer hegemonic as smaller group demands are not adequately met because of the unevenness in the developmental process. The long history of intervention in the domain of education and affirmative action has fostered a growing elite from within the backward castes that no longer identify their stakes with Dravidian common-sense. Entering into the upper end of the labour market both within India and globally, their demands are unlikely to be met through this identity. Simultaneously, there are also efforts to confine Tamil identity within the Hindu fold thereby marginalising the positions of Tamil Christians and Muslims who were key constituents of the subaltern that the Dravidian movement mobilised.

GOVERNANCE SLIPPAGES

The state ranks at the top with regard to several indicators of governance. We pointed out how health and education outcomes have been better than in most states despite moderate resource allocations. The state also has arguably the most efficient PDS system in the country, with minimal leakages. The bureaucracy in the state is known for designing and implementing innovative social sector programmes. A senior bureaucrat explains this as follows. 'If a transgender in Theni district goes to the local authorities with a problem that they face, the solution may well become a policy directive for transgenders across Tamil Nadu within a couple of weeks'.[1] According to him, this underscores the institutionalisation of processes through which specific demands are translated into macro policy interventions. He attributes this possibility to not just the bureaucracy but to a political history that has ensured a process of such responsive policy-making. Importantly, it is the embeddedness of a socially diverse bureaucracy in conjunction with a responsive political process that makes this possible.

The state political apparatus, however, has a reputation for corruption and rent-seeking. Walton and Crabtree (2018) have characterised the state as an exemplary case of 'crony populism'. As Jeyaranjan (2019) demonstrates, the Dravidian parties have built a centralised mechanism for extraction of rents from sand mining. The mechanism looks like pork-barrel politics, socially embedded and politically institutionalised. He shows that both collude to build cartels to corner contracts to mine and transport sand. As a result, there has been systemic under-reporting both of sand sold and of the price at which sand is sold (Rajshekhar 2016). One can find similar examples in the case of other natural resources as well. For instance, Tamil Nadu Minerals Limited (TAMIN)—a state-owned corporation established in 1978—was entrusted with the task of mining minerals and granite. The officials in TAMIN were accused of collusion with private contractors exporting minerals to siphon off the difference between the book price and the actual price (Jeyaranjan 2019). These trends only suggest the institutionalisation of rent-seeking in the state. Such rent-seeking from natural resource extraction sectors also has a direct bearing on electoral funding. The state has one of the highest election expenditures per candidate in the country.

SOCIAL POPULAR AND ELECTORAL DEMOCRACY

Programmatic interventions may not always yield electoral dividends. In Tamil Nadu, though the DMK has sustained social popular interventions over a longer period, it has not fared as well as the AIADMK on the electoral front. Apart from pioneering innovations in affirmative action and subnational development planning, the DMK-led government also passed laws granting equal inheritance rights to girl children and abolishing hereditary positions in village administration, initiated farmers' markets and made efforts to improve the quality of school education in government schools. The reservation policy was constantly reworked to address caste-based inequalities. It also tried to bring in a policy of reservation to address rural–urban and class-based disparities—by offering preferences to rural students and first-generation graduates, respectively, in higher education. While these policies laid the foundation for economic transformations that become visible in the 1990s, they could not, however, sustain the party's electoral prospects.

Its regime during 1996–2001, for example, was seen by many as one of the best that the state had seen in terms of programmatic interventions to promote economic development, albeit through providing an enabling environment for private capital. When the party lost the elections in 2001, Karunanidhi, the DMK leader, poignantly remarked that he would take it as a prize that the people have given him for five years of his rule. Narayan (2018) points out that since 2006, governments have been indulging excessively in patronage or clientelist measures that may undermine the gains in social justice made by the state. It is therefore important to ask whether such a shift away from long-term social popular interventions is a contingent phenomenon or a necessary outcome of the impulses that propelled such a trajectory. Interestingly, here is a paradox. Chibber and Verma (2018) show that Tamil Nadu's developmental trajectory has less to do with vote-buying, clientelism and patronage and more to do with the embedding of its interventions in political ideology. Patronage-targeted transfers and benefits do not always win elections and they point out that notwithstanding cash transfers during elections and the prevalence of bribes in accessing state resources, there is little evidence of citizens actually offering votes in exchange for such favours (2018: p. 109). To add, a survey experiment in Tamil Nadu reveals that the promise of 'freebies' did not influence voting patterns (Kailash 2020).

To sum up, even as a century of mobilisation and over half a century of institutionalised populist interventions have led to considerable democratisation of opportunities and access to public services like health and education, a set of fissures in the Dravidian popular are also visible. Specific caste groups, Dalits in particular, do not see their demands addressed to the extent others' demands are, even as affirmative action policies are becoming less effective. Despite being the most industrialised, issues persist on the quality and quantum of employment generated in the non-farm sectors. Urban Tamil Nadu that was imagined as a terrain less marked by caste-endorsed hierarchies, continues to be segmented, with caste elites dominating the upper segments of the economy. There are also regional divides that interventions have not been able to redress. In the rest of the chapter, we identify some structural factors that contribute to the unravelling of this bloc and also delineate possibilities. To do that, we bring back two elements of our analytical framework. The first is the nature of the limits to institutionalised populism and social popular interventions. And the second is the limit posed by the dynamic of late-modern industrialisation and developmentalism to ensuring social justice. In addition, we also highlight the role of federal relations and the macro-economic regulatory shifts at the national and the global scale to supplement this explanation.

SOME EXPLANATIONS

POPULISM: FROM THE LOGIC OF EQUIVALENCE TO THE LOGIC OF DIFFERENCE

If non-electoral mobilisation crystallised in building a historic bloc and established a normative common-sense through a critique of structures and ideologies that sustain social injustice, mobilisation for electoral dividends has institutionalised populism in the state. This institutionalisation has in turn led to a series of programmatic interventions that have sought to undermine the prevailing relations of injustice based on caste status. Initially, it therefore took the form of social popular interventions—affirmative action, institutional rights and access to public resources. Within a pan-Indian polity, there are, however, limits to the extent to which such interventions can be carried out. Even if there is a collective will for such interventions, there are limits posed by judicial interpretation of the constitutional framework. In fact, Mehta (2007) draws attention to the growing 'judicialisation' of the Indian state since the economic reforms of the early 1990s. Rendering efforts by the state government to deepen affirmative action as illegal is a case in point. The terrain of the social popular is therefore limited by such factors even in the presence of a political will. This exhaustion of the possibilities of the social popular therefore manifests as a governmental imperative and an electoral imperative operating in the domain of the economic popular. The logic of equivalence across demands made by heterogeneous groups through a Dravidian-Tamil identity is now weakened by the governmental logic of difference. Welfarist interventions are targeted at specific groups and also are not meant to transform the social relations that are generative of relations of power. Importantly, such economic popular welfarism also implies an unevenness and generation of new differences across these heterogeneous groups. Narayan's (2018) characterisation of the post-2006 phase of Dravidian politics in the state suggests this possibility. An inability to expand the terrain of affirmative action due to judicial intervention and the growing privatisation of employment has posed clear limits on that front. Given the need to attract private investments, large-scale interventions in this regard too are less attractive. Wyatt (2013b) also attributes the shift in the DMK's style of appeal to the electorate in 2006 to a crisis on the economic and political front.

LIMITS TO MODERNISATION

The Dravidian ideology was clearly rooted in the high modern with a strong faith in the ability of modernisation of the productive domain to diffuse and undermine social hierarchies. But across most parts of the world, there is a growing recognition that such modernisation can neither absorb the entire 'surplus' labour thrown out of traditional sectors like agriculture nor ensure ecologically sustainable transitions (Dorin 2017). Given the extractivist logic that underpins contemporary urban ecologies, Dorin points out that more intensive urbanisations in highly populous countries like India and China, as dominant economic paradigms prescribe, are likely to generate ecological nightmares. Chatterjee (2017) in fact goes on to suggest that even in early-modern Europe which has served as the template for building a theory of economic modernisation, surplus populations that were dispossessed from land and constituted wage labour for expanding capital accumulation in the urban–industrial sectors, could never be entirely transformed into necessary labour for capital. Rather, the bulk of the population evicted from agriculture was resettled in colonies like the Americas or Australia, while large numbers also succumbed to epidemics and famines. If the original historical model was faulty, the prospects of the Global South imitating this path look even more remote.

As scholars working on India (Sanyal 2007), South Africa (Ferguson 2015) and Indonesia (Li 2010) have been suggesting, sizeable populations in these countries are being rendered surplus to the process of accumulation even as they are being dispossessed from their means of production. Unlike earlier Marxist readings that saw the urban informal as a segment that serves to facilitate accumulation by cheapening the costs of production and reproduction, Sanyal argues that large segments of the urban informal are redundant to the process of accumulation. Li makes a similar point and attributes it to the increasing rate of dispossession of rural populations in conjunction with the growing inability of capital to absorb such labour into its productive circuits. Based on a similar reading, Ferguson therefore makes a strong case for social protection and income provisioning based on citizenship, outside the domain of the workplace. The experience of Tamil Nadu in many ways supports this contention.

Despite having the largest share of its population in manufacturing and a sustained economic dynamism, the state has not been able to increase the share of employment in manufacturing. Further, though the wage share is higher than in other states with a strong manufacturing base, it has not been able to address the question of quality of employment adequately. Standard explanations for this phenomenon that are currently popular in policy circles revolve around two factors. The first pertains to the rigidity of labour laws that render labour relatively more expensive than capital and hence incentivise employers to replace labour with capital-intensive technologies. Second, a narrative that is gaining popularity of late is the quality of skill formation. The entire emphasis on skilling through missions like 'Skill India' reflects this belief that once skilling happens, the issue of both quantity and quality of employment can be addressed. Though labour unions have been able to push back flexibilisation of labour markets to a limited extent in the state, there has been a continuous shift towards use of non-permanent workers in manufacturing. Further, the state is also home to arguably the largest pool of technically skilled labour that is also socially inclusive. The limits to transformation of social relations and caste hierarchies through inclusive modernisation therefore probably lies in the limits posed by the paradigm of modernisation per se. This also explains the expanding domain of economic popular interventions in the state or for that matter in other parts of the Global South as well (Barrientos and Hulme 2009).

DEVELOPMENTAL AUTONOMY AT THE SUBNATIONAL SCALE

Given that macro-economic policy-making is determined at the national level, there is little scope for subnational governments to circumvent the limits set by such measures. Policies such as the extent of trade liberalisation, currency regulation and importantly, the direction of economic growth are decided by the union government. We earlier highlighted the shift from an era of planned industrialisation under the leadership of the public sector towards a macro-regime that privileged the agency of private capital and competitiveness in global markets. Flexibility in labour markets was seen as essential to successfully produce for global markets and states were incentivised to compete with one another through tax concessions, low-cost land, labour and infrastructure. Subnational governments and/or political possibilities are therefore circumscribed or enabled by such shifts and incentivisation. For example, while during the planned era, Dravidian ideologues demanded public sector enterprises (PSEs) and industrial licenses for the state, in the 1990s, the Dravidian parties undertook a series of institutional interventions to attract private capital. As a consequence, even if subnational popular demands seek better employment security or higher wages, there is little that governments can do in this regard. We observed how these demands were partly met through interventions outside the workplace in Tamil Nadu. Given that social services and sectors are under the prerogative of subnational governments, they are in a position to innovate within this domain. To add, the framework that guides the nature of resource transfers between subnational governments and the union government also constrains the ability of the former to undertake autonomous policy interventions.

The framework governing vertical and horizontal resource transfers is seen to undermine the fiscal space available to relatively developed states like Tamil Nadu to expand the domain of welfare interventions. Union governments are also seen to deny resources to subnational governments through levy of taxes that are not meant to be shared with subnational governments. The asymmetrical federal power structure puts a limit on the state's capacity to intervene in the economy both in terms of method and resources. Yet, subnational governments account for 80 per cent of expenditure in social sectors and continue to be the theatre of implementation of central schemes. Over the past two decades, India has witnessed a phenomenon of union governments spending on domains that are the primary responsibility of the state. Conditional transfers that allow subnational governments to access funds only when they spend on programmes and schemes that the union government has drawn up, constitute about 40 per cent of the total transfers in the country. This is largely routed through centrally sponsored schemes (CSS) and is hence outside the constitutionally mandated purview of the finance commission. Hence this distorts states' allocations and limits the autonomy of the latter in prioritising state-specific developmental goals. On the other hand, the expenditure burden on the states has been increasing. States are required to spend about 85 per cent of the total educational expenditure, 82 per cent in health and 78 per cent in agriculture. These three sectors are key to developmental outcomes and constitute about 75 per cent of the total combined expenditure of the union and the states (P. Chakraborty 2019). The introduction of the goods and services tax (GST) and increasing share of various types of cess imposed by the centre have further eroded the fiscal space of states in India. The ability of states like Tamil Nadu to sustain and expand their achievements in human development has to be seen in this context of centralisation.

There are also limits posed by the greater integration with global markets. Increasingly in the Global South, both national and subnational governments rely on global capital flows to access resources for investments unlike in the past when surpluses generated from agriculture were seen to be a critical source for investments and capital accumulation (Bernstein 1996). While such opening up has relieved these governments of resource constraints, reliance on global capital also comes with certain limits to policy-making. As this means a greater reliance on global markets to generate growth, competing with other countries for similar markets places limits on autonomous interventions. There are compulsions to use frontier technologies, lower labour and environmental standards and reduce trade restrictions that may otherwise have been used to build capabilities and provide competitive physical and human infrastructures.

Further, since financial markets are critical institutions through which governments seek to tap resources, creating conducive conditions for financial actors plays a critical role in the growth trajectory of these economies. This financialisation of the growth process not only has implications for real or productive sectors but once again reduces the range of policy levers available. As a result, policy interventions across the Global South have strong homogenising tendencies. This can be best illustrated by recent events in India. Kerala and West Bengal in India best demonstrate how policy interventions tend to assume a 'there is no alternative' position irrespective of the political spectrum. Run by communist parties for long periods, both Kerala and West Bengal are hailed for their better ability to initiate land reforms seen as essential to inclusive transition from out of agriculture. However, Left reformism in Kerala or West Bengal has not managed to generate alternate transition possibilities (Das Gupta 2017). In fact, the Bengal government's efforts to attract a car factory through the offer of subsidised land led to one of the most prolonged agitations against new modes of rural dispossession (Nielsen 2018).

RENT-SEEKING, SLIPPAGE IN LEARNING OUTCOMES AND POSSIBILITIES

While mobilisation against corruption in service delivery may be effective in reducing rent-seeking by state actors through this route, there are also certain incentive structures that may not be easily addressed through subnational resistance. The relationship between growth and corruption is a contested one. While it is generally held to reduce efficiency and be inimical to growth, studies also suggest the possibility that under certain conditions, rent-seeking may also aid the growth process in the Global South (Khan 2000). China, for example, is a case where rapid economic growth has been accompanied by increased levels of rent-seeking (Ngo and Wu 2008). Be that as it may, there is a strong popular sentiment against corruption by political elites in Tamil Nadu, as in the rest of the country. Despite this sentiment and active electoral campaigns based on promises of corruption-free governance, there is little evidence to suggest that corruption levels have reduced. One important imperative for rent-seeking stems from the need for resources to sustain political parties and fund elections.

Gowda and Sridharan (2012) point out that poor regulations that govern the funding of political parties and election campaigns have led to the use of political power by elites to mobilise resources through rent-seeking. Further, this has also led political parties to rely on wealthy candidates to contest as they are likely to spend more. This has in turn has led to the emergence of the 'political entrepreneur' who invests to gain political power so as to access rents. While corporate funding is a significant source of funding for political parties, Kapur and Vaishnav (2011) also point to the growing role of real-estate based financing of parties. Given that corporates are more likely to fund national parties, it is possible to suggest that regional parties will rely more on real estate or other localised sources of rents for sustaining their parties or electoral funding. Reliance on rents from sand mining or other minerals is also therefore unlikely to disappear in this context. This has become a significant source particularly after the real estate boom in both Tamil Nadu and at the national level, given the increase in demand for housing and other construction. In fact, a senior bureaucrat suggests that rents from these natural resources provide relative autonomy from big capital for electoral financing.[2]

While such factors may partly explain the persistence of corruption in certain domains, the poor learning outcomes observed in recent years suggest a corruption of another kind. Despite having better quality and socially inclusive teaching staff and better physical infrastructure for schools, the fact that learning outcomes are poorer compared to many states is clearly a puzzle. This is even more intriguing in a context where social justice was essentially seen in terms of access to education. Though we do not have clear answers, one possibility is that when elites exit from the public system (which is not unique to the state) there is less collective pressure on the system. Rather than exercise their voice, the lower-caste groups who can afford it are also possibly exiting the system. But learning outcomes in private schools are in fact lower than in public schools. According to a senior bureaucrat, the emphasis on scoring high marks in school finals above other objectives to ensure college admissions translates into lesser incentives for teachers to invest in learning. However, a government initiative has been launched earlier this year[3] to address this gap.

POSSIBLE FUTURES

In the context of such structural constraints within and external to the populist domain, the limits and possibilities of the political process in the state can probably be best framed through the lives of Sattanathan and Anitha. As Sattanathan, the lower-caste bureaucrat observes in his autobiography, his mother, an illegitimate daughter of a local patron, did not have the ability to demand or aspire for anything beyond food. He retired as a senior bureaucrat and is popular for having written the first backward classes commission report in the state. His mobility from poverty to becoming a public intellectual may not be an exception as one can find many such examples in the state. The Dravidian movement has provided mobility to people from such modest caste–class backgrounds through access to spaces of entrepreneurship, upper echelons of the bureaucracy and labour markets in the private sector. The state has indeed evolved from being a highly unequal caste society to a relatively inclusive, socially advanced and economically productive. On the other hand, we have Anitha, a Dalit girl who took her life on failing to secure admission to train as a medical doctor despite having the required marks due to a change in the admission criteria. Her failure may suggest the inability or indifference of the subnational political regime or the centre's intransigence. But it also exposes the limits or the fault line of the model. If her aspiration to become a doctor epitomises the promise of the model, her failure to realise it shows its limits.

Does this mean that the future is likely to be a mere continuation of economic popular interventions? It may not be. To begin with, what is seldom acknowledged is the possibility that even economic popular interventions tend to have implications for freedom and social justice. Provision of laptops for students, or mixies and grinders for women does have incremental emancipatory effects. Combined with the broad-basing of education and aspirations, such interventions may well serve to forge a new set of demands. The recent large-scale protests around questions of ecology are reflective of this shift. Three of the largest state-level protests in recent years have been around issues of ecology and livelihoods. In Chapter 2, we have already mapped the terrain of the jallikattu protests that sought to link the agrarian crisis, indigenous livestock economies and Tamil identity. Since then, there were also protests across the state against the union government's permission to a private firm for hydrocarbon exploration in the Cauvery delta. This led to the state declaring the delta a zone exclusively for agriculture though questions continue to be asked on the efficacy of this policy move in protecting the zone from further ecological damage. In May 2018, several protestors were killed in police firing in Tuticorin when they were agitating against pollution from copper smelting by a factory belonging to the Vedanta group. Also since 2011, people from several villages in the same region have been protesting, with support from state- and national-level movements, against the commissioning of a new phase of the Kudankulam Nuclear Power Plant. Apart from such protests, the state is home to one of the largest organic farming and traditional seed preservation movements in the country. A number of civil society initiatives are further underway to restore traditional water bodies and localised irrigation systems. Clearly such concerns stand in contrast to the productivist ethos that informed the making of Dravidian common-sense. The DMK in its recent election manifesto for example promised to explore the possibility of introducing affirmative action policies in private sector employment and also assured state incentives for organic farming. Hence, even when interventions seek to depoliticise and clientelise the 'people', the agency of the people embedded in a longer history of political assertion may work in directions not anticipated by readings of populism that do not adequately take account of people's agency. Chatterjee (2019), for example, does not concede the possibility that even interventions driven by governmental imperatives may produce surplus effects. The spaces of freedom opened by material goods and cash transfers tend to exceed the pure logic of governmental control, especially when other mobilisational logics are at work.

Issues of quality, be it in education or healthcare, and consequent disparities in human development can possibly be addressed within the domain of subnational politics and policy implementation. Expansion of the domain of affirmative action too may continue to be the terrain of politics given the persistence of caste-based inequalities all over the country. The limits of structural transformation and its inability to generate dignified livelihoods for those exiting agriculture, or uneven development generated through processes of modernisation cannot, however, be addressed at the subnational scale. The labour question, going by the experience of states like Kerala or Tamil Nadu, is increasingly being resolved through access to global labour markets. Tamil Nadu has in fact emerged as a major source of remittances in the country, with an expanding regime of labour mobility driven by investments in human development. But with growing restrictions to labour mobility globally, there are clear limits to this process. The extent to which populist mobilisation can re-orient its terrain to forge appropriate demands in the new context will shape the possibilities of further expansion of substantive democracy.

NOTES

1   Personal interview (6 April 2020).
2   Personal interview (12 July 2019).
3   Personal interview (6 January 2020).

BIBLIOGRAPHY

Abegaz, B. 2013. 'Political Parties in Business: Rent Seekers, Developmentalists, or Both?' *Journal of Development Studies 49*(11): 1467–83.

Abraham, V. 2016. 'MGNREGS: Political Economy, Local Governance and Asset Creation in South India' (CDS Working Paper No. 471). Centre for Development Studies, http://cds.edu/wp-content/uploads/2016/10/WP471.pdf (accessed 3 October 2019).

Acharya, D., G. Vaidyanathan, V. R. Muraleedharan, D. S. Dheenadayalan and U. Dash. 2011. 'Do the Poor Benefit from Public Spending on Healthcare in India? Results from Benefit and (Utilisation) Incidence Analysis in Tamil Nadu and Orissa'. Consortium for Research on Equitable Health Systems, London School of Hygiene and Tropical Medicine.

Adiseshiah, M. 1972. *The Perspective Plan for Tamil Nadu: Towards a Learning Society—A Plan for Education, Science and Technology, 1976–1986*. Madras: State Planning Commission, Government of Tamil Nadu.

Agarwal, P. 2006. 'Higher Education in India: The Need for Change' (Working Paper No. 180). Indian Council for Research on International Economic Relations, http://www.icrier.org/pdf/ICRIER_WP180__Higher_Education_in_India_.pdf (accessed 10 July 2019).

Agarwala, R. 2013. *Informal Labor, Formal Politics, and Dignified Discontent in India*. Cambridge: Cambridge University Press.

Agarwala, R. and R. Herring 2020. 'Does Class Matter in Politics?: Rethinking "Conditions and Reasons"'. In *Interpreting Politics: Situated Knowledge, India, and the Rudolph Legacy*, edited by John Echeverri-Gent and Kamal Sadiq, pp. 155–89. New Delhi: Oxford University Press.

Aglietta, M. 2000 [1979]. *A Theory of Capitalist Regulation: The US Experience*. London and New York: Verso.

Ahluwalia, M. S. 1978. 'Rural Poverty and Agricultural Performance in India'. *The Journal of Development Studies 14*(3): 298–323.

Alamu, R. 2011. 'It Just Works in TN'. *The Hindu*, 24 September, https://www.thehindu.com/features/magazine/it-just-works-in-tn/article2475948.ece (accessed 28 January 2019).

Alcott, B. and P. Rose. 2017. 'Learning in India's Primary Schools: How Do Disparities Widen Across the Grades?' *International Journal of Educational Development 56*: 42–51.

Alexander, A. 2018. 'What Tamil Nadu, Kerala Can Teach Other States'. *Livemint*, 22 May, https://www.livemint.com/Opinion/qjV2SmyodMJgbGlS6zLnDJ/What-Tamil-Nadu-Kerala-can-teach-other-states.html (accessed 27 January 2019).

Aloysius, G. 2013. *Village Reconstruction*. New Delhi: Critical Quest.

Amirapu, A. and A. Subramanian. 2015. 'Manufacturing or Services? An Indian Illustration of a Development Dilemma' (Working Paper No. 408). Center for Global Development, Washington DC.

Amsden, A. 1989. *Asia's Next Giant: South Korea and Late Industrialization*. New York and Oxford: Oxford University Press.

Anaimuthu, V. 1974. *Periyar Ee Ve Ra Sinthanaikal* [Thoughts of Periyar E. V. R.] (3 Vols). Tiruchirapalli: Thinker's Forum.

Anandhi, S. 2018. 'Education and Dravidian Common Sense', *Seminar, 708* (August), http://www.india-seminar.com/2018/708/708_a_anandhi.htm (accessed 27 March 2019).

———. 1991. 'Women's Question in the Dravidian Movement c. 1925–1948'. *Social Scientist* 19(5/6): 24–41.

Anandhi, S., K. R. Manoharan, M. Vijayabaskar and A. Kalaiyarasan (eds). 2020. *Rethinking Social Justice*. Hyderabad: Orient Blackswan.

Anandhi, S. and M. Vijayabaskar 2013. 'Where Buying a Motorcycle Can Spark a Riot', https://www.thehindu.com/opinion/op-ed/where-buying-a-motorcycle-can-spark-a-riot/article4280216.ece (accessed 27 November 2019).

Annadurai, C. N. 2017 [1949]. *Panathottam* [Garden of Money]. Chennai: Aazhi Publishers.

Anwar, S. 2018. 'Muslims and the Dravidian Movement'. *Seminar*, *708* (August), http://www.india-seminar.com/2018/708/708_s_anwar.htm (accessed 23 February 2020).

Appadurai, A. 2004. 'The Capacity to Aspire: Culture and the Terms of Recognition'. In *Culture and Public Action*, edited by V. Rao and M. Walton, pp. 59–84. Stanford: Stanford University Press.

Arasu, V. 2012. *Madras Secular Society: Collected Articles from an Atheist Journal The Thinker* (6 Vols). Chennai: New Century Book House.

———. 2013. *Aththipakkam A. Venkatachalanaar akkangal thirattu* [Collected Articles of Aththipakkam A. Venkatachalam]. Chennai: New Century Book House.

Arooran, K. N. 1980. *Tamil Renaissance and Dravidian Nationalism, 1905–1944*. Madurai: Koodal Publishers.

Arora, R. U. 2009. 'Globalization and Stages of Development: An Exploratory Analysis'. *Review of Urban & Regional Development Studies 21*(23): 124–42.

Asher, Sam, Paul Novosad and Charlie Rafkin. 2020. 'Intergenerational Mobility in India: New Methods and Estimates Across Time, Space, and Communities', https://www.dartmouth.edu/~novosad/anr-india-mobility.pdf (accessed 17 October 2020).

Athreya, V. B., G. Boklin, G. Djurfeldt and S. Lindberg. 1986. 'Production Relations and Agrarian Change: Some Findings from a Case Study in Tamil Nadu'. *Social Scientist 14*(5): 3–14.

Audretsch, D. B., D. Heger and T. Veith. 2015. 'Infrastructure and Entrepreneurship'. *Small Business Economics 44*(2): 219–30.

Babu, Gireesh. 2009. 'Tamil Nadu Eyes Major Investments in State's Auto, Auto Components Industry', *Business Standard*, 5 January, https://www.business-standard.com/article/economy-policy/tamil-nadu-eyes-major-investments-in-state-s-auto-auto-components-industry-119010400335_1.html (accessed 14 March 2020).

Bagchi A. K. 2012. 'Indian Business History'. *Indian Historical Review 39*(1): 73–91.

Baker, C. J. 1976. *The Politics of South India 1920–1937*. New Delhi: Vikas Publishing House.

Balagopal, G. and M. Vijayabaskar. 2018. *Vulnerability, State and Social Protection in Tamil Nadu: A Life-cycle Perspective*. Report submitted to UNICEF, Chennai.

————. 2019. 'Flaws of Insurance-based Healthcare Provision', *Economic & Political Weekly 54*(2): 18–21.

Balagopal, K. 2009. 'Ideology and Adjudication: The Supreme Court and OBC Reservations'. *Economic & Political Weekly 44*(43): 16–19.

Balakrishnan, P. 2008. 'Visible Hand: Public Policy and Economic Growth in the Nehru Era'. *The Indian Economic Journal 56*(1): 11–35.

Balarajan, Y., S. Selvaraj and S. V. Subramanian. 2011. 'Health Care and Equity in India'. *The Lancet 377*(9764): 505–15.

Banerjee, S. and N. Ghosh. 2018. 'Introduction: Debating Intersectionalities—Challenges for a Methodological Framework'. *South Asia Multidisciplinary Academic Journal*, 19, http://doi.org/10.4000/samaj.4745 (accessed 22 January 2020).

Banerjee, A. and L. Iyer. 2005. 'History, Institutions and Economic Performance: The Legacy of Colonial Land Tenure Systems in India'. *American Economic Review 95*(4): 1190–213.

Bardhan, P. K. 1973. 'On the Incidence of Poverty in Rural India in the Sixties'. *Economic & Political Weekly 8*(4–6): 245–54.

Bardhan, P. 2008. 'Economic Reforms, Poverty, and Inequality in China and India'. In *Arguments for a Better World: Essays in Honour of Amartya Sen*, edited by K. Basu and R. Kanbur, Vol. 2, pp. 49–58. Oxford: Oxford University Press.

————. 2009. 'Notes on the Political Economy of India's Tortuous Transition'. *Economic & Political Weekly 44*(49): 31–36.

————. 2013. 'Inequality, Inefficiency, and the Challenges for Social Democracy in India's Economic Transition'. In *An Indian Social Democracy: Integrating Markets, Democracy and Social Justice*, edited by S. Khilnani and M. Malhoutra, Vol. 2, pp. 17–39. New Delhi: Academic Foundation.

Barnett, M. R. 1976. *The Politics of Cultural Nationalism in South India*. Princeton: Princeton University Press.

Barrientos, A. and D. Hulme. 2009. 'Social Protection for the Poor and Poorest in Developing Countries: Reflections on a Quiet Revolution'. *Oxford Development Studies 37*(4): 439–56.

Basu, R. 2013. 'Leadership in the Health Sector: The Importance of the Tamil Nadu Model for a Universal Public Health Care System in India. Network of Asia Pacific Schools and Institutes of Public Administration and Governance

(NAPSIPAG) Conference, Dehradun, 20–22 June, http://www.napsipag.org/pdf/d_ab_18.pdf (accessed 24 June 2019).

Basu, K. and A. Maertens. 2007. 'Public Health in India'. In *Oxford Companion to Economics in India*, edited by K. Basu, pp. 435–40. Oxford and New Delhi: Oxford University Press.

Benjamin, D., P. Winters, T. Reardon and K. Stamoulis. 2009. 'Rural Nonfarm Employment and Farming: Household-level Linkages'. *Agricultural Economics 40*(2): 119–23.

Berman, P. and R. Ahuja. 2008. 'Government Health Spending in India'. *Economic & Political Weekly 43*(26–27): 209–16.

Bernstein, H. 1996. 'Agrarian Questions Then and Now'. *Journal of Peasant Studies 24*(1–2): 22–59.

Bhagwati, J. and A. Panagariya. 2013. *Why Growth Matters: How Economic Growth in India Reduced Poverty and the Lessons for Other Developing Countries*. New York: PublicAffairs, Perseus Books Group.

Bharadwaj, K. 1982. 'Regional Differentiation in India: A Note'. *Economic & Political Weekly 17*(14–15–16): 605–07+609+611–14.

Bharathidasan, K. 2015. 'Political Biography of Rao Saheb L. C. Guruswamy (1895–1960)'. Presented at MIDS, Chennai.

Bhatnagar, R. 2011. 'More than 50% Engineering Colleges Are of Poor Quality: Government of Tamil Nadu'. *Shiksha*, 1 November, https://www.shiksha.com/b-tech/articles/more-than-50-engineering-colleges-are-of-poor-quality-government-of-tamil-nadu-blogId-4019 (accessed 14 May 2020).

Bonner, K., J. Daum, J. Duncan, E. Dinsmore, K. Fuglesten, L. Lai, J. Lee, K. Manchester, F. Tadesse and R. Quinn. 2012. *MGNREGA Implementation: A Cross-state Comparison* (The Woodrow Wilson School's Graduate Policy Workshop). Princeton: Princeton University.

Carswell, G. and G. De Neve. 2014. 'MGNREGA in Tamil Nadu: A Story of Success and Transformation?' *Journal of Agrarian Change 14*(4): 564–85.

Cassen, R. 1978. *India: Population, Economy, Society*. London: Macmillan.

Chakraborty, A. 2019. 'Inter-state Variations in Infrastructure and Social Service Delivery' (Paper Presentation). National Conference on Growth and Regional Development in India, 13–15 May. Institute for Human Development, New Delhi.

Chakraborty, P. 2019. 'Fiscal Federalism in India: Who Should Do What?'. *The India Forum*, April, https://www.theindiaforum.in/article/fiscal-federalism-india (accessed 27 March 2020).

Chakravarty, P. and V. Dehejia. 2016. 'The Gap between Rich and Poor States'. *The Hindu*, 5 September, https://www.thehindu.com/opinion/op-ed/The-gap-between-rich-and-poor-States/article14623327.ece (accessed 23 December 2018).

Chakravorty. S. 2013. *The Price of Land: Acquisition, Conflict, Consequence*. New Delhi: Oxford University Press.

Chandrasekhar, C. P. and Jayati Ghosh. 2011. 'Public Works and Wages in Rural India', https://www.nregaconsortium.in/download/articles/jayati%20and%20chandrashekhar%2011-jan-11.pdf (accessed 12 December 2019).

———— 2011. 'Self-Employment as Opportunity or Challenge'. *Macrossan*, http://www.macroscan.org/fet/mar07/pdf/Self_employment.pdf (accessed 12 October 2019).

Chari, S. 2004. *Fraternal Capital: Peasant-workers, Self-made Men, and Globalization in Provincial India*. Stanford: Stanford University Press.

Chatterjee, P. 2004. *The Politics of the Governed: Reflections on Popular Politics in Most of the World*. New Delhi: Permanent Black.

————. 2008. 'Democracy and Economic Transformation in India'. *Economic & Political Weekly* 43(16): 53–62.

————. 2011. *Lineages of Political Society: Studies in Postcolonial Democracy*. New York: Colombia University Press.

————. 2017. 'Prelude: Land and the Political Management of Primitive Accumulation'. In *The Land Question in India: State, Dispossession, and Capitalist Transition*, edited by P. D'Costa Anthony and Achin Chakraborty, pp. 1–15. Oxford: Oxford University Press.

————. 2019. *I am the People: Reflections on Popular Sovereignty Today*. New York: Ccolumbia University Press.

Cherodian, R. and A. P. Thirlwall. 2015. 'Regional Disparities in Per Capita Income in India: Convergence or Divergence?' *Journal of Post Keynesian Economics* 37(3): 384–407.

Chhibber P. K. and R. Verma 2018. *Ideology and Identity: The Changing Party Systems of India*. New York: Oxford University Press.

Choudhury, P. K. 2016. 'Role of Private Sector in Medical Education and Human Resource Development for Health in India'. *Economic & Political Weekly* 51(3): 71–79.

Coe, N. M., M. Hess, H. W. Yeung, P. Dicken and J. Henderson. 2004. '"Globalizing" Regional Development: A Global Production Networks Perspective'. *Transactions of the Institute of British Geographers* 29(4): 468–84.

Cornwell, E. Y. and B. Cornwell. 2008. 'Access to Expertise as a Form of Social Capital: An Examination of Race- and Class-based Disparities in Network Ties to Experts'. *Sociological Perspectives* 51(4): 853–76.

Crouch, C. and W. Streeck. 1997. 'Introduction: The Future of Capitalist Diversity'. In *Political Economy of Modern Capitalism: Mapping Convergence and Diversity*, edited by C. Crouch and W. Streeck, pp. 1–18. London: Sage Publications.

Cullen, W. J. 2019. *A Comparative Analysis to Understand the Subnational Motivations for Renewable Energy Development in India*. Unpublished senior thesis, Claremont McKenna College, Claremont, CA.

Damodaran, H. 2008. *India's New Capitalists: Caste, Business, and Industry in a Modern Nation*. Basingstoke: Palgrave MacMillan.

———. 2016. 'How Tamil Nadu's Rural Industry Model Can Keep Farm Unrest at Bay'. *Indian Express*, 27 September, https://indianexpress.com/article/explained/tamil-nadu-farmers-protests-maratha-protests-patel-protests-kapu-protests-3051642/ (accessed 21 October 2019).

Dasgupta, A. 2017. 'Land Reform in Kerala and West Bengal: Two Stories of Left Reformism and Development'. In *The Land Question in India: State, Dispossession, and Capitalist Transition*, edited by P. D'Costa Anthony and Achin Chakraborty , pp. 242–64. Oxford: Oxford University Press.

Das Gupta, M. 2005. 'Public Health in India: Dangerous Neglect'. *Economic & Political Weekly* 40(49): 5159–65.

Das Gupta, M., B. R. Desikachari, R. Shukla, T. V. Somanathan, P. Padmanaban and K. K. Datta. 2010. 'How Might India's Public Health Systems Be Strengthened? Lessons from Tamil Nadu'. *Economic & Political Weekly* 45(10): 46–60.

Datta, K. K. 2009. 'Public Health Workforce in India: Career Pathways for Public Health Personnel' (Background Paper). National Consultation on Public Health Workforce in India, 24–25 June. Ministry of Health & Family Welfare (Government of India) and WHO Country Office for India, New Delhi, https://pdfs.semanticscholar.org/6c0e/be6f693456ec8947a67cb02c5417089b2b43.pdf (accessed 22 July 2019).

Davis, J. R. and D. J. Bezemer. 2004. *The Development of the Rural Non-farm Economy in Developing Countries and Transition Economies: Key Emerging and Conceptual Issues*. Chatham: Natural Resources Institute, http://projects.nri.org/rnfe/pub/papers/keyissues.pdf (accessed 8 February 2020).

D'Costa, Anthony P. and A. Chakraborty (eds). 2019. 'Changing Contexts, Shifting Roles, and the Recasting of the Role of the Indian State: An Introduction'. In *Changing Contexts and Shifting Roles of the Indian State: New Perspectives on Development Dynamics*, edited by Anthony P. D'Costa and A. Chakraborty, pp. 1–21. Singapore: Springer.

De Silva, I. and S. Sumarto. 2015. 'Dynamics of Growth, Poverty and Human Capital: Evidence from Indonesian Sub-national Data'. *Journal of Economic Development* 40(2): 1–33.

Deshpande, A. and S. Sharma 2013. 'Entrepreneurship or Survival? Caste and Gender of Small Business in India'. *Economic & Political Weekly* 48(28): 38–49.

Dewey, J. 1993. *The Political Writings*. Cambridge: Hackett Publishing Company.

Dholakia, A. R. and R. H. Dholakia. 2004. 'Expenditure Allocation and Welfare Returns to Government: A Suggested Model'. *Economic & Political Weekly* 39(24): 853–56.

Dorin, B. 2017. 'India and Africa in the Global Agricultural System (1960–2050): Towards a New Sociotechnical Regime'. *Economic & Political Weekly* 52(25–26): 5–13.

Doval, N. 2017. 'Tamil Nadu's Amma Canteen Concept Catches On in Other States'. *Livemint*, 27 March, https://www.livemint.com/Politics/pHvjY4PHykVOy7irb8H2cO/Tamil-Nadus-Amma-canteen-concept-catches-on-in-other-states.html (accessed 12 March 2019).

Down to Earth. 2019 'Renewable Energy in India: Tamil Nadu One of the World's Top 9 Green Markets'. 20 January, https://www.downtoearth.org.in/news/energy/renewable-energy-in-india-tamil-nadu-one-of-the-world-s-top-9-green-power-markets-62887 (accessed 17 March 2020).

Drèze, J. and A. Sen. 2011. 'Putting Growth in Its Place'. *Outlook*, 14 November, https://www.outlookindia.com/magazine/story/putting-growth-in-its-place/278843 (accessed 18 December 2018).

―――. 2013. *An Uncertain Glory: India and Its Contradictions*. Princeton, NJ: Princeton University Press.

Drèze, J. and R. Khera. 2013. 'Rural Poverty and the Public Distribution System'. *Economic & Political Weekly 48*(45–46): 55–60.

―――. 2012. 'Regional Patterns of Human and Child Deprivation in India'. *Economic & Political Weekly 47*(39): 42–49.

Drèze, J. 2006. 'Universalization with Quality ICDS in a Rights Perspective'. *Economic & Political Weekly 41*(34): 3706–15.

Drèze, J. and C. Oldiges 2011. 'NREGA: The Official Picture'. In *The Battle for Employment Guarantee*, edited by R. Khera, pp. 21–39. Delhi: Oxford University Press.

Dubbudu, R. 2017. 'Karnataka, Tamil Nadu & Telangana Together Make Up for More than 60% of IT Exports'. *Factly*, 26 October, https://factly.in/karnataka-tamil-nadu-telangana-together-make-60-exports/ (accessed 12 April 2019).

Eaton, K. 2004. *Politics beyond the Capital: The Design of Subnational Institutions in South America*. Stanford: Stanford University Press.

Energy Department, Government of Tamil Nadu. 'Power for All-Tamil Nadu', https://powermin.nic.in/sites/default/files/uploads/Power_For_All_Tamilnadu_Signed.pdf (accessed 23 December 2019).

Evans, P. 1995. *Embedded Autonomy: States and Industrial Transformation*. Princeton: Princeton University Press.

Evans, P. and P. Heller. 2015. 'Human Development, State Transformation and the Politics of the Developmental State'. In *The Oxford Handbook of Transformations of the State*, edited by S. Leibfried, F. Nullmeier, E. Huber, M. Lange, J. Levy and J. D. Stephens, pp. 691–713. Oxford: Oxford University Press.

―――. 2018. 'The State and Development' (Working Paper 2018/112). United Nations University World Institute for Development Economics Research.

Ferguson, J. 2015. *Give a Man a Fish: Reflections on the New Politics of Distribution*. Durham: Duke University Press.

Fitjar, R. D. 2010. 'Explaining Variation in Sub-state Regional Identities in Western Europe'. *European Journal of Political Research 49*(4): 522–544.

Forgacs, D. 1993. 'National–Popular: Genealogy of a Concept'. In *The Cultural Studies Reader*, edited by S. During, pp. 177–190. London: Routledge.

———. 2000. *The Antonio Gramsci Reader: Selected Writings 1916–1935*. New York: New York University Press.

Fuller, C. J. and H. Narasimhan. 2014. *Tamil Brahmans: The Making of a Middle-Class Caste*. Chicago and London: University of Chicago Press.

———. 2006. 'Engineering Colleges, "Exposure" and Information Technology: Professionals in Tamil Nadu'. *Economic & Political weekly 41*(3): 258–62, 288.

Galanter, M. 1984. *Competing Equalities: Law and the Backward Classes in India*. Berkeley: University of California Press .

Garretsen, H., P. McCann, R. Martin and P. Tyler. 2013. 'The Future of Regional Policy'. *Cambridge Journal of Regions, Economy and Society 6*(2): 179–86.

Geetha, V. and S. V. Rajadurai 2008. *Towards a Non-Brahmin Millennium: From Iyothee Thass to Periyar*, 2nd edn. Kolkota: Samya.

Ghani, E., A. G. Goswami and W. R. Kerr. 2012. 'Is India's Manufacturing Sector Moving Away from Cities?' (Working Paper No. 12-090). Harvard Business School, Boston.

Ghosh, M. 2012. 'Regional Economic Growth and Inequality in India during the Pre- and Post-reform Periods'. *Oxford Development Studies 40*(2): 190–212.

Giraudy, A., E. Moncada and R. Snyder. 2019. 'Introduction'. In *Inside Countries: Subnational Research in Comparative Politics*, edited by A. Giraudy, E. Moncada and R. Snyder, pp. 3–54. Cambridge: Cambridge University Press.

Gopalakrishnan, R. 2015. 'Labour Jurisprudence of the Supreme Court: Recent Trends'. In *Labour, Employment and Economic Growth*, edited by K. V. Ramaswamy, pp. 292–318. New Delhi: Cambridge University Press.

Gough, K. 1981. *Rural Society in Southeast India*. Cambridge: Cambridge University Press.

Government of India. 2014. *Annual Survey of Industries*. 2014. New Delhi: Central Statistics Office (Industrial Statistics Wing), Ministry of Statistics & Planning, Government of India.

———. 2018a. *All India Survey on Higher Education 2017–18*. New Delhi: Department of Higher Education, Ministry of Human Resource Development, Government of India.

————. 2018b. *Periodic Labour Force Survey 2018*. New Delhi: Ministry of Statistics and Programme Implementation, Government of India.

Gorringe, H. 2017. *Panthers in Parliament: Dalits, Caste, and Political Power in South India*. New Delhi: Oxford University Press.

Government of Tamil Nadu. 1975a. *Report of the Committee to Go into the Living Conditions of Workers in Beedi and Other Unorganised Industries in Tamil Nadu*. Chennai: Office of the Commissioner of Labour.

————. 1975b. *Tamil Nadu State Administration Report, 1972–73*. Madras.

————. 1976. *Tamil Nadu State Administration Report, 1974–75*. Madras.

————. 1993. *Tamil Nadu: An Economic Appraisal 1992–93*. Madras: Department of Evaluation and Applied Research.

————. 1998. *Report of the Committees Constituted to Study the Problems and Issues of Unorganised Labour in Tamil Nadu*. Chennai: Office of the Commissioner of Labour.

————. 2008a. *Monitoring Report for Welfare Boards for Unorganized Workers*. Chennai: Tamil Nadu Construction Workers Welfare Board, Department of Labour and Employment.

————. 2008b. *Monitoring Reports on Tamil Nadu Construction Workers Welfare Board*. Chennai: Tamil Nadu Construction Workers Welfare Board, Department of Labour and Employment.

————. 2014. 'Implementation of the Tamil Nadu Industrial Policy'. G.O. (Ms.) No. 101. Industries (MIB.1) Department, 4 August, http://cms.tn.gov.in/sites/default/files/go/ind_e_101_2014.pdf (accessed 12 January 2020).

————. 2017. *Tamil Nadu Human Development Report*. New Delhi: Academic Foundation.

————. 2019. *Transport Department Policy Note 2018–2019*, https://cms.tn.gov.in/sites/default/files/documents/transport_e_pn_2018_19.pdf (accessed 29 January 2020).

Gowda, M. R. and E. Sridharan. 2012. 'Reforming India's Party Financing and Election Expenditure Laws'. *Election Law Journal 11*(2): 226–40.

Goyal, J. and D. P. Singh 2014. 'Academic Performance of OBC Students in Universities: Findings from Three States'. *Economic & Political Weekly 49*(5): 55–62.

Guhan, S. and J. P. Mencher. 1983a. 'Iruvelpattu Revisited: I'. *Economic & Political Weekly 18*(23): 1013–15 and 1017–22.

———.1983b. 'Iruvelpattu Revisited: II'. *Economic & Political Weekly 18*(24): 1063–74.

Gupta, S. 2013. *Economic History of Bengal Presidency*. Patna: Asian Development Research Institute (ADRI).

Hardgrave, R. L. 1969. *The Nadars of Tamilnad: The Political Culture of a Community in Change*. Berkeley and Los Angeles: University of California Press.

Harriss, J. 1999. 'Comparing Political Regimes Across Indian States: A Preliminary Essay'. *Economic & Political Weekly 34*(48): 3367–77.

———. 2002. 'The Great Tradition Globalises: Reflections on Two Studies of "the Industrial Leaders" of Madras'. *Modern Asian Studies 37*(2): 327–62.

———. 2017. 'Universalizing Elementary Education in India: Achievements and Challenges' (Working Paper No. 2017–3). United Nations Research Institute for Social Development, Geneva.

Harriss, J. and A. K. J. Wyatt. 2019. 'Business and Politics: The Tamil Nadu Puzzle'. In *Business and Politics in India*, edited by C. Jaffrelot, A. Kohli and K. Murali, pp. 234–59. New York: Oxford University Press.

Harriss, J. and J. Jeyaranjan. 2016. 'Rural Tamil Nadu in the Liberalization Era'. In *The Changing Village in India: Insights from Longitudinal Research*, edited by Himanshu, P. Jha and G. Rodgers, pp. 263–88. New Delhi: Oxford University Press.

Harriss, J., J. Jeyaranjan and K. Nagaraj. 2010. 'Land, Labour and Caste Politics in Rural Tamil Nadu in the 20th Century: Iruvelpattu 1916–2008'. *Economic & Political Weekly 45*(31): 47–61.

———. 2012. 'Rural Urbanism in Tamil Nadu: Notes on a "Slater Village": Gangaikondan, 1916–2012'. *Review of Agrarian Studies 2*(2): 29–59.

Harriss-White, B. 1984. 'Meals and Noon Meals in South India: Food and Nutrition Policy in the Rural Food Economy of Tamil Nadu State' (Occasional Paper 31). School of Development Studies, East Anglia.

———. 1996. *A Political Economy of Agricultural Markets in South India: Masters of the Countryside*. New Delhi: Sage.

———. 2002. *India Working: Essays on Society and Economy*. Cambridge: Cambridge University Press.

Harriss-White, B., E. Basile, A. Dixit, P. Joddar, A. Prakash and K. Vidyarthee. 2013. *Dalits and Adivasis in India's Business Economy: Three Essays and an Atlas*. Gurgaon: Three Essays Collective.

Harvey, D. 2005. *Spaces of Neoliberalization: Towards a Theory of Uneven Geographical Development*. Stuttgart: Franz Stenier Verlag.

Hasan, R., S. Lamba and A. Sen Gupta. 2015. 'Growth, Structural Change and Poverty Reduction'. In *Labour, Employment and Economic Growth in India*, edited by K. V. Ramasamy, pp. 91–126. New Delhi: Cambridge University Press.

Hay, C. 2000. 'Contemporary Capitalism, Globalisation, Regionalisation and the Persistence of National Variation'. *Review of International Studies 26*(4): 509–31.

Heller, P. 1999. *The Labor of Development: Workers and the Transformation of Capitalism in Kerala, India*. Ithaca: Cornell University Press.

Heyer, J. 2010. 'Improving Labour Standards: Lessons from the Tiruppur Region' (Paper Presentation). 21st European Conference on Modern South Asian Studies, 26–29 July, University of Bonn.

———. 2016. 'Rural Gounders on the Move in Western Tamil Nadu: 1981–2 to 2008–9'. In *The Changing Village in India: Insights from Longitudinal Research*, edited by Himanshu, P. Jha and G. Rodgers, pp. 327–56. New Delhi: Oxford University Press.

Himakiran, A. and S. Nirmala. 2020. *The Jallikattu Movement, Tamil Nadu, India: A Case Study of Grassroots Activism and People's Politics*. New Delhi: Rajiv Gandhi Institute for Contemporary Studies.

Ho, C-Y. and D. Li. 2007. 'Rising Regional Inequality in China: Policy Regimes and Structural Changes' (WP2007–014). Department of Economics, Boston University, http://ideas.repec.org/p/bos/wpaper/wp2007-014.html (accessed 20 September 2019).

———. 2008. 'Rising Regional Inequality in China: Policy Regimes and Structural Changes'. *Papers in Regional Science 87*(2): 245–59.

Hodges, S. 2013. '"It All Changed after Apollo": Healthcare Myths and Their Making in Contemporary India'. *Indian Journal of Medical Ethics 10*(4): 242–49.

Howarth, D. (ed.). 2015. *Ernesto Laclau: Post-Marxism, Populism and Critique*. London and New York: Routledge.

Huang, X. 2015. 'Four Worlds of Welfare: Understanding Subnational Variation in Chinese Social Health Insurance'. *The China Quarterly 222*: 449–74.

Indian Express. 2013. 'Incentive Scheme to Attract Private Investment in Medical Education'. 18 June, https://indianexpress.com/article/cities/

lucknow/incentive-scheme-to-attract-private-investment-in-medical-education/ (accessed 24 July 2019).

Indo Asian News Service. 2018. 'Kerala Tops Governance Index, Tamil Nadu Ranks Second: Report'. *Hindustan Times*, 22 July, https://www.hindustantimes.com/india-news/kerala-tops-governance-index-tamil-nadu-ranks-second-report/story-z9woJuypL16iaO8XUu9x5H.html (accessed 8 June 2020).

Ingleby, J. C. 1998. *Education as a Missionary Tool: A Study in Christian Missionary Education by English Protestant Missionaries in India with Special Reference to Cultural Change.* Unpublished doctoral dissertation, Oxford Centre for Mission Studies, Oxford, UK.

International Labour Organization and Organisation for Economic Co-operation and Development (ILO and OECD). 2015. 'The Labour Share in G20 Economies'. Report prepared for the G20 Employment Working Group, 26–27 February, Antalya, Turkey.

Irschick, E. F. 1969. *Politics and Social Conflict in South India: The Non-Brahman Movement and Tamil Separatism, 1916–1929.* Berkeley and Los Angeles: University of California Press.

Iyer, L., T. Khanna and A. Varshney 2013. 'Caste and Entrepreneurship in India'. *Economic & Political Weekly* 48(6): 52–60.

Jaffrelot, C and A. Kalaiyarasan. 2019. 'Most Marginalised of Them All'. *Indian Express*, 1 November, https://indianexpress.com/article/opinion/columns/muslim-community-youth-india-marginalisation-6096881/ (accessed 25 November 2019).

Jaffrelot, C. 2000. 'The Rise of the Other Backward Classes in the Hindi Belt'. *Journal of Asian Studies* 59(1): 86–108.

Jain, P. and T. S. Maini. 2017. 'India's Subnational Governments Foray into the International Arena'. *Japanese Journal of Political Science* 18(2): 286–312.

Jeffery, C., N. M. Pamphilis, C. Rowe and E. Turner. 2014. 'Regional Policy Variation in Germany: The Diversity of Living Conditions in a "Unitary Federal State"'. *Journal of European Public Policy* 21(9): 1350–66.

Jeffery, R. 1988. *The Politics of Health in India.* Berkeley: University of California Press.

Jenkins, R. 2000. *Democratic Politics and Economic Reform in India.* Cambridge: Cambridge University Press.

————. 2004. *Regional Reflections: Comparing Politics Across India's States*. New Delhi: Oxford University Press.

Jenkins, R., L. Kennedy and P. Mukhopadhyay (eds). 2014. *Power, Policy and Protest: The Politics of India's Special Economic Zones*. New Delhi: Oxford University Press.

Jessop, B., N. Brenner and M. Jones. 2008. 'Theorizing Sociospatial Relations'. *Environment and Planning D: Society and Space 26*(3): 389–401.

Jeyaranjan, J. 2011. 'Women and Pro-poor Policies in Rural Tamil Nadu: An Examination of Practices and Responses'. *Economic & Political Weekly 46*(43): 64–74.

————. 2019. 'Sand and the Politics of Plunder in Tamil Nadu'. In *The Wild East: Criminal Political Economies in South Asia*, edited by B. Harriss-White and L. Michelutti, pp. 92–114. London: UCL Press.

————. 2020. 'Tenancy Reforms in Tamil Nadu: A Study from the Cauvery Delta Region'. In *Rethinking Social Justice*, edited by S. Anandhi, K. R. Manoharan, M. Vijayabaskar and A. Kalaiyarasan, pp. 255–83. Hyderabad: Orient Blackswan.

Jha, P. 2009. 'The Well-being of Labour in Contemporary Indian Economy: What's Active Labour Market Policy Got to Do with It?' (Employment Working Paper No. 39). Employment Analysis and Research Unit, Economic and Labour Market Analysis Department, International Labour Organization.

Joshi, D. K. and K. McGrath. 2015. 'Political Ideology, Public Policy and Human Development in India: Explaining the Gap between Gujarat and Tamil Nadu'. *Journal of Contemporary Asia 45*(3): 465–89.

Kaali, S. 2018. 'Making of a New Public Sphere'. *Seminar, 708* (August), http://www.india-seminar.com/2018/708/708_sundar_kaali.htm (accessed 22 February 2020).

Kabeer, N. 2012. 'Women's Economic Empowerment and Inclusive Growth: Labour Markets and Enterprise Development' (Discussion Paper No. 29/12). Centre for Development Policy & Research, School of Oriental & African Studies, University of London, https://www.soas.ac.uk/cdpr/publications/papers/file80432.pdf (accessed 19 January 2020).

Kailash, K. K. and M. Rasaratnam. 2015. 'The Policy-Shaping Capacity of States: Publicly Funded Health Insurance in Tamil Nadu and Kerala'. In

Politics of Welfare: Comparisons across Indian States, edited by L. Tillin, R. Deshpande and K. K. Kailash, pp. 40–68. New Delhi: Oxford University Press.

Kailash, K. K. 2020. 'Giving Agency to Political Parties'. *Economic & Political Weekly* 55(8): 23–26.

Kalaiyarasan, A. 2014. 'A Comparison of Developmental Outcomes in Gujarat and Tamil Nadu'. *Economic & Political Weekly* 49(15): 55–63.

———. 2017a. 'NEET Could Undo Tamil Nadu's Achievements in Public Health'. *Economic & Political Weekly* 52(38), https://www.epw.in/node/149907/pdf (accessed 29 September 2019).

———. 2017b. 'Populism and Party Society: Development Regimes in Tamil Nadu and West Bengal'. In *Political Economy of Contemporary India*, edited by R. Nagaraj and Sritpad Motiram, pp. 99–124. New Delhi: Cambridge University Press.

———. 2020. 'Structural Change in Tamil Nadu, 1980–2010: Limits of Subnational Development' (Working Paper). Madras Institute of Development Studies, Chennai.

Kannan, A. 2017. 'Tamil Pride beyond TN: Punjabis, Rajasthanis Join Jallikattu Protests in Coimbatore'. *The News Minute*, 21 January, https://www.thenewsminute.com/article/tamil-pride-beyond-tn-punjabis-rajasthanis-join-jallikattu-protests-coimbatore-56053 (accessed 24 March 2020).

Kannan, R. 2017. *Anna: The Life and Times of C. N. Annadurai*. New Delhi: Penguin.

Kapur, D. 2007. 'International Migration from India: Economic Impact'. In *The New Oxford Companion to Economics in India*, edited by Kaushik Basu and Annemie Maertens. New York: Oxford University Press, 414–17.

———. 2010. 'Indian Higher Education'. In *American Universities in a Global Market*, edited by C. Clotfelter, pp. 305–34. Chicago: National Bureau of Economic Research and University of Chicago Press.

Kapur, D. and M. Vaishnav. 2011. 'Quid Pro Quo: Builders, Politicians, and Election Finance in India'. Center for Global Development Working Paper (276), Washington D.C.

Kapur, D. and P. B. Mehta. 2007a. 'Higher Education'. In *Oxford Companion to Economics in India*, edited by K. Basu, pp. 248–51. New Delhi: Oxford University Press.

———. 2007b. 'Mortgaging the Future'. *India International Centre Quarterly* 34(3/4): 154–66.

Kar, S. and S. Sakthivel. 2007. 'Reforms and Regional Inequality in India'. *Economic & Political Weekly* 42(47): 69–73, 75–77.

Kawlra, A. 2018. *We Who Wove with Lotus Thread: Summoning Community in South India*. Hyderabad: Orient Blackswan.

Keating, M. 2013. *Rescaling the European State: The Making of Territory and the Rise of the Meso*. Oxford: Oxford University Press.

Kennedy, L. 2004. 'The Political Determinants of Reform Packaging: Contrasting Responses to Economic Liberalisation in Andhra Pradesh and Tamil Nadu'. In *Regional Reflections: Comparing Politics Across India's States*, edited by R. Jenkins, pp. 29–65. Oxford: Oxford University Press.

———. 2014. *The Politics of Economic Restructuring in India: Economic Governance and State Spatial Rescaling*. London and New York: Routledge.

Khan, M. H. 2000. 'Rents, Rent-seeking and Economic Development: An Introduction'. In *Rents, Rent-Seeking and Economic Development*, edited by M. H. Khan and K. S. Jomo, pp. 1–20. Cambridge: Cambridge University Press.

Khera, R. 2011a. 'Trends in Diversion of Grain from the Public Distribution System'. *Economic & Political Weekly* 46(21): 106–14.

———. 2011b. 'Revival of the Public Distribution System: Evidence and Explanations'. *Economic & Political Weekly* 46(44–45): 36–50.

Kochhar, K., U. Kumar, R. Rajan, A. Subramaniam and I. Tokatlidis. 2006. 'India's Pattern of Development: What Happened, What Follows?' (Working Paper No. WP/06/22). International Monetary Fund.

Kohli, A. 2012. *Poverty Amidst Plenty in the New India*. Cambridge: Cambridge University Press.

Krishnan, R. K. and R. Sriramachandran. 2018a. 'Dravidian Futures'. *Seminar*, *708* (August): 62–68, http://www.india-seminar.com/2018/708/708_rajan_kurai_krishnan.htm (accessed 22 December 2019).

———. 2018b. 'The Problem' (Dravidianism: A Symposium on the Legacy of the Non-Brahmin Movement in Tamil Nadu). *Seminar*, *708* (August), http://www.india-seminar.com/2018/708/708_the_problem.htm (accessed 22 February 2020).

Krugman, P. 1991. 'Increasing Returns and Economic Geography'. *Journal of Political Economy 99*(3): 483–99.

Kumar, A. S., L. C. Chen, M. Choudhury, S. Ganju, V. Mahajan and A. Sinha. 2011. 'Financing Health Care for All: Challenges and Opportunities'. *The Lancet 377*(9766): 668–79.

Kumar, J. and C. Chandra 2003. 'Back Series of SDP Estimates in Domestic Product of States of India 1960–61 to 2000–01'. Economic and Political Weekly Research Foundation (EPWRF), Sameeksha Trust, Mumbai.

Kumaradoss, Y. V. 2004. 'Kamaraj Remembered'. *Economic & Political Weekly 39*(17): 1655–57.

Laclau, E. 2005. *On Populist Reason*. London and New York: Verso.

———. 2006. 'Why Constructing a People Is the Main Task of Radical Politics'. *Critical Inquiry 32*(4): 646–80.

Laclau, E. and C. Mouffe. 2014. *Hegemony and Socialist Strategy: Towards a Radical Democratic Politics*, 2nd edn. London:Verso.

Lakshman, N. 2011. *Patrons of the Poor: Caste Politics and Policymaking in India*. New Delhi: Oxford University Press.

Lalitha, N. 2008. 'Tamil Nadu Government Intervention and Prices of Medicines'. *Economic & Political Weekly 43*(1): 66–71.

Lanjouw, J. O. and P. Lanjouw. 2001. 'The Rural Non-farm Sector: Issues and Evidence from Developing Countries'. *Agricultural Economics 26*(1): 1–23.

Lewis, A. 1954. 'Economic Development with Unlimited Supplies of Labour'. *The Manchester School* 22: 139–191, reprinted in A. N. Agarwala and S. P. Singh (eds), *The Economics of Underdevelopment*, pp. 400–49 (London: Oxford University Press).

Li, T. M. 2010. 'To Make Live or Let Die? Rural Dispossession and the Protection of Surplus Populations'. *Antipode 41*(S1): 66–93.

Lobao, L., R. Martin and A. Rodríguez-Pose. 2009. 'Rescaling the State: New Modes of Institutional–Territorial Organization'. *Cambridge Journal of Regions, Economy and Society 2*(1): 3–12.

Madras Institute of Development Studies. 1988. *Tamil Nadu Economy: Performance and Issues*. New Delhi: Oxford and IBH Publishing.

Mahadevan, R. 1978. 'Immigrant Entrepreneurs in Colonial Burma: An Exploratory Study of the Role of Nattukottai Chettiars of Tamil Nadu, 1880–1930'. *The Indian Economic and Social History Review 15*(3): 329–58.

———. 1992. 'Process of Manchesterisation in Colonial South India: A Study of the Pattern of Textile Investment and the Growth of Indigenous Capitalists in Coimbatore' (Paper Presentation). 12th European Conference on Modern South Asian Studies, Berlin.

———. 2017. 'Chettiars, Big and Small, of Tamil Nadu'. *Outlook*, 18 September, https://www.outlookindia.com/magazine/story/chettiars-big-and-small-of-tamil-nadu/299290 (accessed 7 July 2020).

Mahadevan, R. and M. Vijayabaskar. 2014. 'Understanding the Making of Non-corporate Capital: Entrepreneurial Narratives from Tiruppur, Tamil Nadu' (Occasional Paper No. 33). Nehru Memorial Museum and Library.

Mahendra Dev, S. 2018. 'Growth, Inclusiveness and Sustainability'. Presidential address, 78th Annual Conference of the Indian Society of Agricultural Economics, 1–3 November, New Delhi.

Malmberg, A. and P. Maskell. 2002. 'The Elusive Concept of Localization Economies: Towards a Knowledge-based Theory of Spatial Clustering', *Environment and Planning A: Economy and Space 34*(3): 429–49.

Manian, S. S. and A. G. Sampath. 2017. *Kolgai kundru A. Govindasami: Sattamandra uraigal* (A. Govindasami: Assembly Speeches) (2 Vols). Villupuram: A. G. S. Pathippagam.

Manoharan, K. R. 2017. '"Anti-casteist Casteism?" A Fanonist Critique of Ramasamy's Discourse on Caste'. *Interventions 19*(1): 73–90.

———. 2020a. 'An Ethic beyond Anti-colonialism: A Periyarist Engagement with Fanonism'. In *Rethinking Social Justice*, edited by S. Anandhi, K. R. Manoharan, M. Vijayabaskar and A. Kalaiyarasan, pp. 159–78. Hyderabad: Orient Blackswan.

———. 2020b. 'In the Path of Ambedkar: Periyar and the Dalit Question'. *South Asian History and Culture 11*(2): 1–14, https://doi.org/10.1080/19472498.2020.1755127.

Marvel, M. R., J. L. Davis and C. R. Sproul. 2016. 'Human Capital and Entrepreneurship Research: A Critical Review and Future Directions'. *Entrepreneurship Theory and Practice 40*(3): 599–626.

Mehrotra, S. 2006. 'Well-being and Caste in Uttar Pradesh: Why UP Is Not Like Tamil Nadu'. *Economic & Political Weekly 41*(40): 4261–71.

Mehrotra, S., J. Parida, S. Sinha and A. Gandhi. 2014. 'Explaining Employment Trends in the Indian Economy: 1993–94 to 2011–12'. *Economic & Political Weekly 49*(32): 49–57.

Mehta, P. B. 2007. 'India's Unlikely Democracy: The Rise of Judicial Sovereignty'. *Journal of Democracy 18*(2): 70–83.

Mencher J. P. 1975. 'Land Ceilings in Tamil Nadu: Facts and Fictions'. *Economic & Political Weekly* 10(5/7): 241, 243, 245, 247, 249, 251, 253–54.

Menon, J. 2006. 'Tamil Nadu Set to Bring Bill Scrapping CET'. *Indian Express*, 13 November, http://archive.indianexpress.com/news/tamil-nadu-set-to-bring-bill-scrapping-cet/16566/ (accessed 3 January 2019).

Ministry of Finance. 2018. *Economic Survey 2017–18*, Vol. 1. New Delhi: Government of India.

Moncada, E. and R. Snyder. 2012. 'Subnational Comparative Research on Democracy: Taking Stock and Looking Forward'. *CD–APSA: The Newsletter of the Comparative Democratization Section of the American Political Science Association 10*(1): 4–9.

Mooij, J. 2003. 'Smart Governance? Politics in the Policy Process in Andhra Pradesh, India' (Working Paper 228). Overseas Development Institute, London.

Morrison, C. J. and A. E. Schwartz. 1996. 'State Infrastructure and Productive Performance'. *American Economic Review 86*(5): 1095–111.

Mouffe, C. 2018. *For a Left Populism.* London and New York: Verso.

Mukherjee, A. 2011. 'Mass-produced Engineers from Private Colleges with No Quality Are of No Use'. *Outlook*, 27 June, https://www.outlookindia.com/magazine/story/mass-produced-engineers-from-private-colleges-with-no-quality-are-of-no-use-to/277221 (accessed 4 May 2020).

Mundle, S., S. Chowdhury and S. Sikdar. 2016. 'Governance Performance of Indian States'. *Economic & Political Weekly 51*(36): 55–64.

Mundle, S. 2018. 'The Development of Education and Health Services in Asia and the Role of the State' (Working Paper No. 239). National Institute of Public Finance and Policy.

Munshi, K. 2014. 'Community Networks and the Process of Development'. *Journal of Economic Perspectives 28*(4): 49–76.

Muraleedharan, V. R. 1992. 'Professionalising Medical Practice in Colonial South-India'. *Economic & Political Weekly 27*(4): PE27–PE30 and PE35–PE37.

Mykhnenko, V. and A. Swain. 2010. 'Ukraine's Diverging Space-economy: The Orange Revolution, Post-Soviet Development Models and Regional Trajectories'. *European Urban and Regional Studies 17*(2): 141–65.

Myrdal, G. 1957. *Economic Theory and Underdeveloped Regions*. London: G. Duckworth.

Nagaraj, K. 2006. 'Tamil Nadu Economy: Contours of Change: A Secondary Data Exploration'. Mimeo, Madras Institute of Development Studies.

Nagaraj, R. and S. Pandey. 2013. 'Have Gujarat and Bihar Outperformed the Rest of India? A Statistical Note'. *Economic & Political Weekly* 48(39): 39–41.

Naidu, T. V. (ed.). 2010 [1932]. *The Justice Movement: 1917*. Madras: Dravidar Kazhagam.

Naig, U. 2015. 'Tamil Nadu Has Most Number of Dalit Entrepreneurs'. *The Hindu*, 11 September, https://www.thehindu.com/news/cities/chennai/state-has-most-number-of-dalit-entrepreneurs/article7639437.ece (accessed 25 October 2019).

Narasimhan, T. E. 2015. 'Amma Canteens for Aam Aadmis'. *Business Standard*, 20 July, https://www.business-standard.com/article/politics/amma-canteens-for-aam-aadmis-115072000413_1.html (accessed 6 August 2019).

Narayan, S. 2018. *The Dravidian Years: Politics and Welfare in Tamil Nadu*. New Delhi: Oxford University Press.

National Commission for Enterprises in the Unorganised Sector (NCEUS). 2008. *Report on Definitional and Statistical Issues Relating to Informal Economy*. New Delhi: Academic Foundation.

———. 2009. *Report of the National Commission for Enterprises in the Unorganised Sector*, Vol. 1. New Delhi: Academic Foundation.

National Sample Survey Office. 2012. *Survey on MGNREGA (July 2009–June 2011): Report 2*. New Delhi: Ministry of Statistics and Programme Implementation, Government of India, http://mospi.nic.in/sites/default/files/publication_reports/MGNREG_Report_8sep15_II_0.pdf (accessed 22 January 2019).

———. 2016. *Education in India* (Report No. 575[71/25.2/1]). NSS 71st round (January–June 2014). New Delhi: Ministry of Statistics and Programme Implementation, Government of India, http://mospi.nic.in/sites/default/files/publication_reports/nss_rep_575.pdf (accessed 8 May 2019).

Neelakantan, S. 1996. 'Change and Continuity: A Contrasting Account of Urban and Rural Transformation' (Working Paper No. 139). Madras Institute of Development Studies, Chennai.

Ngo, T. W. and Y. Wu (eds). 2008. *Rent Seeking in China*. London and New York: Routledge.

Nielsen, A. G. and S. Roy. 2015. *New Subaltern Politics: Reconceptualizing Hegemony and Resistance in Contemporary India*. New Delhi: Oxford University Press.

Nielsen, K. B. 2018. *Land Dispossession and Everyday Politics in Rural Eastern India*. London: Anthem Press.

Omvedt, G. 2011. *Understanding Caste: From Buddha to Ambedkar and Beyond*. Hyderabad: Orient Blackswan.

Pai, S. (ed.). 2007. *Political Process in Uttar Pradesh: Identity, Economic Reforms, and Governance*. New Delhi: Pearson/Longman.

Pandian, M. S. S. 1993. '"Denationalising" the Past: "Nation"' in E. V. Ramasamy's Political Discourse'. *Economic & Political Weekly 28*(42): 2282–87.

———. 1994. 'Notes on the Transformation of "Dravidian" Ideology: Tamil Nadu, c. 1900–1940'. *Social Scientist 22*(5–6): 84–104.

———. 1995. 'Beyond Colonial Crumbs: Cambridge School, Identity Politics and Dravidian Movement(s)'. *Economic & Political Weekly 30*(7–8): 385–91.

———. 1996. 'Towards National–Popular: Notes on Self-respecters' Tamil'. *Economic & Political Weekly 31*(51): 3323–29.

———. 2000. 'Dalit Assertion in Tamil Nadu: An Exploratory Note'. *Journal of Indian School of Political Economy* 12(3 and 4): 501–17.

———. 2007. *Brahmin and Non-Brahmin: Genealogies of the Tamil Political Present*. Ranikhet: Permanent Black.

———. 2011. 'New Times in Tamil Nadu'. *Seminar, 620* (April), https://www.india-seminar.com/2011/620/620_m_s_s_pandian.htm (accessed 15 March 2020).

———. 2012. 'Being "Hindu" and Being "Secular": Tamil "Secularism" and Caste Politics'. *Economic & Political Weekly 47*(31): 61–67.

———. 2013. 'Caste in Tamil Nadu-II: Slipping Hegemony of Intermediate Castes'. *Economic & Political Weekly 48*(4): 13–15.

Pandian, Punitha. 2017a. 'It Makes No Sense to Celebrate Ambedkar and Vilify Periyar'. *The Wire*, 15 October, https://thewire.in/caste/periyar-ambedkar-punitha-pandiyan-caste-brahmins-hindutva (accessed 15 April 2020).

———. 2017b. 'Rejecting Commonalities Between Ambedkar and Periyar Is Equivalent to Denying Facts'. *The Wire*, 17 November, https://thewire.in/caste/periyar-amberdkar-common-dalit-politics (accessed 15 April 2020).

Panneerselvan, A. S. 2017. 'Relentless Legislator'. *Frontline*, 23 June, https://frontline.thehindu.com/the-nation/relentless-legislator/article9719331.ece (accessed 12 February 2020).

———. 2018. 'Indian Federalism: An Innovative Response'. *Seminar*, *708* (August), http://www.india-seminar.com/2018/708/708_as_panneerselvan.htm (accessed 26 September 2019).

Pareto, V. 1968 [1901]. *The Rise and Fall of Elites: An Application of Theoretical Sociology*. Totowa, NJ: Bedminster Press.

Periyar. 1992 [1926]. 'Pirappurimayum Thadaigalum' (Talk on 29 December). Reprinted from *KudiArasu* (9 January 1927) in V. Anaimuthu (ed.) (1974), *Periyar E V R Sinthanaigal (Collected Works)*, Vol. 1, pp. 3–8 (Tiruchirapalli: Thinkers Forum).

Piketty, T. 2020. *Capital and Ideology*. Cambridge: Harvard University Press.

Prabhu, K. S. 2007. 'Social Sectors during Economic Reforms: The Indian Experience', *Oxford Development Studies 27*(2): 187–210.

Prabhu, K. S. and V. Selvaraju 2006. 'Public Financing for Health Security in India: Issues and Trends'. In *Securing Health for All: Dimensions and Challenges*, edited by S. Prasad and C. Sathyamala, pp. 410–14. New Delhi: Institute for Human Development.

Prakash, A. 2012. 'Caste and Capitalism', *Seminar*, *633* (May), https://www.india-seminar.com/2012/633/633_aseem_prakash.htm (accessed 9 December 2019).

Radcliffe, S. A. 2015. *Dilemmas of Difference: Indigenous Women and the Limits of Postcolonial Development Policy*. Durham: Duke University Press.

Radice, H. 2000. 'Globalization and National Capitalisms: Theorizing Convergence and Differentiation'. *Review of International Political Economy 7*(4): 719–42.

Raghaviah, J. 2014. *Basel Mission Industries in Malabar and South Canara (1834–1914): A Study of Its Social and Economic Impact*. New Delhi: Gyan Publishing House.

Rajadurai, S. V. 2012. *Periyar: August 15*, 3rd edn. Coimbatore: Vidiyal Pathippagam.

Rajadurai, S. V. and V. Geetha. 1996. *Periyar: Suyamariyadhai samadharmam*. Coimbatore: Vidiyal Pathippagam.

———. 2009. *Periyar: Suyamariyadhai samadharmam*, expanded edn. Coimbatore: Vidiyal Pathippagam.

Rajivan, A. K. 2006. 'ICDS with a Difference'. *Economic & Political Weekly 41*(34): 3684–88.

Rajshekhar, M. 2016. 'Politicians Aren't Only Messing with Tamil Nadu's Water—They're Making Rs 20,000 Crore from Sand'. *Scroll.in*, 19 September, https://scroll.in/article/815138/tamil-nadus-political-parties-are-making-money-from-sand-worth-a-whopping-rs-20000-crore-a-year (accessed on 30 August 2020).

Ramachandran, S. 1975. *Anna Speaks: At the Rajya Sabha 1962–66*. New Delhi: Orient Longman.

Ramakrishnan, H. 2018. 'Tamil Nadu Power Sector: The Saga of the Subsidy Trap'. In *Mapping Power*, edited by N. Dubash, S. Kale and R. Bharvirkar, pp. 255–73. New Delhi: Oxford University Press.

Raman, B. 2017. 'Practices of Territory in Small and Medium Cities of South India'. In *Subaltern Urbanisation in India*, edited by E. Denis and M-H. Zérah, pp. 235–60. New Delhi: Springer.

Ranjan, R. 2019. 'NEET in Focus Again after 3 Teenage Girls Commit Suicide in 2 Days in Tamil Nadu'. *The Citizen*, 7 June, https://www.thecitizen.in/index.php/en/NewsDetail/index/9/17072/NEET-in-Focus-Again-After-3-Teenage-Girls-Commit-Suicide-in-2-Days-in-Tamil-Nadu (accessed 4 May 2020).

Rao, M., K. D. Rao, A. K. Shiva Kumar, M. Chatterjee and T. Sundararaman. 2011. 'Human Resources for Health in India'. *The Lancet 377*(9765): 587–98.

Rao, S. 2017. *Do We Care: India's Health System*. New Delhi: Oxford University Press.

Rasathurai, P. 2009. *Needhik Katchi arasin sadhanaigal* [Justice Party's Achievements in Government]. Chennai: Dravidar Kazhagam.

Ravikumar, N. 2017. 'Tamil Nadu Shuts Down for Jallikattu'. *Deccan Chronicle*, 21 January, https://www.deccanchronicle.com/nation/current-affairs/210117/tamil-nadu-shuts-down-for-jallikattu.html (accessed 8 May 2020).

Reddy, K. S. 2017. 'Beyond the Lament'. *Indian Express*, 17 August, https://indianexpress.com/article/opinion/columns/gorakhpur-hospital-tragedy-health-of-children-in-india-beyond-the-lament-4799968/ (accessed 20 August 2019).

Rostow, W. W. (1959). 'The Stages of Economic Growth'. *The Economic History Review* 12(1): 1–16.

Rosanvallon, P. 2008. *Counter-Democracy: Politics in an Age of Distrust*. Cambridge: Cambridge University Press.

Rothboeck, S., M. Vijayabaskar and V. Gayathri 2001. *Labour in The New Economy: The Case of The Indian Software Industry*. New Delhi: International Labour Organization.

Rukmani, R. 1993. 'The Process of Urbanisation and Socioeconomic Change in Tamilnadu, 1901–81'. Unpublished doctoral dissertation, University of Madras.

———. 1994. 'Urbanisation and Socio-economic Change in Tamil Nadu, 1901–91'. *Economic & Political Weekly* 25(51–52): 3263–72.

Sample Registration System (SRS). 'Compendium of India's Fertility and Mortality Indicators, 1971–2013'. Ministry of Home Affairs, Government of India, https://censusindia.gov.in/vital_statistics/Compendium/Srs_data.html (accessed 20 August 2019).

Sanyal, K. 2007. *Rethinking Capitalist Development: Primitive Accumulation, Governmentality and Post-colonial Capitalism*. New Delhi: Routledge.

Sarkar, S. and A. K. Karan 2005. 'Status and Potential of Village Agro-Processing Units/Industries' (Occasional Paper 37). NABARD, Mumbai.

Sattanathan, A. N. 2007. *Plain Speaking: A Sudra's Story*. New Delhi: Permanent Black.

Selvaraj, S., D. Abrol and K. M. Gopakumar 2014. *Access to Medicines in India*. New Delhi: Academic Foundation.

Selvavinayagam, T. S. 2016. 'Learning from Chennai Floods to Mitigate Epidemic'. *International Journal of Health Systems and Disaster Management* 4(4): 114–19.

Sennett, R. 2012. *Together: The Rituals, Pleasures and Politics of Cooperation*. New Haven and London: Yale University Press.

Shyam Sundar, K. R. 2009. 'The Current State of Industrial Relations in Tamil Nadu'. Asia–Pacific Working Paper Series, International Labour Organization, New Delhi.

Singh, Pritam. 2008. *Federalism, Nationalism and Development: India and the Punjab Economy*. Oxon: Routledge.

Singh, Prerna. 2015. *How Solidarity Works for Welfare: Subnationalism and Social Development in India*. New York: Cambridge University Press.

Singh, S. K. 2000. 'Productive Efficiency Across Firms: State Road Transport Undertakings'. *Economic & Political Weekly* 35(48): 4269–75.

Sinha, A. 2003. 'Rethinking the Developmental State Model: Divided Leviathan and Subnational Comparisons in India'. *Comparative Politics* 35(4): 459–76.

———. 2006. *The Regional Roots of Developmental Politics in India: A Divided Leviathan*. New Delhi: Oxford University Press.

Sinha, D. 2016. *Women, Health and Public Services in India: Why Are States Different*. New Delhi: Routledge.

Slater, G. 1918. *Some South Indian Villages*. Oxford: Oxford University Press.

Snyder, R. 2001. 'Scaling Down: The Subnational Comparative Method'. *Studies in Comparative International Development 36*(1): 93–110.

Sotiris, P. 2018. 'Gramsci and the Challenges for the Left: The Historical Bloc as a Strategic Concept'. *Science & Society 82*(1): 94–119.

Spencer, J. W., T. P. Murtha and S. A. Lenway. 2005. 'How Governments Matter to New Industry Creation'. *Academy of Management Review 30*(2): 321–37.

Spratt, P. 1970. *D.M.K in Power*. Bombay: Nachiketa Publications.

Srinivasan, V. 2010. 'Understanding Public Services in Tamil Nadu: An Institutional Perspective'. Unpublished doctoral dissertation, University of Syracuse, New York.

Sriramachandran, R. 2018. 'Pluralization of Political Identity'. *Seminar, 708* (August), http://www.india-seminar.com/2018/708/708_ravindran_srirama chandran.htm (accessed 22 February 2020).

Storper, M. 1997. *The Regional World: Territorial Development in a Global Economy*. London and New York: Guilford Press.

Subagunarajan, V. M. S. (ed.). 2018. *Namakku yen indha izhinilai? Jaathi magaanaadukalilum jaathi ozhippu magaanaadukalilum Periyar* [Why Are We in This Degraded Position? Periyar's Speeches at Caste and Caste Abolition Conferences]. Chennai: Kayal Kavin Books.

Subramanian, N. 1999. *Ethnicity and Populist Mobilization: Political Parties, Citizens, and Democracy in South India*. New York: Oxford University Press.

Sud, N. 2012. *Liberalization, Hindu Nationalism and the State: A Biography of Gujarat*. New York: Oxford University Press.

Sumarto, S. and I. de Silva. 2014. 'Being Healthy, Wealthy, and Wise: Dynamics of Indonesian Subnational Growth and Poverty' (TNP2K Working Paper 09-2014). Tim Nasional Percepatan Penanggulangan Kemiskinan (The National Team for the Acceleration of Poverty Reduction).

Suntharalingam, R. 1980. *Politics and Nationalist Awakening in South India, 1852–1891*. New Delhi and Jaipur: Rawat.

Suryanarayana, M. H. 1986. 'The Problem of Distribution in India's Development: An Empirical Analysis'. Unpublished doctoral dissertation, Indian Statistical Institute, Bangalore.

Sushma, U. N. 2018. 'How Tamil Nadu Became One of the World's Leading Renewable Energy Markets'. *Quartz India*, 19 February, https://qz.com/india/1208222/how-tamil-nadu-became-one-of-the-worlds-leading-renewable-energy-markets/ (accessed 10 December 2019).

Swaminathan, P. 1991a. 'Evolution of Industrial Policy in Madras Presidency, 1900–1947' (Working Paper No.105). Madras Institute of Development Studies, Chennai.

———. 1991b. 'State Intervention in Industrialization: A Case Study of Madras Presidency' (Working Paper No.99). Madras Institute of Development Studies, Chennai.

———. 1992. 'Technical Education in Madras Presidency' (Working Paper No. 106). Madras Institute of Development Studies, Chennai.

———. 1994. 'Where Are the Entrepreneurs? What the Data Reveal for Tamil Nadu'. *Economic & Political Weekly 29*(22): M64–M74.

Swamy, Arun R. 1998. 'Parties, Political Identities and the Absence of Mass Political Violence in South India'. In *Community Conflicts and the State in India*, edited by Amrita Basu and Atul Kohli, pp. 108–48. New Delhi: Oxford University Press.

Taeube, Florian A. 2004. 'Proximities and Innovation: Evidence from the Indian IT Industry in Bangalore' (Working Paper No 04–10). Danish Research Unit For Industrial Dynamics (DRUID), Copenhagen.

Tamil Nadu Construction Workers Welfare Board. 2008. *Monitoring Reports on Tamil Nadu Construction Workers Welfare Board*. Chennai: Tamil Nadu Construction Workers Welfare Board.

Taylor, C. 1992. *Multiculturalism and the Politics of Recognition: An Essay*. Princeton: Princeton University Press.

Thangaraj, M. 1995. 'Trends in Fragmentation of Operational Holdings in India: An Exploratory Analysis'. *Indian Journal of Agricultural Economics 50*(2): 176–84.

Thirumavelan, P. 2018. *Adhika saadhigalukku mattume avar Periyaraa?* [Is He Periyar Only for the Dominant Castes?]. Chennai: Natrinai Publishers.

Thirunavukkarasu, K. 2013. *The History of Justice Party (1916–1944)*, 3rd edn. Chennai: Nakkeeran Publishers.

Thiruneelakandan, A. 2017. *Niitaamankalam caatiyak kotumaiyum tiraavita iyakkumam* [Needamangalam: Caste Oppression and the Dravidian Movement]. Nagercoil: Kalachuvadu Publications.

Tilly, C. 1998. 'How to Hoard Opportunities'. In *Durable Inequality*, pp. 147–69. Berkeley, Los Angeles and London: University of California Press.

TNM. 2018 'Anitha's Family Inaugurates Library in Her Memory, Year after Suicide over NEET'. *The News Minute*, 2 September, https://www.thenewsminute.com/article/anitha-s-family-inaugurates-library-her-memory-year-after-suicide-over-neet-87664 (accessed 4 May 2020).

Trautmann, T. R. 2006. *Languages and Nations: The Dravidian Proof in Colonial Madras*. New Delhi: Yoda Press.

Tyabji, N. 1988. 'State Aid to Industry: Madras 1921–37'. *Economic & Political Weekly 23*(31): PE51–PE62.

United Nations Population Fund. 2018. 'The State of World Population 2018'. Press release, 17 October, https://www.unfpa.org/press/state-world-population-2018 (accessed 13 May 2019).

Upadhya, C. 2007. 'Employment, Exclusion and "Merit" in the Indian IT Industry'. *Economic & Political Weekly 42*(20): 1863–68.

Vaidyanathan, G. 2014. 'How Has Tamil Nadu Fared under NRHM: An Introspection'. In *India Social Development Report 2014: Challenges of Public Health*, pp. 101–12. New Delhi: Council for Social Development and Oxford University Press.

Varrel, A. and M. Vijayabaskar. 2019. 'The De-metropolitisation of Software Services in India: An Institutional Understanding of IT Cluster in Coimbatore, Southern India' (Paper Presentation). 11th International Convention of Asian Scholars, 15–19 July, Leiden, Netherlands.

Varshney, A. 2012. 'Two Banks of the Same River? Social Order and Entrepreneurialism in India'. In *Anxieties of Democracy: Tocquevillean Reflections on India and the United States*, edited by P. Chatterjee and I. Katznelson, pp. 225–56. New Delhi: Oxford University Press.

———. 1995. *Democracy, Development, and the Countryside: Urban-Rural Struggles in India*. Cambridge: Cambridge University Press.

Venkatachalapathy, A. R. 1995. 'Dravidian Movement and Saivites: 1927–1944'. *Economic & Political Weekly 30*(14): 761–68.

———. 2018. 'DK and DMK: The Double-barrelled Gun'. *Seminar*, *708* (August), http://www.india-seminar.com/2018/708/708_ar_venkatachalapathy.htm (accessed 22 February 2020).

Venkatasubramanian, A. K. 2006. 'The Political Economy of the Public Distribution System in Tamil Nadu'. In *Reinventing Public Service Delivery in India*, edited by V. K. Chand, pp. 266–93. New Delhi: Sage.

Vidiyal. 2017. *Periyar indrum yendrum: Periyarin thernthedukapatta katuraigal* [Periyar Today and Forever: Selected Essays], 3rd edn. Coimbatore: Vidiyal Pathippagam.

Vignesh Karthik, K. R. and J. Karunanithi. 2018. 'Dravidian Movement and M. Karunanidhi: A Tale of Fostering a Fraternal Society'. https://indian culturalforum.in/2018/08/17/dravidian-movement-and-m-karunanidhi-a-tale-of-fostering-a-fraternal-society (accessed 5 March 2020)

Vijayabaskar, M. 2011. 'Global Crises, Welfare Provision and Coping Strategies of Labour in Tiruppur'. *Economic & Political Weekly 46*(22): 38–45.

———. 2014. 'The Politics of Silence'. In *Power, Policy and Protest: The Politics of India's Special Economic Zones*, edited by R. Jenkins, L. Kennedy and P. Mukhopadhyay, pp. 304–31. New Delhi: Oxford University Press.

———. 2017. 'The Agrarian Question amidst Popular Welfare: Interpreting Tamil Nadu's Emerging Rural Economy'. *Economic & Political Weekly 52*(46): 67–72.

——— 2001. 'Industrial Formation under Conditions of Flexible Accumulation: The Case of a Global Knitwear Node in Southern India'. Unpublished Ph.D dissertation submitted to Jawaharlal Nehru University, New Delhi.

Vijayabaskar, M. and A. Kalaiyarasan. 2014. 'Caste as Social Capital: The Tiruppur Story'. *Economic & Political Weekly 49*(10): 34–38.

Vijayabaskar, M. and G. Balagopal. 2019. 'Politics of Poverty Alleviation Strategies in India' (Working Paper No. WP 2019–7). United Nations Research Institute for Social Development.

Vydhianathan, S and R. K. Radhakrishnan. 2010. 'Behind the Success Story of Universal PDS in Tamil Nadu', *The Hindu*, 10 August, http://www.thehindu.com/opinion/op-ed/behind-the-success-story-of-universal-pds-in-tamil-nadu/article562922.ece (accessed 2 June 2014).

Vivek, S. 2014. *Delivering Public Services Effectively: Tamil Nadu and Beyond*. New Delhi: Oxford University Press.

Wade, R. 1990. *Governing the Market: Economic Theory and the Role of Government in East Asian Industrialization*. Princeton: Princeton University Press.

Walton, M. and J. Crabtree 2018. 'Crony Populism'. Talk at the Centre for Policy Research (CPR)and the Trivedi Centre for Political Data (TCPD), Dialogues on Indian Politics, New Delhi, https://cprindia.org/events/7099 (accessed 19 January 2020).

Washbrook, D. A. 1977. *The Emergence of Provincial Politics: The Madras Presidency 1870–1920*. New Delhi: Vikas Publishing House.

Weiner, M. 1990. *The Child and the State in India: Child Labor and Education Policy in Comparative Perspective*. New Jersey: Princeton University Press.

Witsoe, J. 2013. *Democracy Against Development: Lower-Caste Politics, and Political Modernity in Postcolonial India*. Chicago: University of Chicago Press.

World Bank. 2009. *Reshaping Economic Geography: World Development Report*. Washington DC.

Wyatt, A. K. J. 2013a. 'Combining Clientelist and Programmatic Politics in Tamil Nadu, South India'. *Commonwealth and Comparative Politics 51*(1): 27–55.

———. 2013b. 'Populism and Politics in Contemporary Tamil Nadu'. *Contemporary South Asia* 21(4): 365–81.

Yelery, A. 2014. 'China's "Going Out" Policy: Sub-national Economic Trajectories' (ICS Analysis No. 24). Institute of Chinese Studies, https://www.icsin.org/publications/chinas-going-out-policy-sub-national-economic-trajectories (accessed 8 April 2019).

INDEX

capacity to aspire, 46, 52–53, 79

capital accumulation, 1–2, 4–6, 10–13, 23, 28, 39–40, 48, 79, 112–14, 122–23, 125, 130, 139, 144, 147, 158, 174, 193, 217, 222–23, 225

caste solidarities, 11, 42–43, 51, 107, 114, 186, 188

caste status, 33, 121, 183, 211, 217, 221

Centre of Indian Trade Unions (CITU), 187, 207n18

centre–state relations, 114

Chatterjee, P., 1, 4, 20, 28, 43–44, 222, 229

Chetty, Theagaraya, 62, 73, 128

circulating elites, 140

civil society, 1, 30, 41, 64, 131, 174, 184, 229

claim-making, 29, 45, 105, 185, 188

clientelism, 220

clientelist, 46, 48, 220

clusters, 17, 118, 133, 135, 142n15

Coimbatore District Small Scale Industries Association (CODISSIA), 139

collective action, 11, 105, 148, 159, 165

collective bargaining, 188, 192

Common sense, 23, 26–27, 29, 40–43, 45, 52–53, 76–77, 130–31, 173–74, 216, 218, 221, 229

Communist Party of India-Marxist (CPI-M), 148–49

Community Health Centre (CHC), 90

Conferment of Ownership of Homestead Act, 149

Congress (party), 37, 39, 63, 77, 114, 129, 131, 133, 142n7, 148–49, 187, 216

connectivity, rural–urban, 165, 214

Contract Labour (Regulation and Abolition) Act, 185

contractualisation, 173, 177, 179, 185

cooperatives, 39, 130, 134–35, 160, 195, 208n25

corruption, 75, 219, 226–27

crony populism, 219

cultivators, 17, 125, 128, 130, 147, 153, 155

Dalit Indian Chamber of Commerce and Industry (DICCI), 17, 122

Dalits, 49, 75, 119, 121–22, 130, 136, 139, 147, 149–50, 155–57, 162, 164–65, 171n1, 171n6–7, 180, 182–83, 216–18, 220

Damodaran, H., 17, 112–13, 118–19, 125, 130, 137–39, 142n5, 217

delta, 148–49, 171n2–3, 229

demand, social, 27, 29

demand, popular, 23, 27, 29, 114, 131, 211, 224

Dewey, J., 81n14

Dharmambal Ammaiyar Memorial Widow Remarriage Scheme, 47

diversification, economic, 157

Dravida Munnetra Kazhagam (DMK), 38, 46–47, 49, 50n2, 62–64, 74–75, 77, 99, 114, 125–26, 131–33, 142n7, 147–50, 160, 174, 187–88, 190–91, 193, 207n18, 216, 219–20, 222, 229

Dravidar Kazhagam, 50n2, 74, 114,

148. See also Dravida Munnetra
Kazhagam
Dravidar Vivasaya Thozhilalar
Sangam (DVTS), 148
Dravidian common sense, 26–27,
40–43, 45, 52, 76, 173–74, 216, 218,
229
Dravidian-Tamil, 10, 27, 29, 33, 40,
42–44, 106, 210, 214, 218, 222

ecology, 228
economic popular, 29, 45–48, 53, 65,
79, 83, 107, 145, 149, 159, 163, 166,
189–90, 192–95, 214–15, 221–22,
224, 228
education, primary, 34, 46, 53, 58–61, 63,
66, 80n4, 212
education, tertiary, 21, 53, 65, 71, 75, 79,
80n5,181–83, 212–13
educational attainment, 57, 75, 101, 105,
215, 217
election manifesto, 160, 188, 229
electoral funding, 219, 227
elite bias, 42, 71–72, 75, 82, 96, 211–12
elites, caste, 30–33, 36–37, 39–41, 43, 79,
87, 113, 122, 130, 133, 137, 143n23,
147–48, 150, 180, 183, 211, 215,
220
embedded autonomy, 2–3, 24n2
embedded labour, 187, 214
entrepreneurship, 12, 17, 23, 112, 115,
119–24, 136–37, 139, 217, 228
equivalence, demand, 27, 29, 32–33, 38,
43–46, 48, 114, 218, 221–22
Evans, P., 1–2, 24n2, 82

federal, 3, 225
federal relations, 221
female labour force participation rate
(FLFPR), 176
Food Corporation of India (FCI), 160
food security, 162
Forum for IT Employees
(FITE), 188

Galanter, M., 41
Geetha, V., 26, 32, 35–36, 39, 49, 73,
129
governance, 3, 5, 17–18, 36, 83, 123,
218–19, 226
governmentality, 48
Gramsci, A., 29, 45, 50n5
gross attendance ratio, 67–68
gross enrolment ratio, 21–22, 57, 66
Gurusami, L. C., 129

Harriss, B., 103–04
Harriss, J., 3, 9, 12, 49, 59, 112, 145, 147,
150–51, 153, 157
Harriss-White, B., 1, 28, 119, 125
healthcare system, 16, 83, 97, 213
health insurance, 7, 83, 107, 191
hegemony, 26, 28, 33, 36, 148, 216
Heller, P., 1–2, 13, 82
Herfindahl–Hirschman Index
(HHI), 118
Heyer, J., 125, 194
Hindu Succession Act, 47
horizontal solidarities, 43, 51, 107
human capital, 7, 10, 24n8, 47, 53, 68,
72–73, 124, 136, 216

social justice, 9, 23, 26–27, 38–41, 47, 52,
61, 73, 76–78, 107, 112, 114, 131, 139,
144, 159, 179, 196, 210, 220–221,
227–228
social Left, 186
social networks, 106, 119, 111n19, 180,
207n7
social popular, 29, 45–48, 53, 79, 83, 105,
114, 145, 163, 189–90, 219–21
social protection, 161–62, 165, 173, 189,
194, 196, 214, 223
software services, 16, 119, 137, 174, 196
solidarities, 42–43, 51, 107, 114, 186, 188
Southern Question, 132
Sriramachandran, R., 26–27, 43
State Aid to Industries Act, 129
State Industries Promotion
Corporation of Tamil Nadu
(SIPCOT), 133
State Investment Potential Index, 123
state planning commission, 83, 89, 124
status-based inequality, 41, 211
structural transformation, 4, 13–18,
23, 39, 46, 48, 115–19, 144, 165, 176,
195–96, 211, 214–16, 229
Subagunarajan, V. M. S., 49
subnational, 1–13, 23, 24n2, 24n4–5,
26, 40, 70, 108–09, 111n18, 114, 133,
138, 144, 196, 210–12, 219, 224–26,
228–29
Subramanian, N., 10, 15, 49, 82–83,
144, 193
subsidies, 53, 110n9, 125, 135, 160, 169,
195
Suntharalingam, R., 30–33

Swaminathan, P., 112, 128–29, 142

TAHDCO Kamarajar Adi Dravidar
housing, 158
Tamil-Dravidian. See Dravidian-
Tamil
Tamil Maanila Kattida Thozhilalar
Panchayat Sangam (TMKTPS),
190
Tamil Nadu Agricultural Lands
(Record of Tenancy Rights) Act,
147, 149
Tamil Nadu Backward Classes
Commission, 78
Tamil Nadu Civil Supplies
Corporation (TNCSC), 160, 195
Tamil Nadu Co-operative Milk
Producers' Federation
(TCMPF), 135
Tamil Nadu Cultivating Tenants
(Payment of Fair Rent) Act,
148
Tamil Nadu Cultivating Tenants
Protection Act, 148
Tamil Nadu Dairy Development
Corporation, 135
Tamil Nadu Energy Development
Agency (TEDA), 124
Tamil Nadu Housing Board
(TNHB), 193
Tamil Nadu Human Development
Report (TNHDR), 2–3, 58, 80n7,
109n5, 216
Tamil Nadu Industrial Development
Corporation (TIDCO), 133

Tamil Nadu Manual Workers (Regulation of Employment and Conditions of Work) Act, 189–190

Tamil Nadu Manual Workers Welfare Board, 189, 203

Tamil Nadu Medical Services Corporation (TNMSC), 84, 102

Tamil Nadu Public Service Commission (TNPSC), 99, 150

Tamil Nadu Road Development Company (TNRDC), 135

Tamil Nadu Slum Clearance Board (TNSCB), 193

Tamil Nadu Small Industries Corporation Limited (TANSI), 133

Tamil Nadu State Development Finance Corporation, 126

Tamil Nadu State Transport Corporation (TNSTC), 126

Tamil Nadu Textile Corporation, 134

Tamil Nadu Urban Development Fund (TNUDF), 135

Taylor, C., 78

technical education, 16, 23, 69, 71, 73, 76, 80n78, 124, 128–29, 131, 142n15, 213

tenancy, 47, 147–50

tertiary education, 21, 53, 65, 71, 75, 79, 80n5, 181–83, 212–13

Thanjavur Tenants and Pannaiyals Protection Act, 1952, 148

Thoss, Pundit Iyothee, 33

'the people', 26–29, 210, 229

Theosophists, 31–33

Thirumavelan, P., 49, 150, 171n2

Thiruneelakandan, A., 148

Thirunavukkarasu, K., 73

total fertility rate (TFR), 22, 84–85

trade union, 173, 185–90, 208n21

transgenders, 192, 218

transport, 18, 64, 66, 123, 126, 158, 160, 165, 214, 219

tripartite committee, 188

under-nutrition, 86

under-five mortality rate (U5MR), 22, 84, 86–87

universal progamme/welfare, 46, 162

urbanisation, 171n7, 175, 216, 222

Vaishya Vacuum, 130

Venkatachalapathy, A. R., 37, 131

village health nurses (VHNs), 89, 92–93, 100

Vivek, Srinivasan, 11, 159, 162, 165

wage differentials, gender, 58

wage rates, 153, 158, 163, 174, 179

wage share, 177–79, 189, 214, 223

weak ties, 84, 105–07

Weiner, M., 58–59, 94–96

welfare boards, 174, 189–92, 203–05, 214

welfare interventions, 10, 13, 47, 82, 145, 159, 164, 166, 174, 189–95, 214, 224

welfare state, 10, 12, 48–49

Western Tamil Nadu, 130, 138, 142n10, 193

Witsoe, J., 9, 13, 42

Wyatt, A., 3, 12, 46, 49, 112, 139, 222

Milton Keynes UK
Ingram Content Group UK Ltd.
UKHW012106240823
427464UK00011B/138